SCOTTISH WILD COUNTRY BACKPACKING

30 weekend and multi-day routes in the Highlands and Islands

by Stefan Durkacz, Peter Edwards and David Lintern

© Stefan Durkacz, Peter Edwards and David Lintern 2022

First edition 2022

ISBN: 978 1 85284 904 7

Printed in Singapore by KHL Printing

A catalogue record for this book is available from the British Library.

Route mapping by Lovell Johns
www.lovelljohns.com

All photographs are by the authors unless otherwise stated.

Photos for Routes 1, 2, 3, 7, 9, 10, 13, 15, 16, 17, 18, 20, 21, 24 and 25 (except page 174) and on pages 2, 3, 12, 15, 18 (bottom left), 22 (bottom), 23, 26, 27, 30, 32, 33, 34 (top), 36, 37, 40, 77, 87, 107 and 199 are by David Lintern. Photos for Routes 8 (except page 87), 11, 12, 14 and 19 (except page 144) and on page 16 are by Stefan Durkacz. Remaining photos are by Peter Edwards.

© Crown copyright 2022 OS PU100012932.
NASA relief data courtesy of ESRI

◄◄ *Front cover:* A Coigach camp (Route 21)

◄ *Pages 2–3:* Summit of Lurg Mhòr (Route 16)

▶ *This page:* The ridge towards Sgùrr Ghiubhsachain (Route 2)

▶▶ *Page 7:* By the Scavaig River - the outflow of Loch Coruisk (Route 6)

CONTENTS

Route summary table 8
Map key 10
Overview map 11

INTRODUCTION 13

The Scottish Highlands 14
Wildness and wilderness in a Scottish context 14
Wildlife 17
Plants and flowers 21
Geology 21

Backpacking in the Highlands 25
Getting there 25
Getting around 26
Equipping for Scotland's backcountry 27
Using bothies 34
Backpacking with dogs 35
Environmental impact and Leave No Trace 36
Maps and route-finding 37
Safety and emergencies 39
Using this guide 41

WESTERN HIGHLANDS AND INNER HEBRIDES 45

Route 1	The Glen Etive Five	46
Route 2	Fort William to Glenfinnan via north Ardgour	50
Route 3	Streap and Braigh nan Uamhachan	55
Route 4	The west coast of Jura	59
Route 5	Around the coast of Rùm	66
Route 6	Isle of Skye: Glen Sligachan, Loch Coruisk and Camasunary	72

CENTRAL AND EASTERN HIGHLANDS 77

Route 7	Ben Alder: Tour of the ridges	78
Route 8	Blair Atholl to Kingussie	83
Route 9	The Mòine Mhòr Munros	89
Route 10	Ben Avon and Beinn a' Bhuird	95
Route 11	Northeast Cairngorms	99

NORTHWEST HIGHLANDS 107

Route 12	Inverinate Forest and the Gates of Affric	108
Route 13	Affric Haute Route	112
Route 14	Killilan Forest: Sgùman Còinntich, Faochaig, and Aonach Buidhe	117
Route 15	The Applecross Peninsula: Sgùrr a' Chaorachain and Beinn Bhàn	121
Route 16	Achnashellach, Bendronaig and West Monar	125
Route 17	Coulin Forest	132
Route 18	The Fannichs	137
Route 19	Fisherfield and Letterewe	141
Route 20	Flowerdale Three: Beinn Eoin, Beinn Dearg and Baosbheinn	145

THE FAR NORTH 151

Route 21	The Postie's Path and the Coigach group	152
Route 22	Glencoul, Gleann Dubh and Beinn Leòid	156
Route 23	Ben Klibreck and the Ben Armine Forest	160
Route 24	Around Strath Dionard	166
Route 25	Cape Wrath, Sandwood Bay and the Parph	170

OUTER HEBRIDES 177

Route 26	A circuit of Mingulay	178
Route 27	Hecla, Beinn Mhòr and South Uist's wild east coast	181
Route 28	Harris Hills, Loch Rèasort and Cravadale	185
Route 29	Isle of Lewis: Uig Hills and coast	190
Route 30	Isle of Lewis: Pairc Peninsula	194

Appendix A	Table of Munros and Corbetts	200
Appendix B	Glossary	202
Appendix C	Further reading	203

UPDATES TO THIS GUIDE

While every effort is made by our authors to ensure the accuracy of guidebooks as they go to print, changes can occur during the lifetime of an edition. Any updates that we know of for this guide will be on the Cicerone website (www.cicerone.co.uk/904/updates), so please check before planning your trip. We also advise that you check information about such things as transport, accommodation and shops locally. Even rights of way can be altered over time. We are always grateful for information about any discrepancies between a guidebook and the facts on the ground, sent by email to updates@cicerone.co.uk or by post to Cicerone, Juniper House, Murley Moss, Oxenholme Road, Kendal, LA9 7RL.

Register your book: To sign up to receive free updates, special offers and GPX files where available, register your book in your Cicerone library at www.cicerone.co.uk.

SCOTTISH WILD COUNTRY BACKPACKING

ROUTE SUMMARY TABLE

ROUTE NO.	ROUTE TITLE	START
1	The Glen Etive Five	Glen Etive road NN 136 468
2	Fort William to Glenfinnan via north Ardgour	Camusnagaul Pier NN 095 750
3	Streap and Braigh nan Uamhachan	Car park A830 NM 929 798
4	The west coast of Jura	Kinuachdrachd Harbour NR 705 982
5	Around the coast of Rùm	Dibidil Pony Path NM 404 911
6	Isle of Skye: Glen Sligachan, Loch Coruisk and Camasunary	Sligachan NG 487 298
7	Ben Alder: Tour of the ridges	Dalwhinnie station NN 634 849
8	Blair Atholl to Kingussie	Blair Atholl station NN 870 653
9	The Mòine Mhòr Munros	Achlean Glen Feshie NN 850 983
10	Ben Avon and Beinn a' Bhuird	Car park by Tomintoul NJ 164 176
11	Northeast Cairngorms	Tomintoul NJ 169 186
12	Inverinate Forest and the Gates of Affric	Parking off A87 NG 947 212
13	Affric Haute Route	Car park for Loch Beinn a' Mheadhain NH 243 262
14	Killilan Forest: Sgùman Còinntich, Faochaig, and Aonach Buidhe	Parking at road end Killilan NG 939 303
15	The Applecross Peninsula: Sgùrr a' Chaorachain and Beinn Bhàn	Bridge over the River Kishorn NG 836 423
16	Achnashellach, Bendronaig and West Monar	Parking just off A890, Craig NH 038 493
17	Coulin Forest	Achnashellach station NH 002 484
18	The Fannichs	Car park on A832 NH 313 626
19	Fisherfield and Letterewe	Layby on A832 at Corrie Hallie NH 114 850
20	Flowerdale Three: Beinn Eoin, Beinn Dearg and Baosbheinn	Car park on the A832 called 'Red Stable' NG 856 720
21	The Postie's Path and the Coigach group	Road end parking off A835, Blughasary NC 134 014
22	Glencoul, Gleann Dubh and Beinn Leòid	Parking by A894 NC 240 292
23	Ben Klibreck, and the Ben Armine Forest	The Crask Inn NC 524 247
24	Around Strath Dionard	Parking on A838 west of Carbreck House NC 330 591
25	Cape Wrath, Sandwood Bay and the Parph	Parking at Blairmore NC 194 600
26	A circuit of Mingulay	Landing place NL 567 828
27	Hecla, Beinn Mhòr and South Uist's wild east coast	Parking Loch Sgioport road NM 827 386
28	Harris Hills, Loch Rèasort and Cravadale	Amhuinnsuidhe NB 053 077
29	Isle of Lewis: Uig Hills and coast	Brèinis NA 993 264
30	Isle of Lewis: Pairc Peninsula	Parking near Eishken Lodge NB 325 124

ROUTE SUMMARY TABLE

FINISH	DISTANCE	TIME	ASCENT	DESCENT	PAGE
Glen Etive Road NN 136 468	26.5km (16½ miles)	2 days	2485m (8150ft)	2485m (8150ft)	46
Glenfinnan station NM 899 810	43km (26¾ miles)	2-3 days	2585m (8480ft)	2455m (8055ft)	50
Car park A830 NM 929 798	23km (14½ miles)	2 days	1775m (5825ft)	1775m (5825ft)	55
A846 at Tarbert NR 606 823	50km (31 miles)	4 days	2210m (7250ft)	2210m (7250ft)	59
Kinloch Castle NM 401 995	40km (25km)	3 days	1295m (4250ft)	1295m (4250ft)	66
Elgol NG 520 139	21.25km (13¼ miles)	2 days	775m (2545ft)	715m (2345ft)	72
Dalwhinnie station NN 634 849	61km (38 miles)	3 days	2620m (8595ft)	2620m (8595ft)	78
Kingussie station NH 756 004	52.5km (32½ miles)	2-3 days	2270m (7450ft)	2150m (7055ft)	83
Achlean Glen Feshie NN 850 983	49km (30½ miles)	2-3 days	2250m (7380ft)	2250m (7380ft)	89
Car park by Tomintoul NJ 164 176	50km (31 miles)	2 days	1625m (5330m)	1625m (5330m)	95
Tomintoul NJ 169 186	93.5km (58 miles)	3-4 days	2230m (7315ft)	2230m (7315ft)	99
Parking off A87 NG 947 212	39km (24¼ miles)	3-4 days	3110m (10,205ft)	3110m (10,205ft)	108
Car park for Loch Beinn a' Mheadhain NH 243 262	50km (31 miles)	3 days	3860m (12,665ft)	3860m (12,665ft)	112
Parking at road end Killilan NG 939 303	39.5km (24½ miles)	2-3 days	2010m (6595ft)	2010m (6595ft)	117
Bridge over the River Kishorn NG 836 423	27.5km (17 miles)	2-3 days	1420m (4660ft)	1420m (4660ft)	121
Parking just off A890, Craig NH 038 493	41km (25½ miles)	2-3 days	2785m (9140ft)	2785m (9140ft)	125
Achnashellach station NH 002 484	36km (22½ miles)	3 days	2990m (9810ft)	2990m (9810ft)	132
Car park on A832 NH 313 626	57km (35½ miles)	2-3 days	3275m (10,745ft)	3275m (10,745ft)	137
Layby on A832 at Corrie Hallie NH 114 850	39.75km (24¾ miles)	2-3 days	2865m (9400ft)	2865m (9400ft)	141
Car park on the A832 called 'Red Stable' NG 856 720	35km (21¾ miles)	2-3 days	2375m (7795ft)	2375m (7795ft)	145
Road end parking off A835, Blughasary NC 134 014	33km (20½ miles)	3 days	2610m (8565ft)	2610m (8565ft)	152
Parking by A894 NC 240 292	41.5km (25¾ miles)	2-3 days	2170m (7120ft)	2170m (7120ft)	156
The Crask Inn NC 524 247	56.5km (35 miles)	3 days	2360m (7745ft)	2360m (7745ft)	160
Parking on A838 west of Carbreck House NC 330 591	37.5km (23¼ miles)	2 days	2250m (7380ft)	2250m (7380ft)	166
Parking at Blairmore NC 194 600	55km (34 miles)	4 days	1425m (4675ft)	1425m (4675ft)	170
Landing place NL 567 828	13km (8 miles)	5-6hr	825m (2705ft)	825m (2705ft)	178
Parking Loch Sgioport road NM 827 386	34km (21 miles)	2 days	1915m (6285ft)	1915m (6285ft)	181
Amhuinnsuidhe NB 053 077	36km (22½ miles)	2-3 days	1860m (6100ft)	1860m (6100ft)	185
Brèinis NA 993 264	24km (15miles)	2 days	1830m (6005ft)	1830m (6005ft)	190
Parking near Eishken Lodge NB 325 124	45.5km (28¼ miles)	3 days	2155m (7070ft)	2155m (7070ft)	194

SCOTTISH WILD COUNTRY BACKPACKING

SYMBOLS USED ON ROUTE MAPS

- (SF) start/finish point
- (S) start point
- (F) finish point
- (S) alternative start point
- → direction of route
- route (Day 1)
- alternative route (Day 1)
- route (Day 2)
- alternative route (Day 2)
- route (Day 3)
- alternative route (Day 3)
- route (Day 4)
- alternative route (Day 4)
- footpath
- track
- water feature
- peak
- building
- = bridge
- P parking
- railway station
- youth hostel
- bothy
- shelter
- castle
- lighthouse
- ferry

N SCALE: 1:100,000

0 kilometres 1 2
0 miles 1

Contour lines are drawn at 50m intervals and labelled at 100m intervals.

GPX files for all routes can be downloaded free at www.cicerone.co.uk/904/GPX.

MOUNTAIN SAFETY

Every mountain walk has its dangers, and those described in this guidebook are no exception. All who walk or climb in the mountains should recognise this and take responsibility for themselves and their companions along the way. The author and publisher have made every effort to ensure that the information contained in this guide was correct when it went to press, but, except for any liability that cannot be excluded by law, they cannot accept responsibility for any loss, injury or inconvenience sustained by any person using this book.

International distress signal (emergency only)
Six blasts on a whistle (and flashes with a torch after dark) spaced evenly for one minute, followed by a minute's pause. Repeat until an answer is received. The response is three signals per minute followed by a minute's pause.

Helicopter rescue
The following signals are used to communicate with a helicopter:

Help needed:
raise both arms above head
to form a 'Y'

Help not needed:
raise one arm above head,
extend other arm downward

Emergency telephone numbers
999

Weather reports
The Mountain Weather Information Service (MWIS)
www.mwis.org.uk
The Scottish Avalanche Information Service (SAIS)
www.sais.gov.uk

Mountain rescue can be very expensive – be adequately insured.

10

INTRODUCTION

The Highlands and Islands of Scotland are home to the most ruggedly beautiful, expansive and challenging backpacking country in the British Isles. Out among the mountains, moors, glens and along the wild coastline it is still possible to walk for days without encountering roads, settlements and other people. Herein lies the purpose of this guidebook: the unifying theme for the 30 backpacking routes gathered here is that they are designed to make the best of the wildest, most remote and most spectacular landscapes the Highlands and Islands have to offer.

Of course, the Highlands and Islands are an immensely popular destination attracting a wide range of visitors, including many hillwalkers, climbers, cyclists, kayakers and other outdoor enthusiasts, drawn by the near-limitless possibilities for adventures great and small. There are, however, places that remain accessible only on foot, which may take days of walking to reach and require resourcefulness and planning to do so. Such places are the preserve of those willing and able to carry their own shelter and supplies, with enough experience and self-reliance to navigate proficiently and otherwise stay safe in an environment which can easily become inhospitable.

Proper equipment, careful planning and grounded experience open the way to the joys of backpacking in those less-visited hinterlands of the Highlands and Islands. This then is not a guidebook of routes for beginners; rather, our aim is to appeal to more experienced backpackers and those who want to work up to the challenging routes included here. For the latter, this guidebook includes comprehensive yet concise sections on the various practicalities of backpacking in Scotland's wild backcountry. Equipment, access, weather, safety and first aid are all covered, while sections on wildlife, geology and plants and flowers are intended to enhance readers' appreciation of the environments they are walking in.

For some of us, few things are as exciting and liberating as packing your rucksack ready for a backpacking trip. Obviously, planning your own routes is one of the most enjoyable parts of the whole deal for many backpackers and, although the routes included here are real gems polished over many years of experience backpacking throughout the Highlands and Islands, most include plenty of scope for adapting, expanding or curtailing to fit your own agenda. In this sense the routes are intended as an inspirational template – there to be modified at will.

The routes are spread throughout the region, covering geologically and topographically diverse landscapes, from the jagged gabbro peaks of Rùm and Skye to the whale-backed massifs and tundra-like plateaux of the Cairngorms; from the vast raised beaches and cave-riddled cliffs of Jura to the *lochan*-speckled blanket bog of the Flow Country. The routes are of varying lengths with at least one night out and as many as five, though the majority are one or two nights and therefore two or three days' walking. In several cases routes can be combined with a little adaptation here and there. Many of the routes include overnighting at a bothy or two as an option – see the section on mountain bothies, below. In all cases the overnighting options for camping and bothying are intended to make the most of some exceptionally beautiful landscapes, but also to avoid undue exposure to the elements. Fine-weather options for bivouacs on mountaintops or **bealachs** are included in some cases.

Because of the challenges involved, these routes are, by definition, less-frequented – with less livestock and land management, fewer roads, hill tracks or other infrastructure – and therein lies a significant part of the appeal. The kind of infrastructure we prefer is a crystal-clear burn for your water supply, a beach or loch to pitch your tent by or a mountain bothy for shelter.

Having used these terms several times in this introduction it's worth noting here that at present the words 'remote' and 'wild' in the Scottish context are freighted with cultural and environmental controversy – with good reason, as described in the following section.

◂ Foinaven's finely sculpted ridge (Route 24)

THE SCOTTISH HIGHLANDS

WILDNESS AND WILDERNESS IN A SCOTTISH CONTEXT

Picture the scene. We stand on the edge of a crag, high above a landscape untroubled by tower blocks and traffic, studded with sunlight-jewelled *lochans* (small lochs) threaded with a sinuous, silvered river flowing through a vast sea of dusty purple heather. Further up, our mountain's slopes are bronzed and treeless, before giving way to sharp, angular granite shadows. Our gaze is soundtracked by only the wind, the caw of a raven, the chatter of ptarmigan and the sharp bark of a hind. These sunlit uplands are ours and ours alone. The difference to our urban life could not be more marked. Is this not a timeless wilderness?

Forgive the slightly formulaic setup. There's a tension in writing a book like this one, a tension in the language we will use to describe the experience of being out there in Scotland's backcountry. The concept of wilderness is particularly controversial in the Scottish Highlands. The wild and remote places we visit in this book have their roots in the history and politics of the past.

The Clearances

From around 1740 to 1880, at least 170,000 crofters and small tenant farmers were forcibly evicted from their homes by their landowners to be replaced by sheep. It's likely to have been many thousands more. The beginning of the Clearances marks the end of the clan system and the expansion of enclosure to land north of the border. Common law rights were replaced by the arrival of industrial capitalism in the Scottish countryside, but it was pre-existing feudal landownership that allowed that to happen.

This period also marks the beginning of the modern Scottish diaspora. Thousands were indentured to colonial landowners and sold onto ships bound for the New World, while others were burnt out of their homes. The people were replaced by an industrial-scale sheep economy, at least until the global wool market collapsed.

There followed a period of attrition, with the sheep replaced by deer for 'sport' and many of the remaining inhabitants experiencing disease and famine on poorer reservation-like plots after relocation. It might be tempting to attribute this all to the English, but Scottish lairds, lawyers, clergy and soldiery were often the executors and sometimes the beneficiaries of this upheaval. It is a gruesome period in the history of not just Scotland, but the whole of Britain.

Alongside this grew an idealised vision of Scotland as 'wilderness', popularised by Queen Victoria's visits to her Balmoral holiday home, which helped sell it as a retreat to the old elites and a newly wealthy industrial middle class. Sometimes referred to as Balmoralisation, this legacy still fuels much of our tourism today.

The concept of 'wilderness'

The concept of wilderness as 'pure' and without people that we often use in the UK is heavily borrowed from the North American writings of Muir, Thoreau and others, but more recently has been questioned there and elsewhere. Historians are demonstrating that indigenous Americans were cleared into reservations to facilitate the first national parks, and ethnographers are unearthing new evidence showing the farming of rainforests dating back thousands of years. We continue to learn more about landscape terraforming by native peoples using fire and controlled grazing, from the great plains of Missouri to the even greater plains of Mongolia.

In Scotland, as elsewhere, the vast majority of the highest, most mountainous land was always free of any full-time settlement – it simply isn't productive enough to support human life in large numbers. That is not to say that humans never visited these places, or left a mark, or that they do not bear our signature in name, trail, shieling, song and story. This specific intertwining of natural and cultural history is the reason many conservationists in Scotland make a distinction between wildness and wilderness.

Who owns Scotland?

Some of these tensions and inequities remain today. According to historian Jim Hunter, Scotland still has "the most concentrated pattern of land ownership in the developed world", with over 50% owned by fewer than 450 people. There's a growing call for land redistribution and resettlement in places that were previously cleared, as well as a thriving community land movement. Community-owned land now makes up at least 2.5% of the total and continues to grow.

On the other hand, some traditional estates are using their power and influence to repair and restore land in their care.

A brief history of access in Scotland

These days, Scotland has some of the most enlightened access laws in the world. The Land Reform (Scotland) Act (2003) enshrined in law the right to roam, camp and use lochs and rivers for boating and swimming. So not only does Scotland boast

WILDNESS AND WILDERNESS IN A SCOTTISH CONTEXT

▲ Abandoned croft house, Samhnan Insir, Rùm (Route 5)

spectacular scenery, it affords the self-powered traveller the freedom to explore it fully.

The modern struggle for access rights has its roots in the broader social upheavals occurring around 250 years ago. The pacification of the Highlands after Culloden and the development of a road network helped facilitate the birth of tourism, and interest in exploring the Highlands grew. However, the Highland Clearances soon began and a centuries-old way of life vanished, replaced by sheep farming and deer stalking. Landowners jealously guarded this newly emptied 'wilderness', and conflict inevitably developed on two fronts: access to ancient through-routes and, later, open access to mountains and moorland.

In 1845 the Scottish Rights of Way Society was formed, leading to many legal actions that secured access to a number of ancient tracks. Key battles occurred in 1847, when the Duke of Atholl was prevented from blocking access through Glen Tilt after a confrontation with a professor and his botany students, and in 1888, when local shepherd Jock Winter defied the landowner over access to the drovers' route between Glen Doll and Braemar. This latter confrontation demonstrated it wasn't always the prosperous urban establishment fighting for access – the ensuing legal case relied heavily on shepherds' testimonies.

Establishing a right to roam off the path took much longer. Tolerance prevailed in many areas with a tradition of open access developing organically, but ultimately access still depended on landowners' whims. The formalisation of rights via the 2003 Act was hugely significant and long overdue.

Nowadays, Scotland still has a highly concentrated pattern of land ownership; some landowners try to defy the Act and seasonal restrictions on camping in Loch Lomond and Trossachs National Park are seen by some as an erosion of rights. Eternal vigilance is undoubtedly the price of freedom regarding access.

SCOTTISH WILD COUNTRY BACKPACKING

Scotland's access laws are predicated on responsible access. We'd recommend studying the Scottish Outdoor Access Code before undertaking the routes in this guidebook. The Code is based on three key principles:

▶ Respect the interests of others
▶ Care for the environment
▶ Take responsibility for your own actions

This guidebook's approach to 'wild country'

Where does all this leave you, the reader? The title of this book uses the words 'wild country', and in choosing the routes, we've focused on a feeling of wildness. Wild country is land that is more or less self-willed; where nature can often be more in charge than we are. Scotland may lack toothy carnivores and by comparison to other places not constitute 'wilderness', but where there are places where a subjective feeling of wildness exists, we have tried to include them.

We have also tried to include a few places where there are attempts to improve the so-called 'wild' qualities of the land, for example by reforesting and reducing deer numbers and therefore improving biodiversity.

Wherever we pass by signs of our human past we make mention of them, because it is important to acknowledge the ways in which our ancestors made their mark, as well as to note that a place can feel 'wild' even with these marks.

We have considered distance from high-density infrastructure (though not necessarily from other people or their historical presence) and prioritised routes 'off the beaten track'. Where there is a choice, we will turn away from the well-trodden... and we might well choose not to take a path at all!

In the context of this book, wildness is about being at one with a place on its terms, not ours, about encouraging self-reliance and resilience in an environment we do not individually control, and the renewed perspective and broadened outlook and skill-set that comes from those experiences. We have discovered that these wild places are not barren or empty, they are rich and full.

Scotland is a country like any other, managing many contemporary ups and downs alongside a sometimes troubled past, but the authors are still very much in love with those mountainous folds and inky black lochs, and there is still untold wildness to be found there, of a character unique in the world. Come along in – the water's cold, deep and lovely.

▲ Sgùrr Gaorsaic and Sgùrr nan Ceathreamhnan from the eastern spur of Beinn Fhada (Route 12)

▲ Foraging stag, north-east Jura

WILDLIFE

The Highlands and Islands' diverse terrain, including large tracts of undeveloped land, together with areas of sensitive land management and regeneration, provides an abundance of natural habitats allowing many species to thrive. Opportunities for encountering wildlife at close quarters are plentiful for those venturing into the hills and hinterlands or along the wild coastline.

Deer are the region's largest mammals with red deer being the biggest and most numerous. Fallow deer and roe deer are also relatively common in some areas. The red deer population grew exponentially with the expansion of 'deer forests' for commercial sport in the 19th century.

However, beautiful and emblematic as they are, sheer weight of numbers (approximately 700,000 in Scotland) has a deleterious impact on the environment and on the health of the herd. Overgrazing, especially of native woodland, has contributed to the 'wet desert' of Scotland's uplands. A lack of natural predators is a key factor and although culling – including commercial stalking – helps to keep the numbers down, more extensive intervention is needed to keep the herd within sustainable numbers.

Wild goats are found in upland and coastal areas of Scotland, including many Inner Hebridean islands. They are likely to have descended from domestic animals abandoned by crofters during the Clearances. Wild goats are usually dark brown with white patches or else entirely dark brown. They have long, shaggy coats and the billy goats have curving, swept-back horns.

Foxes, badgers and pine martens are found throughout the Highlands and also on Skye, while pine martens are also found on Mull. Other predatory land mammals include brown and black rats, feral cats, mink, polecats and hedgehogs. Among other land mammals, mountain hares and red and grey squirrels are found throughout the Highlands and some Inner Hebridean islands. Pipistrelle bats are found throughout the Highlands, Inner Hebrides and on Lewis, while long-eared and Natterer's bats are present in the Highlands and parts of the Inner Hebrides.

Commonly found are three amphibians – common frogs, common toads and newts (smooth and palmate) – and three reptiles – the slow worm, common lizard and the adder (which is the only snake found in the Highlands and the Inner Hebrides – there are none present in the Outer Hebrides).

SCOTTISH WILD COUNTRY BACKPACKING

▲ *Clockwise from top:* Atlantic grey seals, Mingulay; Otter, Loch Seaforth, Lewis and Harris; Mountain hare in winter coat, Monadhliath mountains

WILDLIFE

Invertebrates include earthworms, snails, grasshoppers, flies, spiders and harvestmen, numerous species of damselfly, dragonfly, beetle, butterfly and moth as well as several species of bumblebee, which thrive particularly well in areas with low-intensity crofting agriculture.

Otters are present throughout the islands and coastal areas. Breeding pairs usually have a coastal territory of around 5km in length. There are good chances of seeing otters when walking along uninhabited or sparsely populated stretches of coastline. They are most often seen when hunting just offshore.

Atlantic grey and common seals are abundant throughout the islands and coastal areas of the western and northern mainland particularly and are frequently seen basking on offshore rocks and skerries or observing onshore activity from the sea. A variety of cetaceans frequent the seas around the Highlands and Islands, including minke whales, pilot whales, orcas, porpoises and various dolphins. Basking sharks are summer visitors to the Hebridean waters particularly, though seasonal distribution is related to availability of zooplankton.

Among the freshwater fish species present in the Highlands and Islands' lochs and burns are brown trout, salmon, grayling, char, European eels and three-spined sticklebacks.

Birds

The birdlife of the region is rich, diverse and often spectacular. There are small to robust populations of various raptors distributed among the Highlands and Islands, including merlins, kestrels, hen harriers, golden and white-tailed eagles as well as tawny, short-eared and barn owls.

A number of rare and uncommon species are found only in very specific habitats, such as the corncrake – present in the islands and far northwest mainland – and the chough, which is found only on Islay and Colonsay. Both species are endemic to types of low-intensity crofting farmland. The Scottish crossbill is unique to the Scots pine woods of the central and eastern Highlands. The endangered capercaillie, a huge woodland grouse, is found only in native and plantation pine woods in the eastern Highlands. The ptarmigan – also a member of the grouse family – is found only in the high mountains of the Highlands.

The red grouse, however, is problematic. The maintenance of drained shooting moors increases the risk of flooding, water pollution, smoke pollution from muir burning and transforms moorland into a mono-cultural environment. Crows and stoats, which prey on grouse eggs, are trapped and killed, albeit legally, while birds of prey, including hen harriers and eagles, have been persecuted illegally, with few successful prosecutions of offending gamekeepers or estates.

The seabird populations of certain islands and mainland coastal areas are quite spectacular – including photogenic species such as the razorbill and puffin – and are internationally important in several cases, such as Rùm's migrant population of Manx shearwater and the gannet colonies of the Hebridean archipelago. Guillemots, storm petrels, skuas and terns are

▲ Puffins, Mingulay

distributed around mainland coastal regions and the islands. Various gulls are also present including great black-backed, herring and Iceland gulls.

Waders, divers and ducks variously populate sand flats, salt marshes, freshwater and sea lochs, machair and sandy shorelines – including sandpiper, lapwing, turnstone, dunlin and oystercatcher; great-crested and Slavonian grebes; red-throated, black-throated and great northern divers; red-breasted merganser, eider, teal and goldeneye. The grey heron, mute and whooper swan also haunt lochs, coastline and rivers.

Insects
Among the highlights of the Highlands and Islands' abundant insect life are a variety of bumblebees, butterflies and dragonflies. Watch out for the blaeberry bumblebee (*Bombus monticola*) on the high moors. There are 30 species of butterfly in the Highlands, including the familiar peacock, red admiral and small tortoiseshell, and several species of fritillary, skipper and hairstreak. Encountering a large, shimmering dragonfly hunting over the heather is a special treat in summer. Again, species are abundant with 29 recorded in Scotland, three of which breed only here: the northern damselfly, azure hawker and the northern emerald.

Biting beasties
Deer are commonplace everywhere other than a few islands, therefore ticks are often picked up when walking through bracken and long grass from early spring through to late autumn. Wearing shorts increases your chances of picking them up. These miniscule beasties burrow their heads into the flesh and are best removed with tweezers, but you must ensure that you remove the head when extracting them. Some ticks carry Lyme disease, which can become seriously debilitating if undiagnosed and untreated. Removing infected ticks within 36 hours greatly reduces the risk of contracting Lyme disease. A red ring around a bite is an indicator of infection, but this doesn't always occur. Lyme disease can be effectively treated with antibiotics if caught early. A variety of tick-removal tweezers and forks are available from outdoor pursuits retailers.

The hugely irritating midge (*Culicoides impunctatus*), a small biting gnat, is abundant throughout the Highlands and Islands between late spring and autumn. Carry some insect repellent, antihistamines and a midge net for your head. Don't pitch your tent near standing water or completely sheltered from any breeze.

The cleg – an aggressive horse fly – tends to hang around in gangs during the spring and summer months and can deliver a painful bite, which can swell up.

Adders are common in parts of the Highlands and on some islands, though they are unlikely to bother you unless you bother them first. Be aware, however, as a bite can cause dizziness, vomiting, painful swelling and immobility of an affected limb – which can be a serious problem if you're a long and difficult walk away from treatment. Jellyfish are common in the seas

▲ Atlantic grey seals on the beach at Bàgh Mhiùghalaigh, Mingulay

GEOLOGY

around the islands and some mainland coastal areas in summer so be vigilant when enjoying a swim.

PLANTS AND FLOWERS

The diverse range of landscapes found in the Scottish Highlands is matched by a corresponding diversity of temperate ecologies. These include coniferous and deciduous woodlands, coastal and estuarine, oceanic and tundra landscapes. Without centuries of human activity, much of the Highlands would be covered by forest dominated by the Scots or Caledonian pine (*Pinus sylvestris*), especially towards the east, with birch dominating in the west. The finest fragments of the old Caledonian pine forest can be found in Glen Affric and the Cairngorms.

In the hills, the main vegetation in the lower moorland zones includes heather, sedge, rushes, bog asphodel and a range of grasses. On the deepest peat, cotton grass often grows in abundance. Heather is most dominant in the drier east. The most common species is *Calluna vulgaris*. It flowers in August, turning swathes of the Cairngorms foothills a distinctive purple-pink. Above, on the high plateaux, the Cairngorms boast a range of arctic-alpine vegetation unique in Britain.

Blaeberry, crowberry and cowberry often carpet the ground in the Caledonian pine forests, open moorland and some higher mountain areas. In late summer they produce a profusion of berries, a vital food source for the many birds and animals preparing for winter.

Some coastal areas in the northwest and especially the Hebrides boast fertile, low-lying grasslands known as machair, a unique habitat part natural, part shaped by generations of crofting and grazing. In summer the machair is covered in a colourful variety of flowers, including, among many others, bird's foot trefoil, red clover, poppies, yarrow and daisies. Beds of flag irises often thrive in wetter hollows.

GEOLOGY

The fantastically varied landscapes and landforms you'll encounter on the routes in this book are fragments of the 3000 million-year story of how the land of Scotland came to be as it is now. Being able to piece together and interpret some of that story as you walk these routes can add great depth to your enjoyment of the Scottish uplands and islands.

It's perhaps not surprising that one of the greatest figures of the Scottish Enlightenment was James Hutton, often described as the father of modern geology. Through studying rock formations, Hutton came to understand that the planet is much older than was commonly believed. At that time, centuries of religious dogma insisted that the Earth was only 6000 years old. Hutton challenged that with his theory of uniformitarianism, which proposed that the natural processes we see in action today are those which have always operated and have shaped the world as we see it now.

So, we'd argue that geology provides a healthy dose of perspective on human life and endeavour, a glimpse of the

▲ *Left:* Marsh orchid, Jura; *Right:* Rock rose, Mingulay

SCOTTISH WILD COUNTRY BACKPACKING

vastness of the processes that shape our world, and demonstrates the transience of even the most immutable reference points in the landscape – the mountains themselves. If backpacking in the Scottish Highlands is a feast for the soul, then geology provides the raw ingredients.

Three billion years of geology

In geological terms, 3000 million years is a very long time – long enough to produce the varied landscapes we see in the Highlands today, from the rounded, billowing plateaux of the Cairngorms and the sharp ridges and deep glens of the west, to the eerie, isolated hulks of the far northwest on their plinth of watery moorland. Two key processes have driven the formation of the Highland landscape: the shifting of the Earth's tectonic plates and, later on, the action of glaciers and ice sheets that periodically extended across Scotland within the last one million years.

The oldest rocks belong to the Lewisian Complex, largely composed of gneiss, a type of metamorphic rock – that is, rock which has been crushed and contorted. These date back to between 2900 and 1700 million years ago and can be found in the far northwest and the Outer Hebrides.

The Highlands were born during Scotland's most significant mountain-building episode, the Caledonian Orogeny, which happened between 490 and 390 million years ago. As the ancient Iapetus Ocean closed, the continents of Laurentia (including Scotland's oldest rocks), Avalonia (including much of the rest of what is now the UK) and Baltica were involved in a complex collision. This created the Caledonian mountain range. It was Himalayan in proportions but eroded quickly as Scotland drifted north over the equator. The final period of rock creation occurred 60 million years ago as the North Atlantic Ocean began to open. The Earth's crust was ripped apart, triggering volcanic activity along Scotland's west coast. Enormous volcanoes and lava flows made their mark especially on what are now the Inner Hebrides. Subsequent erosion of overlying rocks has exposed the volcanic chambers where the molten magma pooled after rising through the Earth's crust. Scotland's most spectacular and technically difficult mountain range for climbers, the Black Cuillin of Skye, was born during this period.

Things were fairly quiet for many millions of years after the volcanoes died out. Erosion carried on its relentless work, and sedimentary rocks continued to accumulate in some areas. The final sculpting of the Highland landscape we know today occurred over the last million years as ice sheets and glaciers advanced and retreated across Scotland several times. The tremendous weight of ice that built up during periods of glaciation

▲ *Top*: Weathered Torridonian sandstone, Rùm; *Bottom:* Sandstone tors on Beinn Dearg

gouged and scoured the land, creating that familiar landscape of corrie, glen and loch you'll encounter on your Highland journeys.

That said, there's ample variety within that template, as noted earlier. Different areas of the Highlands have their own unique character, reflecting the localised impacts of the processes described above. Scotland's wildest areas, where you'll find the routes we've included in this book, are in the Northwest Highlands, the Islands, and, over in the east, the Cairngorms and surrounding hill country.

The Northwest Highlands

The very wildest land in Scotland lies north and west of the Great Glen fault, the deep loch-filled trough cutting diagonally across the mainland from Fort William and Inverness. The landscape character of the far northwest differs greatly from that of the rest of the area. This is due to a low-angled fault known as the Moine Thrust, which resulted in a sheet of metamorphic rocks (Moine schists) pushing northwest over younger sedimentary rocks. Southeast of the Moine Thrust, the rocks were severely metamorphosed during the Caledonian Orogeny. Stand on a peak in Knoydart, Affric or Kintail and the views positively jostle with mountains often linked by long, high ridges.

Northwest of the Moine Thrust, things are a little different. The rocks here were unaffected by these events, and the landscape is characterised by strange, often isolated mountain bastions surrounded by miles of rough *lochan*-studded moors. Three distinct rock groups make up this northwestern 'foreland'. Firstly, the really ancient rock, Lewisian gneiss, impervious to water, underlying the miles of '*cnoc* and *lochan*' moorland. Secondly, sedimentary deposits known as Torridonian Sandstone, laid down between 1000 and 800 million years ago. These have eroded, leaving isolated, spectacular remnants, characterised by horizontal terraces, rounded buttresses and pinnacle ridges. The mountains of Applecross, Torridon, An Teallach and Suilven are among the best known of these peaks.

▲ Looking north from the approach to spot height 808m on Foinaven (Route 24)

A third layer, the Cambro-Ordovician sediments, was deposited around 570 million years ago as the sea began to cover the land. Some of the mountains in the far northwest are capped by light-coloured Cambrian quartzites, contrasting starkly with the red Torridonian sandstone underneath. Foinaven and Arkle in the far north of Sutherland are rare examples of mountains composed mostly of Cambrian quartzite.

Grampians and Cairngorms

The Dalradian Supergroup may sound like a Scottish folk music collective, but is in fact the name for the thick pile of volcanic and sedimentary rocks laid down between 700 and 600 million years ago that was later 'metamorphosed' by crushing and folding during the Caledonian Orogeny. It underlies most of the area between the Great Glen in the northwest and the Highland Boundary Fault in the southeast.

The Caledonian Orogeny also caused molten magma to rise from deep inside the Earth and pool underneath these contorted rocks. The magma cooled to form erosion-resistant granite, which was exposed as the Caledonian mountains wore away. Thus, the Cairngorms were born, a range characterised by its extensive high plateaux littered with pink granite. The Scots Gaelic name for the range is Am Monadh Ruadh, the red mountains, and you'll see why if you view the Cairngorms from afar, bathed in sunlight on a summer evening.

Glaciation over the last million years has left profound marks on the Cairngorms. Although the summits are fairly unchanged, the contrast with the deep, eroded glens is dramatic. Here, powerful and fast-moving glaciers gouged out spectacular troughs such as the Loch Avon basin and Gleann Einich, cutting through watersheds to form glacial breaches (most notably in the Lairig Ghru and Ryvoan Pass), and diverting the headwaters of some rivers into new courses. The high plateaux are scalloped by deep corries, and there is much speculation about just how recently places like the Northern Corries of Cairngorm and An Garbh Choire of Braeriach harboured remnant glaciers.

The geological processes described have bequeathed a monumental landscape. Nowhere else in Scotland is there the sense of space encountered on those rolling, sub-arctic plateaux, and glaciation has created some of the longest and finest through-routes in the land. It is, in short, perfect backpacking country.

The Islands

Depending on where you go in the Hebrides, you'll encounter the youngest, or the oldest, rocks in Scotland. The Outer Hebrides are composed mostly of Lewisian gneiss, while the most recent rock creation took place in the Inner Hebrides during the period of volcanic activity 60 million years ago as Western Europe separated from North America. Much of the mountainous terrain of Rùm, Skye and Mull is the remains of volcanic complexes and lava flows. As elsewhere, more recent glaciation has scoured and shaped the landscape.

Turning north, much of the Orkney Islands is formed of sandstones laid down between 400 and 360 million years ago, when rivers from the north of Scotland drained into a low-lying area known as the Orcadian Basin. Shetland, however, is geologically very diverse, comprising Lewisian gneiss, and Moine and Dalradian rocks. This is due to a number of north–south faults which have brought together different rocks in a narrow zone. Shetland also shows more evidence of glaciation than Orkney, although glacial valleys and corries can be found in Orkney's Hoy Hills.

▲ Nearing the summit of Taran Mòr (Route 28)

BACKPACKING IN THE HIGHLANDS

GETTING THERE

Unless you live locally, getting to the Highlands and Islands can often be a demanding trek in itself. The relative remoteness of many of the routes included here only adds to the challenge. However, a little judicious planning goes a long way.

Inverness is the main transport hub for the Highlands with good air, rail and road links from points south, including Glasgow, Edinburgh and London. North of Inverness the public transport infrastructure is reasonable in some areas, patchy in others, with the far northwest having particularly sparse coverage.

Other hubs such as Fort William, Kyle of Lochalsh and Oban are linked to the cities of Scotland's south and east by rail and coach routes, also making them accessible from further afield. Intermediate points along the main transport arteries are equally accessible and those in the heart of hill country, such as Crianlarich, Glencoe or Aviemore make good bases for walkers without cars.

As well as the above-mentioned air links, the Hebrides are served by an extensive network of ferry services operated by Caledonian MacBrayne – otherwise known as CalMac. For timetables and information go to www.calmac.co.uk. The west coast ferry ports of Oban and Mallaig have good rail and coach links while Ullapool and Kennacraig have the latter only. Train routes and timetables are available at www.scotrail.co.uk, while coach travel is covered at www.citylink.co.uk.

Many walkers drive to the hills and hinterlands of the Highlands and Islands, and not without good reason as many areas are not accessible by public transport alone – including a good proportion of the walks in this book. Travelling by car

▲ Caledonian MacBrayne ferry en route to Islay with Beinn a' Chaolais, Jura, beyond

SCOTTISH WILD COUNTRY BACKPACKING

provides a certain amount of freedom and flexibility and can be easier on cost and carbon footprint if shared among several people.

However, there are challenges for those not used to driving on Highland and Island roads. Firstly, there is a great preponderance of single-track road once you're off the arterial roads. These are often rustic by nature and are given to winding tortuously through unforgiving geography. An understanding of the use of passing places should be acquired in advance. Driving conditions can be difficult during the Scottish winter, which can last from September until May, and in the summer months the volume of traffic – including convoys of gigantic motorhomes travelling at 20mph – will add to your journey times significantly.

Glasgow, Edinburgh, Inverness and Aberdeen are the principal airports used by those travelling from outwith Scotland and there are a number of smaller airports and airfields around the country – in the Hebrides in particular, including Campbeltown and Oban in Argyll, Stornoway, Benbecula and Barra in the Outer Hebrides, and Colonsay, Islay, Broadford (Skye) and Tiree in the Inner Hebrides. The Highlands and Islands Airports website is a useful resource: www.hial.co.uk.

A really useful website for all Scottish travel information is www.visitscotland.com.

GETTING AROUND

Public transport is sketchy in some areas of the Highlands and Islands, so if you're getting around without a car then it's worth doing a bit of advance planning with bus and train timetables.

Hitch-hiking remains viable in the Highlands and Islands though it's probably best not to depend on getting lifts in remote places – especially if you have a train, bus or ferry to catch.

By bike

Cycling can be a hugely enjoyable way of getting around on quieter Highland roads (though narrow, busy roads are no fun, sometimes verging on the dangerous), but a minimalist approach to packing is required if you're going to be carrying all your backpacking kit in panniers. Leaving your bike somewhere safe and secure – and ideally protected from the elements – is also a logistical issue if you're cycling to the start of a route and heading off into the hills for some days.

'Bikepacking' has become relatively popular in recent years and increasing numbers of folk are to be seen dotting around on fat-tyred mountain bikes with all their kit strapped to the frame, handlebars and saddle in cleverly designed purpose-made bags/packs – eschewing panniers and racks. Bikepackers can essentially go where any other mountain-bikers

▲ Climbing Garbh Choireachan (Route 21)

EQUIPPING FOR SCOTLAND'S BACKCOUNTRY

▲ Cycling in to upper Glen Nevis (Route 1)

go, though the extra weight will lead to more 'hike-a-bike' as it's known in Scotland.

The great advantage to bikepacking or transporting a mountain bike by car is in being able to pedal in and out of those routes with a long 'walk-in' on track roads, hill tracks and otherwise bike-negotiable paths. The greatest benefit is usually felt when coasting back along the inevitably downhill route on the return.

By boat

A couple of the routes in this guidebook include options to use 'water taxis' to get to and from the start and finish of walks and there are certainly a couple of other routes that can be adapted to do so.

None of the routes included here requires the use of a kayak, canoe or packraft to navigate coastal or inshore waters at the start/finish of a walk, although there is scope for adapting some of the routes. There is so much water in and around the Highlands and Islands that it makes sense to think about water-borne approaches when planning your own routes. Obviously, a necessary degree of competence, experience and proper equipment are required before tackling coastal waters, freshwater lochs and other bodies of water under your own steam, so to speak.

EQUIPPING FOR SCOTLAND'S BACKCOUNTRY

For many of the more remote routes in this book, we'd hope that you'd already have some experience in clothing, self-reliance and camp-craft for Scottish conditions. That said, it might be useful to share some thoughts on general principles.

Clothing and equipment should reflect the expected conditions and terrain.

Conditions

In general terms, the Scottish climate is temperate and Atlantic facing. For those new to the country, that translates as cold, wet and windy! Prolonged exposure to our climate carries a higher risk of hypothermia, which can and does kill.

It's a truism that Scotland only has two seasons: winter, and the other three. 'Three-season' Scottish weather is temperamental – sunny one minute, hailing the next, so keeping warm and dry can be challenging, especially on multi-day routes. On the highest ground, wind speeds can achieve 100mph or more, and it can snow at any time of the year.

▲ Looking east from the Bealach a' Bhuirich (Route 22)

Winter begins in earnest in January and could last through until June on the tops. Prior to that, October to December will often see fierce storms and this, alongside much shorter daylight hours, can make for difficult and uncomfortable backpacking. March, May and September are often fairer months, with longer hours of daylight and without bothersome insects.

The winter season, especially off trail, requires mountaineering equipment, skills and experience.

Terrain

Much of the terrain covered in this book is rough and off trail, and you should equip with that in mind. You will meet river crossings without bridges, steep ground, bog, snow and ice. Your kit should be tried and tested, wind and water resistant, and durable. It needn't be heavy, but given how far you might be from help, you'll need to trust it and have the skills to use it. On a more reassuring note, the country's Ordnance Survey mapping is generally very accurate.

Three-season clothing

Feet and legs

Some prefer trail shoes, others prefer boots. Scottish conditions and terrain mean it's almost impossible to keep your feet completely dry over a number of days, so bear in mind that simple leather boots or unlined trail shoes will drain more quickly than those lined with a (so-called) 'waterproof' membrane. A lined shoe doesn't prevent water ingress forever, but it does prevent its escape, and this can cause blisters and infection.

EQUIPPING FOR SCOTLAND'S BACKCOUNTRY

▲ Crossing a burn, Jura (Route 4)

If you opt for leather boots, then full gaiters can be useful to slow down the inevitable. Even those wearing trail shoes may find low-profile running gaiters useful to prevent gravel and heather entering shoes and socks.

Wool socks are usually best, perhaps with a synthetic liner in winter. Wool retains some insulating properties when wet or damp, and will also resist odour, at least for a day or two. Trail shoe wearers may find a pair of thin neoprene socks worn over their wool socks a useful way of preventing frost nip in early spring and late autumn.

Layering

Practise a layering system. Layers allow you to regulate your temperature, remain drier (from either rain or sweat) for longer and reduce your risk of hypothermia through evaporation, by controlling the breathability of your clothing and reducing wind-chill.

The layering system requires a baselayer, a midlayer (fleece or other insulator) and an outer shell (waterproof). Increasingly the science recommends a fourth, windproof layer as well, placed between the insulator and shell layers. Add or remove layers as required during the day.

It's helpful to know that natural and synthetic materials have different properties. Synthetics generally dry faster and are cooler, so may suit high summer and deep winter (for different reasons). For longer trips, merino wool will resist odour for longer and cover a wider range of temperatures, but takes a little longer to dry.

Head and hands

Hats and gloves may seem basic but are essential in reducing wind-chill. It's useful to have at least a couple of sets as they are easily lost or blown away. The layering system can also be applied to gloves – a liner and an outer or mitt – to improve protection from the elements. 'Beanie' hats are useful as they sit well under a shell hood, and peaked caps can provide structure to the same and shield the eyes from bright sun or heavy rain.

Camp clothes

It's useful to have a complete dry set of clothes for camp – thermals, socks (including perhaps another waterproof pair to wear inside wet footwear, in case of a call of nature), and perhaps an additional insulation layer. Being cold and wet overnight is not an option.

EQUIPPING FOR SCOTLAND'S BACKCOUNTRY

Drybags

A backpacking essential. Pack your sleeping bag and sleeping clothes into these, and make sure they are fully waterproof. Don't expect items stored in plastic bags to stay dry in a downpour. A drybag is your last line of defence between some level of basic comfort and abject misery, or worse.

Walking poles

Walking poles or a walking stick can be useful for river and bog crossings, to 'feel out' terrain you cannot see with the naked eye. They also help maintain an upright posture when carrying a heavy pack and reduce the risk of knee injury from prolonged descents.

Three-season camping

Tents

These vary wildly in design, price, weight and weatherproofness. Whatever you use, make sure it's wind resistant and waterproof – in short suited to the conditions in which you want to take it!

Pitch the narrow end of your tent or shelter into the wind, with the doorway facing away. Note that in high corries or glens, the wind direction may change overnight (or every ten minutes in the Hebrides!).

A mixed tent peg set can be useful for the wide range of ground (from boggy to stony) that you'll experience in Scotland – don't expect the 'toothpicks' supplied with some lightweight models to work every time.

Sleeping mats and bags

A sleeping mat reduces heat conduction, the greatest source of heat loss when you are in your tent or shelter. The good ones will have an 'R value'. Look for R1.5–3 for three-season conditions, and above that for winter. Mats can be stacked to improve protection from cold ground.

Sleeping bags sadly lack a uniform gauge of warmth across brands, but most will have a 'comfort' and a 'limit' rating. Again, there are natural or synthetic options, and both have pros and cons, but don't expect to have a comfortable night sleeping at your bag's 'limit'!

It may be worth spending a little more on a solid shelter and warmer sleeping bag, so as to enjoy rather than endure your wild camp.

◀ A bealach bivi north of Loch Mullardoch

SCOTTISH WILD COUNTRY BACKPACKING

Hot food and drink

While the authors have very different gear lists, we are all great fans of hot food and drink while backpacking! Given sometimes challenging weather and terrain, hot food and drink is not only a way to replenish lost calories but a huge morale boost – something to look forward to at the end of a tiring day in the open.

Everyone's preferences are different, but wet food is heavy. While there is a bewildering array of dehydrated meals on offer from outdoor shops, simple things like noodles, couscous, quick-cook rice or pasta plus a little olive oil and spices can go a long way. This can be augmented with dried meat (such as chorizo), cheese and vegetables. Porridge or muesli for breakfast can be made with dried milk or water. Flatbreads or oatcakes with salami and/or cheese work fine for lunch. Sachets of soup are excellent to replenish salts and can be drunk as usual or used to make a sauce for a main meal.

How to cook? One of the joys of this simple food is that backcountry 'cooking' can be limited to boiling water. As with everything, there's a wide array of stoves available, from gas to alcohol, petrol to wood.

However, please make 100% sure the hot parts of your stove are completely isolated from the ground, as wildfires are increasingly common. Use a foil tray or a flat stone to do this.

Under no circumstances should you use any wood found locally – either alive or dead. Scotland's tree cover is woefully depleted and even deadwood supplies valuable habitat and nutrients for invertebrates and birdlife. The only exception to this might be for some of the coastal routes in this book, when tidal driftwood could be used for a small fire. It is not sensible to rely on its availability though, so plan to bring your own fuel.

WATER

Scotland is blessed with abundant and mostly very clean natural water. Sometimes you will curse how abundant it is! This means purification is rarely needed, except when near agricultural land or urban settlements. However, it is useful to have the ability to carry water. You may want to camp high on a mountain without a stream (or 'burn') nearby or be walking one of the coastal routes where fresh water is scarcer. If you are eating dehydrated food, then access to water is even more important.

Be prepared to carry an additional 2–3 litres in capacity for such circumstances. Useful for this are the folding plastic water containers which pack down small and weigh very little.

▲ Cooking by headtorch, Bearnais bothy

EQUIPPING FOR SCOTLAND'S BACKCOUNTRY

▲ Descending to the arete of Stob Coire Dheirg (Route 1)

In addition
You will also need a headtorch (fully charged if rechargeable and spare batteries otherwise), a small first-aid kit (see 'Safety and emergencies') and the ability to use it, plus a map and compass and the ability to use it. Do not exclusively rely on smartphone mapping or GPS units, as they can suffer from power loss and failure. Part of enjoying remote wild places is in becoming self-sufficient – don't self-sabotage or short change your own experience.

Backpacking in winter
You will need axe, crampons and ski goggles, as well as additional insulating layers, and extra pairs of gloves. For the routes presented here, you should be well versed in how to use this extra equipment.

Winter travel may demand warmer, stiffer footwear, and full gaiters are recommended to prevent snow and water entering your boots. Winter backpacking is the fine art of keeping dry. Sweat will make clothing damp and snow will melt next to your skin – both can refreeze and markedly reduce the effectiveness of your layering and insulation, especially over a few days.

For camping, an avalanche shovel and a few wide-profile snow stakes can prove invaluable. Consider whether your sleeping bag is warm enough for minus double digits and whether your shelter can withstand 50mph winds or several inches of overnight snowfall. As always, equip and plan according to prevailing conditions.

SCOTTISH WILD COUNTRY BACKPACKING

USING BOTHIES

There are a number of bothies included in the routes in this book. Bothies are 'simple shelters provided for the use and benefit of all those who love wild and lonely places', says the Mountain Bothy Association (MBA). They are basic and privately owned buildings, repaired and maintained by volunteers and fellow hill-goers. Don't expect running water, flushing toilets or electricity. If you are lucky there will be a good roof and windows. Some of them may have a fireplace or stove, but you'll need to bring in your own wood or coal.

When using them, please obey the following code:

Respect Other Users Please leave the bothy clean and tidy with dry kindling for the next visitors. Make other visitors welcome and be considerate to other users.

Respect the Bothy Tell the MBA about any accidental damage. Don't leave graffiti or vandalise the bothy. Please take out all rubbish which you can't burn. Avoid burying rubbish; this pollutes the environment. Please don't leave perishable food as this attracts vermin. Guard against fire risk and ensure the fire is out before you leave. Make sure the doors and windows are properly closed when you leave.

Respect the Surroundings If there is no toilet at the bothy please bury human waste out of sight. Use the spade provided, keep well away from the water supply and never use the vicinity of the bothy as a toilet. Never cut live wood or damage estate property. Use fuel sparingly.

Respect Agreement with the Estate Please observe any restrictions on use of the bothy, for example during deer stalking or at lambing time. Please remember bothies are available for short stays only. The owner's permission must be obtained if you intend an extended stay.

Respect the Restriction on Numbers Because of overcrowding and lack of facilities, large groups (6 or more) should not use a bothy. Bothies are not available for commercial groups.

▲ *Top*: The new Camasunary bothy at the foot of Blàbheinn's north-west ridge (Route 6); *Bottom:* Drying out at Ruantallain bothy, Jura (Route 4)

BACKPACKING WITH DOGS

Some dogs love backpacking and having your furry friends along on a trip can really enhance the experience. However, there are a few points to remember when hitting the trails with canine companions.

Dogs need to be on a lead and/or under close control in the vicinity of livestock. Ewes in lamb can be stressed to the point of aborting if worried by dogs, and cows with calves can become dangerously aggressive.

Even where there is no livestock you will likely encounter wild animals such as deer and goats. Again, keep your dog leashed/under close control as it could kill or maul a wild animal or it may itself get injured or lost in pursuit. Be aware of seals also; very occasionally dogs are killed by seals in the water. In remote coastal areas you may encounter female seals hauled out on the shore with their pups, usually between October and December. In Scotland, feral goat kids are usually born in January and fallow, roe and red deer calve variously between mid-May and mid-July. Ground-nesting birds are particularly vulnerable to curious dogs so you are wise to keep dogs on a lead in upland and coastal areas during the spring months.

An adder bite could kill a small dog or immobilise a larger beast. Antihistamines help to slow the spread of venom and certain brands can be administered according to the dog's relative weight. Check with a vet. Deer ticks are found where there are deer – so almost everywhere in the Highlands and on many islands also. Your dog may be treated already or you may want to use a spot-on repellent or tick collar. Otherwise feel through their coats regularly and remove any attached ticks with tick tweezers or thumb and index fingernails. Dunking your dog in the sea/river/loch at the end of the day will help.

When off the lead your dog will cover many more miles than you – don't let them overdo it. Though characteristically robust, dogs will suffer from prolonged exposure to heat, cold and wet; make sure they have frequent access to water and that they can be kept warm at rest.

Bury your dog's poos away from water courses.

▲ *Top*: Backpacking doggo; *Bottom*: Icy conditions, falling snow and poor visibility, Uig Hills, Lewis (Route 29)

▲ A bealach camp on Streap (Route 3)

ENVIRONMENTAL IMPACT AND LEAVE NO TRACE

There is no excuse whatsoever for littering wild places. That includes ALL food and drink wrappers and containers, which should be 'packed out' with you.

This also includes going to the toilet in the hills. In some places, groundwater may be contaminated by bad practice. The solution is to carry a trowel (or use a tent peg or walking pole) dig a deep hole at least 75m away from running water, do your worst and then completely bury it. Plan ahead, and don't get caught short – it can take some time to find a place that suits. Remove all toilet paper and carry it out in a bespoke bag or container. Burning it with a lighter rarely works in our windy, rainy weather, and if it's dry enough to burn, 1) you might start a ground fire, and 2) you are dehydrated! If you are making use of the bothies, a spade and instructions are usually provided. Use both.

When cleaning cups, pans or yourself, do not wash directly in running water, as others may need to drink from the source further downstream. Wash away from the stream or river and dispose of the grey water away from the source. Use organic and biodegradable soaps and toothpaste (or just plain water). Avoid overcooking, and if you do have waste food at the end of a meal, pack all of it out with you in a rubbish sack or zip-lock bag.

Camp on durable, well-drained ground and avoid commonly used campsite areas. Any stones removed to erect a shelter should be replaced when you leave. When you leave, there should be zero trace of you having stayed overnight.

The increased popularity of outdoor activities has led to increased footfall and erosion. We can all help to mitigate some of this damage by wearing lighter footwear, carrying the right amount of kit and practising Leave No Trace.

There is plenty of information online on Leave No Trace principles as they apply in the UK. Please take this as seriously as you plan the rest of your trip; other people's challenge and enjoyment is every bit as important as yours.

MAPS AND ROUTE FINDING

MAPS AND ROUTE-FINDING

It is essential that you carry the relevant maps and a compass (even if you have a GPS) when following the routes in this guidebook. A wristwatch altimeter is also useful for navigation, especially in the hills. There are few waymarkers, signposts or even paths of any kind on many of the walks, making accurate route-finding all the more important. This is particularly the case in mountainous areas of the Highlands and Islands which are prone to mist and cloud cover. It's not quite so easy to get lost when walking along coastline, but it is always worth knowing exactly where you are, particularly in poor weather and low visibility, especially if for any reason you need to head inland or seek shelter.

Anyone attempting the routes in this guidebook should have a good level of navigational competence. If not, do a course or read-up and practise before exposing yourself to unnecessary risk in a challenging environment. A good place to start is Pete Hawkins' *Navigation: Techniques and Skills for Walkers*, Cicerone, 2017.

This guide incorporates 1:100,000 mapping with highlighted routes; these should be used in conjunction with OS 1:25,000 or 1:50,000 maps or Harvey 1:25,000 maps because of the greater topographic detail. Do not rely solely on the maps in this guidebook as it is essential that you can ascertain your position in the wider context, should you need to abandon your walk and make for the nearest road or settlement. The relevant maps are given in the information box for each route.

Deer-stalking season

In those areas where deer are culled it is advisable to contact the estates where you will be walking during the deer-stalking season, which runs from 1 July until 15 February, both for your own safety and as a matter of courtesy. The contact numbers for the relevant estates are included in the information boxes for the routes affected.

▲ *Left*: Planning the way ahead; *Right*: The bypass path on the turrets of Sgùrr a' Chaorachain (Route 15)

CAMPFIRES

After a day of blazing trails through the landscape, the idea of a brew or dram by a crackling campfire, or while gazing at the glowing embers in a bothy hearth can be very appealing. However, there are a number of important considerations to be made before doing so. Few disasters are more avoidable than causing wildfires, burning down bothies or vandalising woodland. Sadly, instances of all of these are on the increase in Scotland's great outdoors.

Because much of Scotland's uplands are cloaked in peat, which is a very combustible soil when dry, there are only a few places where having a campfire is either safe, practical, acceptable or advisable. Beaches, riverbanks and loch edges are preferable, where there is plentiful driftwood and/or you've carried in your own fuel. Never cut live wood and don't use all the dead wood from the ground, as it forms part of habitat lifecycles. If you're planning on firing-up the stove or hearth in a bothy then carry in your own wood and coal – use any driftwood or peats supplied sparingly.

Treating campfires as an occasional luxury rather than a necessity – which it seldom is – already goes some way to making them more sustainable. Being considerate and safety conscious reduces the risk of a fire getting out of control

Here's a handy checklist for al fresco pyrophiles:

- Use a stove whenever possible.
- If you do make a fire, make it on stones, sand or shingle.
- Below the tideline is best.
- Make it small, certainly no bigger than two hand widths long on each square side.
- Always better to make new friends than a new fire circle. Never make a new fire circle when you could use or share another one close by. Never ever cut live trees – they don't burn anyway!
- If you plan on making a fire, always take wood or coal in with you.
- Never make a fire on peaty soil when there is a strong breeze or in periods of dry weather.
- Never ever make fires on the open hillside, high on the hilltops or in woodland.
- Never leave a fire unattended.
- Have a plentiful supply of water to hand to douse the flames.
- Clear all trace of your fire. Scorch marks are to be avoided at all costs. No-one should be able to tell you have had a fire once you leave.

SAFETY AND EMERGENCIES

All the walks in this guidebook are demanding, some extremely so, and arguably are best not attempted alone. They should only be undertaken by fit and experienced walkers and are not suitable for the very unfit, small children or anyone carrying an injury. The degree of difficulty is provided in the information boxes at the beginning of each route.

In the mountains and remote areas, as well as the first-aid kit (see below) you should carry a survival blanket, mobile phone and extra food. Carry spare layers and wear at least one item of high-visibility clothing. A whistle and/or torch are important for attracting attention in case of injury – six blasts on the whistle or six torch flashes should be repeated every minute.

Consider carrying a personal locator beacon (PLB; see Emergencies, below), especially if you are on your own and/or backpacking in a very remote area where mobile phone coverage may be patchy or non-existent: www.mountainsafety.co.uk/EP-PLB.aspx.

Mountain weather

In fine weather the Highlands and Islands may seem like an earthly paradise; however, the onset of high winds and driving rain, sleet or snow can rapidly make the place feel quite hellish, especially if you are exposed to the elements. Becoming cold and wet rapidly drains body heat, which can lead to hypothermia. The early symptoms of exposure are often abbreviated to 'Fumbles, Mumbles and Stumbles' – keep an eye out for shivering, confusion, drowsiness, slurred speech and the onset of clumsiness, in yourself or your companions.

It is very important that you are properly equipped and are able to navigate proficiently in poor visibility. Check weather forecasts before setting out and allow yourself plenty of time to complete your route. Be aware of the available daylight hours. Always let someone know your intended route and estimated time of completion.

Mountaintop views in Scotland combine land, sky, lochs and sea to dramatic effect – handsomely rewarding the effort of climbing. However, mountainous terrain attracts mist and cloud cover, making route-finding difficult – especially where paths are vague or non-existent. Furthermore, high winds and driving rain or snow can blow in with little warning; exposure at altitude can quickly become life-threatening. In winter, if there is more than a dusting of snow on the mountains (which can also occur in autumn and spring) you may need to carry an ice axe and crampons with you (and know how to use them). Be aware of avalanche risk – slopes between 25° and 45° are most at risk – and snow cornices on ridge crests. *Avalanche!* by Roberto Bolognesi (Cicerone, 2007 – out of print) is a useful guide to assessing risk and reducing danger.

The Mountain Weather Information Service (MWIS) provides forecasts for Scotland's mountain areas at www.mwis.org.uk. The Scotland Avalanche Information Service (SAIS) does what the name suggests: www.sais.gov.uk.

River crossings

Heavy rain and snow melt makes burns and rivers run very high with a terrific volume of fast-moving water. This is especially the case in the mountainous areas. Do not attempt to cross rivers in spate – if you are swept away your chances of survival are very small. If you're successful in crossing one river in such conditions you may come up against an impassable torrent further on; if you then attempt to recross the river you previously crossed, you may find that it is running higher and faster than before.

Fast-flowing water deeper than knee depth is dangerous. Never cross upstream of waterfalls or boulders that you might be swept onto. Ensure that essential items – including dry clothes – are sealed in a waterproof bag. Undo your rucksack's hip and chest straps for quick release in case you should fall in. Do not attempt to cross barefoot – if you want to avoid wet boots consider carrying Crocs or trainers for this purpose. If you're not confident of your ability to get across a river safely turn around and live to complete the walk another day.

▶ Stepping stones across a burn, Rùm (Route 5)

If very wet weather is expected when you plan to head out, you should consider adapting your route and seeking alternatives in case you encounter dangerously fast-moving and/or deep river crossings.

First-aid kit
At a minimum this should include a survival blanket, a couple of wound dressings, plasters, antiseptic topical cream, a bandage sling, steri-strips, anti-inflammatory painkillers, Imodium tablets or similar for diarrhoea and electrolyte powder for rehydration. Antihistamine tablets are useful for allergic reactions, all manner of bites and stings, including adder bites, which can be extremely serious if you're in a remote place with a leg that won't work. Some antihistamines can also be given to dogs bitten by adders – dose proportionate to the dog's weight.

Emergencies
There is a long tradition of self-reliance and self-sufficiency in our mountain culture. This is part and parcel of what makes backpacking in the Highlands and Islands such a unique experience. But it also means you should assume that you will have to self-rescue and you should plan and travel accordingly.

It is advisable that you have some practical knowledge of first aid before heading into remote, difficult to access areas. In case of injury or other incident, try to stay calm and assess your situation. Try to ascertain your exact position on the map and consider your options for walking to safety, finding shelter, staying put or seeking help. Remember that it may take an emergency team some hours to reach you, especially in poor conditions in a remote area.

▲ Looking over Loch Shiel, north east of Meall nan Creag Leac (Route 2)

USING THIS GUIDE

Mountain Rescue in the UK hills is undertaken by volunteers – albeit working at a high level of professionalism – who, without payment, help save lives while risking their own. They are organised and assisted by the Police.

Before you set off, register your phone with emergency SMS, and understand how this system works: http://www.emergencysms.org.uk/registering_your_mobile_phone.php.

You may also consider carrying a personal locator beacon (PLB). This is an electronic transmitting device that, once activated, will alert rescue services to a life-threatening situation in the air, on water or in remote areas.

If you or a companion is injured and you need to call for help, call 999 and ask for Police, then MOUNTAIN RESCUE.

Then give the following details:

- Location (with a grid reference if possible)
- Name, gender and age of the casualty
- Nature of injuries or emergency
- The number of people in the group
- Your mobile phone number

Then, stay where you are until you are found.

USING THIS GUIDE

The numbered routes are marked on an overview map at the front of the book.

Maps

This guide incorporates 1:100,000 mapping with highlighted routes; these should be used in conjunction with OS Explorer (1:25,000) or Landranger (1:50,000) maps or Harvey Superwalker (1:25,000) maps – because of the greater topographic detail. Do not rely solely on the maps in this guidebook as it is essential that you can ascertain your position in the wider context, should you need to abandon your walk and make for the nearest road or settlement. The relevant maps are given in the information box for each route.

Route information boxes

The degree of difficulty (in terms of distance, ascent, terrain) of each walk is made clear in the information boxes at the beginning of each route. The maps covering the route and the start/finish points (with grid references) are also given. The total distance (including any variants) of each walk is given in kilometres and miles. A rough timing is given for each route, which is estimated for walkers with a good level of fitness and does not include stopping for breaks – weather and ground conditions will also affect progress on a walk. Total ascents are given in metres and feet and are worth checking and metabolising before you set out. The nature of the terrain is also briefly described in the information boxes and any potential difficulties are flagged up (see also Route introductions, below). Public transport to and from the routes is included where it exists. Other important points to note, such as estate contact details for use during the deer-stalking season, are also included. The boxes also list the summits visited en route: an (M) denotes a Munro, a (C) a Corbett.

Key figures from the route information boxes are also included in the route summary table at the beginning of the book.

WHAT'S IN A NAME? MUNROS AND CORBETTS

The 'Munros' are the 282 Scottish hills over 3000 feet (914.4m), named after Sir Hugh Munro, who first listed them. 'Corbetts' are hills of between 2500 and 3000 feet (762–914.4m) that also have a descent of 500 feet (152.4m) on all sides. There are 222 of them in Scotland, a list named after its compiler, John Rooke Corbett. Corbett went on to explore these mountains after becoming the first Englishman to complete all the 'Munros'.

Corbetts are often more challenging than Munros. They are not as frequently visited and often lack paths altogether, so navigation and terrain can be more demanding. The 500-foot (152.4m) descent on all sides also means they stand alone, sometimes making for tougher going.

Munros and Corbetts visited by these routes are identified in the route information boxes and listed in Appendix A.

USING THIS GUIDE

Route introductions
Each route description is prefaced with an introduction – usually a couple of paragraphs – which gives an overview of the walk and what to expect, including access, the terrain encountered, the degree of strenuousness and any potential difficulties or obstacles – such as river crossings and areas of navigational difficulty. Highlights and points of interest are also covered, variously including sites of historical, geological or botanical interest as well as wildlife that might be encountered en route.

Route descriptions
Most of the routes in this book are without waymarkers of any kind; in some instances paths are vague or even non-existent. Therefore, each of the walks is described in sufficient detail to enable the user to follow the route with relative ease. Natural and man-made features are regularly referenced in the route descriptions. Grid references are also given where deemed useful or necessary in most of the route descriptions; a grid reference for the start/finish points is also given in the information box for each route. Altitudes are given in metres, abbreviated to m, for example '750m'. Distances along the ground are given in metres, fully spelled out, for example '100 metres'.

Appendices
At the back of the book, three appendices provide a table of Munros and Corbetts, a Scottish Gaelic–English glossary and a further reading bibliography.

GPX tracks
GPX tracks for the routes in this guidebook are available to download free at www.cicerone.co.uk/904/GPX. If you have not bought the book through the Cicerone website, or have bought the book without opening an account, please register your purchase in your Cicerone library by logging into your account or registering for one if you have not done so already to access GPX and update information.

A GPS device is an excellent aid to navigation, but you should also carry a map and compass and know how to use them. GPX files are provided in good faith, but in view of the profusion of formats and devices, neither the authors nor the publisher accepts responsibility for their use. We provide files in a single standard GPX format that works on most devices and systems, but you may need to convert files to your preferred format using a GPX converter, such as www.gpsvisualizer.com or one of the many other apps and online converters available.

GAELIC PLACE-NAME ELEMENTS

The following Gaelic terms occur frequently in the route description. For a more comprehensive list of Gaelic place-name elements, see the glossary at the back of the book.

- *bealach* = pass, gap
- *lochan* = a small loch (lake)
- *allt* = burn, stream
- *abhainn* = river

◀ Rugged coastline at Bàgh Uamh nan Giall, northwest Jura (Route 4)

WESTERN HIGHLANDS AND INNER HEBRIDES

◀ Harris Bay with the Rùm Cuillin forming the backdrop (Route 5)

SCOTTISH WILD COUNTRY BACKPACKING

ROUTE 1
The Glen Etive Five

Start/finish	Informal car park on the Glen Etive road (NN 136 468)
Total distance	26.5km (16½ miles)
Total ascent	2485m (8150ft)
Time	1 very long day or 2 more leisurely/winter days
Terrain	Track, rough path, steep slopes and one short but moderately airy scramble.
Key summits	Ben Starav 1078m (M), Beinn nan Aighenan 960m (M), Glas Bheinn Mhòr 997m (M), Stob Coir' an Albannaich 1044m (M), Meall nan Eun 929m (M)
Maps	OS Explorer 377 Loch Etive & Glen Orchy; OS Landranger 50 Glen Orchy & Loch Etive
Note	Work is under way on several run-of-river hydro developments which will impact on the walk in and out, in the future.

Glen Etive is a spectacular and relatively accessible place, and is deservedly popular with walkers, kayakers and campervan enthusiasts, but away from the busy single-track road, there is a palpable sense of remoteness and solitude. Old shielings line the rivers as water tumbles freely through natural gullies and over granite slabs, while birch and pine cling to the steep-sided hills. Go higher and you'll find a wealth of fine, rocky summits linked by short arêtes and *bealaichean* (mountain passes) strewn with glacial erratics, with some of the finest views in the Southern Highlands.

Etive is a great example of Scottish wild country; a tightly woven mix of nature and culture. Alongside the riches described above, it's stuffed full of Irish mythology, old drove roads and song-poems by 18th-century bards (see below). Along with neighbouring Glen Coe, it was originally earmarked as a National Park. Although it is recognised as a National Scenic Area, protected for its 'wild land' qualities as well as for being a breeding ground for golden eagles, it has recently seen the development of run-of-river hydro schemes.

Glen Etive makes an early appearance in Irish mythology as a rich and fertile farming settlement where humans lived in balance with nature. It is described in Deirdre of the Sorrows, a ballad sung by the tragic heroine Deirdre as a "Fruitful glen of pools and fishes… Glen of hawks, blue eyed, crying."

According to Irish literature, Deirdre escaped betrothal to Ulster's King Conchabar by fleeing to Scotland and founding Glen Etive along with her lover, Naoise. They were later joined by Naoise's brothers and their partners, finding peace in the valley. When they eventually returned to Ireland, all were murdered by the king for their disobedience. Deirdre committed suicide rather than marry him.

▶ Showers and a rainbow looking east from camp under Beinn nan Aighenan

ROUTE 1 – THE GLEN ETIVE FIVE

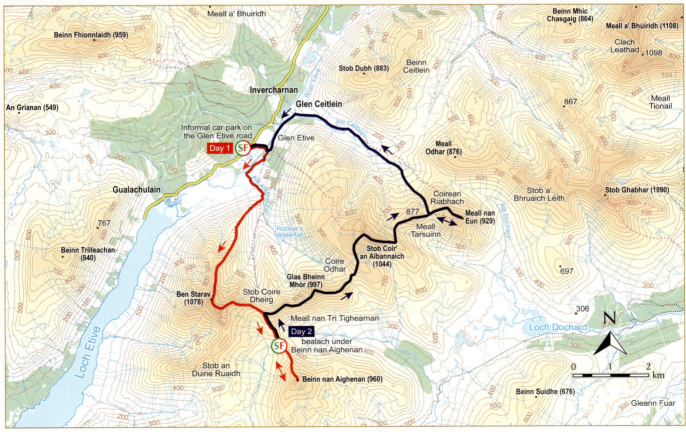

DAY 1
Car park for Ben Starav to bealach camp

Start	Informal car park for Ben Starav (NN 136 468)
Distance	11km (6¾ miles)
Total ascent	1445m (4740ft)
Time	6–8hr
Summits	Ben Starav 1078m (M), Stob Coire Dheirg 998m, Beinn nan Aighenan 960 (M)

Exit right from the small parking area and head towards the loch for a few metres. Take a left through a gate onto a track, which descends to a bridge over the **River Etive**. Cross the bridge and turn right, following signage directing walkers around the fenced enclosure of the smallholding of Coileitir on an extremely boggy path. Relocating the riverside path, follow it to a footbridge over **Allt a' Mheuran**. Cross this and turn left, following the track alongside this river, up towards the enormous north ridge of Ben Starav. There are some beautiful pools here of the kind alluded to in the song-poem Deirdre of the Sorrows.

Where the path splits, take a right fork onto the north ridge and follow it for nearly 3km to the summit.

The corrie bowl to your left was a hiding place for reivers (cattle thieves) who would ambush traders and their herds on the drove road between Fort William and the south – note the Robber's Waterfall marked on the OS map.

It's a long, tiring climb and the final metres to the flat summit of **Ben Starav** (1078m) are stony and steep.

Continue southeast around the head of Coire an Fhir Lèith and descend to a thin, blocky arête which joins Starav with Stob Coire Dheirg. The arête is a moderately exposed but non-technical scramble best tackled with a fair head for heights and with walking poles and cameras stowed away. After the summit of **Stob Coire Dheirg** (998m), descend easily, taking a faint path that forks right onto the *bealach* which adjoins the next Munro of **Beinn nan Aighenan** (960m). Cross here and ascend approximately 300m to its summit, using a rough path tucked in slightly to the east of the mountain's northerly spur. Return to the *bealach* for an atmospheric camp in beautifully remote surroundings. There is usually plentiful water nearby.

▲ Loch Etive from the climb of Beinn nan Aighenan

ROUTE 1 – THE GLEN ETIVE FIVE

▲ The bealach descent to Glen Ceitlein

DAY 2
Bealach camp to car park for Ben Starav

Start	Camp at *bealach* (in the vicinity of NN 143 416)
Distance	16km (10 miles)
Total ascent	1045m (3430ft)
Time	6–8hr
Summits	Meall nan Trì Tighearnan, Glas Bheinn Mhòr 997m (M), Stob Coir' an Albannaich 1044m (M), Meall Tarsuinn 877m, Meall nan Eun 929m (M)

Rejoin the trail to the north and then continue in a northeasterly direction on a broad grassy ridge over **Meall nan Trì Tighearnan**, to the bulky Munro of **Glas Bheinn Mhòr** (997m). Descend east over rockier terrain to the *bealach* at the head of **Coire Odhar**. Climb the switchback path to the north, accessing a large, sloping plateau under our fourth Munro. The summit of **Stob Coir' an Albannaich** (1044m) is a veritable crow's nest, with superlative views back to Ben Starav and the route so far.

Carefully descend its sharp, easterly ridge and, where the slope eases, turn left and descend a clear rake north to another flattened area dotted with pools and glacial erratics, which offers good views southeast to Loch Dochard. Go over **Meall Tarsuinn** (877m) and cross another *bealach*, from which you will shortly make your escape. Climb the slopes of **Meall nan Eun** (929m) and head southeast for its rather nondescript summit.

Return to the *bealach* (between Meall nan Eun and Meall Tarsuinn) and descend northwest, following the burn into **Coirean Riabhach**. The headwaters of Allt Ceitlein are wonderfully dynamic, bubbling vigorously through deep natural channels before dispersing over smooth granite slabs.

Further down the atmospheric Glen Ceitlein you'll find remains of summer shielings. It's here, in the well-known 18th-century song-poem Song of the Ewe that the gamekeeper and bard Donnchadh Bàn Mac an t-soir (anglicised to Duncan Ban Macintrye) partakes of whisky from a scallop shell. His poem is in the tradition of a 'waulking' song, usually sung by women as they washed and compressed woollen cloth at a table. Scotland has one of the largest repertoires of these songs in the world. In 'The Song of the Ewe', Donnchadh Bàn has fallen on hard times. A fox has killed a prize sheep and so he asks his neighbours for their help. The song follows him as he circles the community asking for gifts of wool to make a coat. It's the story of the people he meets and the places he visits on the way – a *songline* in which people and place are completely intertwined.

Crossing the bridge at the foot of **Glen Ceitlein**, head southwest on a track to a wooded junction just before the house at Coileitir. Turn right, cross the bridge over the **River Etive** and return to the car park.

SCOTTISH WILD COUNTRY BACKPACKING

ROUTE 2

Fort William to Glenfinnan via north Ardgour

The mountainous district of Ardgour may be separated from Fort William by a narrow stretch of sea loch, but the contrast between the two shores couldn't be greater. Once across the water on the tiny passenger ferry, the bustling town, the tourist-thronged bulk of Ben Nevis, and the roar of the A82 are left far behind. Here is solitude, peace and many miles of unfrequented mountain country.

There is a wonderful sense of completeness about the landscape. Rugged peaks and ridges are complemented by wide glens, birch-clad hillsides and riotous rivers fringed by fragments of ancient Atlantic oak and Caledonian pine. Deer roam the hills and otters patrol the riverbanks. The views are grand too: gazing south into the heart of Ardgour, you'll see there's much more to explore, and the route described here is but a taste of what this area has to offer.

Finding campsites can be tricky as the terrain is often boggy. Drier ground can often be found higher up the hillsides, or around stands of old Scots pine trees. There are no serious river crossings. The Cona River is spanned by a footbridge that is perfectly placed for this route. It is, however, always a good idea to search online for up-to-date information about the state of local bridges, especially after stormy weather.

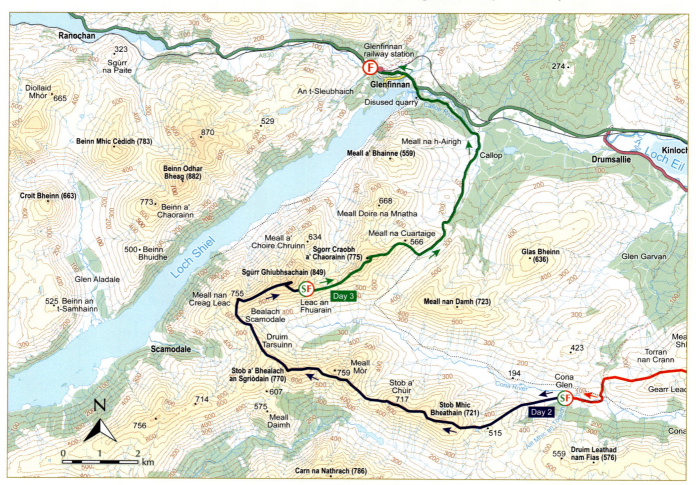

ROUTE 2 – FORT WILLIAM TO GLENFINNAN VIA NORTH ARDGOUR

Start	Camusnagaul Pier (NN 095 750). Caledonian MacBrayne operates a foot passenger ferry between Fort William (pier by the A82 at NN 099 738) and Camusnagaul
Finish	Glenfinnan railway station (NM 899 810) for trains between Mallaig and Fort William
Total distance	43km (26¾ miles)
Total ascent	2585m (8480ft)
Time	2–3 days
Terrain	Good paths and roads for the first and last few miles. Otherwise mainly rough, trackless mountain terrain.
Key summits	Stob Coire a' Chearcaill 771m (C), Stob a' Bhealach an Sgriòdain 770m (C), Sgùrr Ghiubhsachain 849m (C), Sgorr Craobh a' Chaorainn 775m (C)
Maps	OS Explorer 391 Ardgour & Strontian; OS Landranger 40 Mallaig & Glenfinnan and 41 Ben Nevis. The Explorer map names many more landscape features than the Landranger
Note	Strong walkers could complete this over 2 days but, given the need to synchronise with train and ferry timetables, 3 days allows the route to be savoured at an easier pace. Careful scouting along the banks of the Cona River should yield a campsite for the first night, while the shoulder east of Sgùrr Ghiubhsachain makes for a fine high camp on the second night.

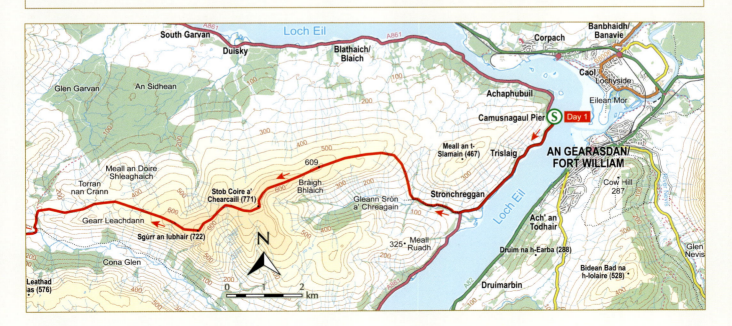

DAY 1
Camusnagaul Pier to Cona Glen

Start	Camusnagaul Pier (NN 095 750)
Distance	18.5km (11½ miles)
Total ascent	885m (2905ft)
Time	6–7hr
Summits	Stob Coire a' Chearcaill 771m (C), Sgùrr an Iubhair 722m

From the **pier**, follow the single-track A861 southwest. Just before the bridge over Abhainn Sròn a' Chreagain, turn right and take the track up the glen with its lively, tree-lined river. Stob Coire a' Chearcaill fills the view ahead. Throughout the day's walk, take time to appreciate the diversity of native woodland, from the Atlantic oakwood remnants around sea level, to the birch-clad hillsides of Coire a' Chearcaill, and Scots pines of Cona Glen.

After crossing the burn that drains Corran Dubh, leave the track and climb northwest up grassy slopes. Follow the easy moorland shoulder of **Bràigh Bhlàich** westwards for 3km, then bear south to climb more steeply to the summit of **Stob Coire a' Chearcaill** (771m).

For the next 6km the route descends gradually west, taking in **Sgùrr an Iubhair** (722m). The mountains of Ardgour fill the view across Cona Glen. To reach the path at the summit of the pass between Loch Eil and Cona Glen, bear west across the streamlets draining Coire Mhic Gill' a' Chamshronaich, between the spurs of **Torran nan Crann** and **Gearr Leachdann**. A couple of streams have carved quite deep gullies which require care in crossing.

Follow the path south to meet the track in **Cona Glen**. Cross the footbridge (NM 958 720) to the south bank and head west over some very boggy ground for 750 metres. There are patches of drier ground for camping among the old Scots pines around **Allt Mhic an Tòisich**.

▲ Descending into Cona Glen from Sgùrr an Iubhair

ROUTE 2 – FORT WILLIAM TO GLENFINNAN VIA NORTH ARDGOUR

DAY 2
Cona Glen to shoulder below Sgùrr Ghiubhsachain

Start	Allt Mhic an Tòisich, Cona Glen (NM 949 720)
Distance	13km (8 miles)
Total ascent	1405m (4610ft)
Time	7–8hr
Summits	Meall Mòr 759m and 763m, Stob a' Bhealach an Sgriòdain 770m (C), Sgùrr Ghiubhsachain 849m (C)

Climb southwest towards Cnap a' Choire Lèith Bhig, then a clutch of tarns at around 500m near the crest of the ridge. The massive pyramid of Sgùrr Dhomhnuill, the highest mountain in Ardgour, appears to the south.

The most testing part of the route lies ahead: around 9km northwest along a ridge with many ups and downs, much exposed rock and a number of tops. The twin summits of **Meall Mòr** (759m and 763m) can be skirted to the south, following faint deer trods across the steep hillside. The highest point, **Stob a' Bhealach an Sgriòdain** (770m; NM 875 727) is unnamed on the OS Landranger and Explorer maps, but has been named by the Scottish Mountaineering Club after the *bealach* 450 metres northwest of the summit. In autumn, during the red deer rut, linger on Stob a' Bhealach an Sgriòdain a while and thrill to the unearthly roars of the stags echoing around the corries.

Beyond Bealach an Sgriòdain, continue northwest over **Druim Tarsuinn** to the deep cleft of **Bealach Scamodale**. The subsequent lung-bursting climb is rewarded by a dramatic view over Loch Shiel to the mountains of Moidart.

On **Meall nan Creag Leac** (755m) the route turns abruptly east. A ridge leads in 1.25km to the rocky summit of **Sgùrr Ghiubhsachain** (849m).

On the way to the summit ridge of Sgùrr Ghiubhsachain, take a few careful steps to the left and trace the 28km length of inky-dark Loch Shiel far below. Only 10 metres above sea level, it was a sea loch until blocked by glacial deposits at the end of the last ice age.

Descending to the wide, level shoulder to the southeast requires care as the slopes immediately below the summit are steep and craggy. Retrace your steps west for 200 metres before descending southeast down easier slopes. Once on more level ground bear east. There is plenty of scope for camping on this shoulder, where some springs provide water.

▲ View from Stob a' Bhealach an Sgriòdain

DAY 3
Shoulder below Sgùrr Ghiubhsachain to Glenfinnan

Start	Leac an Fhuarain (NM 879 749)
Distance	11.5km (7¼ miles)
Total ascent	295m (9680ft)
Time	4–5hr
Summits	Sgorr Craobh a' Chaorainn 775m (C)

From the col east of **Sgùrr Ghiubhsachain**, climb towards **Sgorr Craobh a' Chaorainn** (775m) From the 722m point on the southwest shoulder, the summit appears an impregnable, craggy dome. Aim to the right then clamber up easier slopes to the top.

Descend east-northeast for 800 metres, extremely steeply at first. Before the ground rises again towards **Meall na Cuartaige** (566m), descend right to the path between Cona Glen and **Callop**. This soon becomes a track as you follow it northwards. After 4km, beyond the buildings at Callop, bear left onto a wide forestry road for 1.5km, staying south of the **Callop River**. At a **disused quarry** (NM 910 801) a path branches right and crosses the river by a footbridge, marked only on the OS Explorer map. Reach the A830 and follow it west into **Glenfinnan village**.

Glenfinnan may mark the end of your trip, but over 350 years ago it marked the start of another journey that ended on the battlefield of Culloden and changed the Highlands forever. On 19 August 1745, Prince Charles Edward Stuart, the 'Young Pretender', raised his standard here at the head of Loch Shiel, rallying an army of clansmen in what would prove to be the final attempt to reinstate the exiled Stuarts on the throne of Great Britain and Ireland. For the people of the Highlands, the significance of the Jacobite rebellion of '45 and its ultimate failure reached far beyond the elite politics and power play of the day. It heralded the destruction of the clan system and the end of a centuries-old way of life. Gaelic culture and language were supressed, the clan chiefs became unmoored from their land and people, and the glens were depopulated in the long attrition of the Highland Clearances that followed. There's a straight line between Glenfinnan and lonely grass-grown ruins you'll pass on your Highland journeys. As you cross the Glenfinnan Viaduct on the train back to Fort William, look out on your right for the monument constructed in 1815 to commemorate the raising of the standard, a memorial to beginnings and endings.

▲ Taking a breather overlooking Loch Shiel

ROUTE 3
Streap and Braigh nan Uamhachan

Start/finish	Car park on north side of A830 (NM 929 798)
Total distance	23km (14¼ miles)
Total ascent	1775m (5825ft)
Time	2 days
Terrain	Forestry tracks, intermittent, vague paths, grassy slopes, steep rock with one airy, vertiginous section.
Key summits	Streap 911m (C), Braigh nan Uamhachan 765m (C)
Maps	OS Explorer 398 Loch Morar & Mallaig; OS Landranger 40 Mallaig & Glenfinnan
Note	This route takes in a high camp, but it is also conveniently sized for a more leisurely weekend with a simple evening walk-in to Gleann Dubh Lighe bothy (NM 944 819). (It can also be extended to include the Munro of Gulvain (987m) to the east.) Low mileage and ascent figures belie the rough terrain underfoot.

▲ Streap's final approach

SCOTTISH WILD COUNTRY BACKPACKING

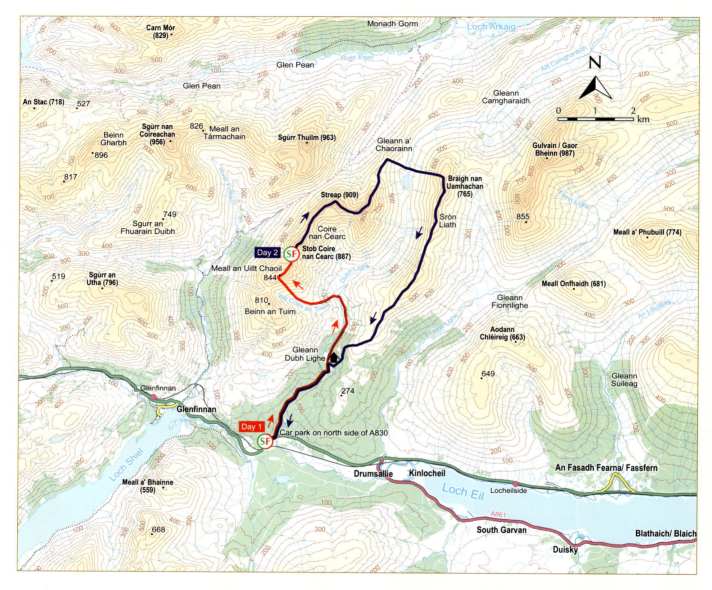

This brace of Corbetts is one of the finest shorter backpacking routes in the Central Highlands. Leaving the crowds of Glenfinnan behind, it incorporates a fine bothy, extensive shieling remains, and the summits of Streap – only five metres short of Munro status – and Braigh nan Uamhachan, one of the smallest Corbetts. Many treat the former as an out-and-back affair, but this is to miss out on an elegant snaking traverse of the entire mountain, a line which ebbs and flows, rises and falls with a rhythmic cadence.

Streap is a hill that deserves more than just a tick. Its Gaelic name means simply, 'climbing' – it's an evocation, a call to adventure. The full traverse of this Alp in miniature, especially in winter conditions, is both remote and challenging, high in ambience but relatively low in technicality. It's partnered here with a characterful but straightforward walk over the lesser top, offering an unusual perspective on Ardgour and Loch Shiel.

ROUTE 3 – STREAP AND BRAIGH NAN UAMHACHAN

DAY 1
Car park north of A830 to Bealach Coire nan Cearc

Start	Cragaig Estate car park (NM 929 798)
Distance	8km (5 miles)
Total ascent	890m (2920ft)
Time	3–4hr
Summits	Meall an Uillt Chaoil (844m)

From the **car park**, return to the road and head east for a short distance before turning left onto the estate track. Go through a gate and continue through forestry, following the course of **Dubh Lighe** with its many picturesque waterfalls. After around 2.5km, turn right at a T-junction for a gate and cross a wide bridge over the river. The track now crosses open ground with the river on your left. Situated just beyond another T-junction, **Gleann Dubh Lighe bothy** provides a good option for an overnight stay should you wish.

Gleann Dubh-Lighe bothy is now very well appointed with a small library, but it was almost completely destroyed by fire in 2011. The fire was caused by a faulty screw on a gas canister, which allowed gas to escape and catch the naked flame of a candle. After the devasting blaze, only the stonework remained. It was rebuilt by Mountain Bothy Association volunteers in close cooperation with Fassfern Estate and in memory of hillwalker Nicholas Randell, who lost his life in the hills near Bridge of Orchy in 2005.

Continue north, leaving the forestry after another 1km and emerging into the open glen. Cross a bridge (not marked on the map) over the River Dubh Lighe, near some ruined shielings at NM 947 837, and head steeply west uphill on rough terraced pasture, keeping right of **Allt Coire an Trium** until it levels off. Now make a direct line northwest to the summit of **Meall an Uillt Chaoil** (844m) on predominantly grassy slopes. From here enjoy the breathtaking views of Eigg and Rùm sighted dramatically at the end of Loch Beoraid.

A camp can be made at **Bealach Coire nan Cearc**, a little way to the north, if desired.

▲ The north ridge traverse after Stob Coire nan Cearc

DAY 2
Bealach Coire nan Cearc to car park north of A830

Start	Bealach Coire nan Cearc (NM 935 848)
Distance	15.5km (9½ miles)
Total ascent	885m (2905ft)
Time	8–9hr
Summits	Stob Coire nan Cearc, Streap 911m (C), Braigh nan Uamhachan 765m (C)

The ridge continues north over complex ground to the first top of **Stob Coire nan Cearc** (887m) where Streap's beautiful zigzag reveals itself fully. Descend north-northeast on a narrowing ridgeline before a short, flat but narrow arête leads to the final climb for Corbett number one on our route – **Streap** (911m). There's a rocky step about two-thirds of the way up which can be bypassed to the left in summer, but in winter may be banked out and may require a little *à cheval* technique (legs astride). A good head for heights is useful for this entire section, regardless of season.

From the summit cairn, descend very steeply southeast to a broader *bealach* before the final ascent to **Streap Comhlaidh** (909m) Continue northeast and then north, initially following a fence line, but exercise caution if there are cornices. Savour the open vistas of Loch Arkaig to the northeast and the more distant hills of Knoydart to the northwest.

Continue steeply down the ridge until you near its lowest point. Then, descend east to the north end of Lochan a' Chomlain.

Cross the remote glen and begin the relentless climb up grassy slopes to the second Corbett – **Bràigh nan Uamhachan** (765m). Aim north of the crags near the top and turn south for the summit itself. Now continue on this fine ridgeline for nearly 5km, soon joining an old dry-stone boundary wall, trending southwest as the ridge slowly loses height. There's ample opportunity to recall the excitement of the earlier traverse and enjoy spectacular views over **Loch Shiel**. At the end of the ridge, descend steeply west over rough ground before scaling a fence (no ladder) and joining an old forestry track at NM 949 823. Follow this down to the bothy T-junction and retrace your steps through the forest to the **car park**.

▲ The spectacular northeast ridge from Streap Comhlaidh

ROUTE 4
The west coast of Jura

Start	Kinuachdrachd Harbour (NR 705 982) or Ardlussa (NR 671 928)
Finish	A846 at Tarbert (NR 606 823)
Total distance	50km (31 miles) or 60km (37.25 miles)
Total ascent	2210m (7250ft) or 2560m (8400ft)
Time	4 days
Terrain	Largely pathless, rough, rocky and boggy. Dense bracken from spring until autumn.
Maps	OS Explorer 355 Jura & Scarba; Harvey Superwalker Jura XT25
Note	During deer-stalking season (1 July–15 February) contact the gamekeepers at: Barnhill, tel 01496 820327, Ardlussa, tel 01496 820321, and Ruantallain, tel 01496 820287, to notify them of your intended route.

▲ Map continues on page 60

SCOTTISH WILD COUNTRY BACKPACKING

▶ *Top:* Fording the outflow of the Shian River
▶ *Middle:* Bracken-infested rocky terrain south of Glendebadel Bay
▶ *Bottom:* Am Miadar, south of Corpach Bay

ROUTE 4 – THE WEST COAST OF JURA

The west coast of Jura is arguably the wildest stretch of coastline in Scotland. A ruggedly beautiful landscape of glacial cliffs, white-sand bays and remarkable geological features. There are no roads, permanent habitations or livestock and the shores and glens teem with wildlife.

This tough four-day, 50km walk takes in the island's entire northwest coast; the terrain is often rough going and largely pathless. But the camping and bothying options are excellent.

To start at Kinuachdrachd, take a water taxi from the mainland. Contact Duncan Philips of Farsain Cruises at Croabh Haven on tel 07880 714165 (at time of writing £90 one way or £15 per person if more than six).

Starting at Ardlussa, the northernmost Jura bus stop (timetable information tel 01436 810200), adds 13km. Alternatively, a small parking area 5.5km beyond Ardlussa at Road End (NR 671 928) is as far north as unauthorised vehicles are permitted. Either way this makes for a tough day's walk to Glengarrisdale; taking an extra day and camping en route at Bàgh Gleann nam Muc is a good option.

SCOTTISH WILD COUNTRY BACKPACKING

DAY 1
Ardlussa or Kinuachdrachd to Glengarrisdale

Start	Ardlussa (NR 671 928) or Kinuachdrachd Harbour (NR 705 982)
Distance	26km (16 miles) or 13km (8 miles)
Total ascent	875m (2870ft) or 525m (1722ft)
Time	8–9½hr or 5–6hr

From **Ardlussa** follow the road past Ardlussa House and continue northeastwards along the track road for 13km, passing **Barnhill** (where George Orwell wrote *Nineteen Eighty-Four*) 2km before Kinuachdrachd.

From **Kinuachdrachd Harbour** continue around the bay, climb towards the farmhouse then take a path climbing left through bracken. Go through a deer fence gate then another after 2km. Cross a stream (NM 701 007) and follow the path northwest a short way to a vantage point.

There are superb views of the Isle of Scarba across the Gulf of Corryvreckan – the narrow strait between the two islands – the often turbulent confluence of the Firth of Lorn and the Sound of Jura with its infamous whirlpool. The tidal convergence of conflicting currents is catalysed by a submerged pyramidal rock, known as Caillich, The Hag, which generates the infamous whirlpool and standing waves of up to nine metres.

In August 1947, when returning from a camping trip on the west coast with his three-year-old son Richard, his sister Avril, two nephews and a niece, George Orwell steered his small boat into the gulf and rapidly got into difficulties. The boat's outboard motor was wrenched off in the violent tumult of water and disaster was narrowly forestalled when the party managed to scramble to safety on a small islet after the boat capsized. Several hours later, they were rescued by a passing fishing boat.

▲ Glengarrisdale bothy at the foot of Ben Garrisdale

Contour west for 200 metres on a vague path, descend a broad gully then continue northwest down another gully through glacial cliffs to the raised shore platform fringing the west coast.

Continue round the coast through boggy ground to **Bàgh Gleann nam Muc**. Cross the sandy beach and continue through rocky, bracken-infested terrain to another beach. At its far side follow a vague path through rocky outcrops around the cave-riddled Àird Bhreacain promontory to Glentrosdale Bay. Continue around the shore platform through rocky, bracken-covered terrain. After 400 metres follow an obvious path up a gully, which levels then descends to Bàgh Uamh Mhòr, dominated by high craggy cliffs. Continue round into **Bàgh Uamh nan Giall**. Cross large, slippery boulders and a beach of large cobbles then continue to a small sandy beach.

Cut across the neck of **Garbh Àird**, continue along the shore before taking to higher ground avoiding a stretch of rocky shoreline. Descend alongside a burn feeding into **Feith a' Chaorainn**. Once beyond the boggy ground continue through rocky terrain above the shore, passing quartz-veined cliffs along the way. Eventually the white walls and red roof of **Glengarrisdale bothy** come into view across Glengarrisdale Bay. On reaching the bay, cross the beach and ford the outflow of the Glengarrisdale River at its shallowest point.

The bothy is an old crofting cottage on the Ardlussa Estate, now maintained by the Mountain Bothy Association (MBA).

DAY 2
Glengarrisdale to Shian Bay

Start	Glengarrisdale bothy (NR 644 969)
Distance	17.5km (10¾ miles)
Total ascent	663m (2175ft)
Time	7–9hr

Head southwest between the bothy and the neighbouring ruin, then up across the boggy neck of **Àird Rachdaig**. Continue west, descending to Bàgh Gleann Speireig. From the bay climb through **Gleann Speireig**, keeping right of Allt Gleann Speireig. From the head of the glen descend towards steep-sided Glen Debadel; make for the point where the Glendebadel Burn reaches the beach (NR 623 951).

Cross the burn and continue along the shore platform. After 1km follow tracks on to a rocky spur (NR 614 950) climbing to higher ground above the cliffs. Contour southwest at 100 metres for 1km, cross a burn and continue until you reach **Cnoc na h-Uamha** (110m, NR 608 941). Descend to cross another burn, climb to 100 metres and contour for 1km before climbing to the landward side of **Stac Dearg** (130m, NR 594 935). Skirt a *lochan*, bear southwest and cross Garbh uisge nan Cad burn before it drops into a steep-sided gorge (NR 591 931).

Climb westwards to level ground crossed by a small burn. Continue southwest for 300 metres then descend towards the shore at **Rubha Lag Losguinn**. Follow tracks southwest through bracken above the shore for 1km, then cross a beach of large pebbles at **Corpach Bay**. Cross the sandy beach and the outflow of **Abhainn na Corpaich**, continue for 1km to Am Miadar with its beaches, arches, caves and dunes. This is a wonderful bivouac site with good camping ground, a burn and driftwood.

At the southwestern end of **Am Miadar** climb the steep-sided gully and continue along the clifftop. After 1.5km descend a spur towards the shore; beneath the spur is a large natural arch with the remnants of a man-made structure protecting its entrance.

The environmental artist Julie Brook (www.juliebrook.com) lived in the natural arch for several periods during the early 1990s, including an entire year between April 1993 and April 1994. Julie had supplies delivered by fishing boat and, apart from occasional forays into the teeming metropolis of Craighouse, she lived a solitary existence with only her cat for company. Julie produced a number of large impressionistic paintings, which she later exhibited in Craighouse, and various ephemeral sculptures including 'firestacks' – driftwood fires set on top of stacks built from large pebbles at low tide, which would appear to become floating islands of fire as the tide came in.

Continue for 1.5km to the waterfall above the outflow of Allt an Tairbh (NR 538 893). Cross **Allt an Tairbh** upstream of the waterfall and descend to the shore further on. Continue for 2.5km to **Shian Bay**, a white-sand crescent fringed with machair and the **Shian River** flowing into the bay. This is a fine bivouac site, though somewhat exposed. In rough weather it may be best to continue to **Ruantallain**, which is 5.25km and 1½–2hr further on.

DAY 3
Shian Bay to Cruib Lodge

Start	Shian Bay NR 531 875
Distance	13km (8 miles)
Total ascent	256m (840ft)
Time	5–6hr

Cross the outflow of the **Shian River** then follow ATV tracks heading inland. After 200 metres turn southwest off the tracks, continuing across country. After 1.5km follow an obvious ATV track southwestwards.

Just north of **Breinn Phort** the track turns sharply southeast for 350 metres before turning southwest along the clifftop above the bay, crossing a raised beach then turning southeast. Leave it here following a faint path southwest past a dry-stone-walled enclosure, descending through rocky outcrops to **Ruantallain bothy**. The bothy is at the eastern end of a building belonging to the Ruantallain Estate. The main part of the house is private and kept locked. The bothy is a single room with a fireplace.

From the bothy, head southeast to **An Sàilean** bay then follow deer tracks across pebble beaches and through bracken to gain the raised shore platform. Continue, through rocky terrain past glacial cliffs perforated with caves.

Continue into **Bàgh Gleann Righ Mòr**, crossing sandy bays, rocky outcrops and raised beaches. Follow deer paths through the rugged terrain of the **Àird Reamhar** promontory and into the next bay. Negotiate your way over a rocky outcrop above the shore. The rocks can be slippery and are pitched steeply enough to be hazardous.

Continue around the bay, cross **Rubha Liath** then work your way around **Port Falaich a' Chumhainn Mhòir**. Where white-painted navigation pillars stand above **Rubha Gille nan Ordag** (NR 543 814), the shoreline becomes estuarine and difficult to negotiate, so climb to higher ground, continuing northeast along a low ridge.

▲ Walking into Bàgh Gleann Righ Mòr on the north shore of Loch Tarbert

ROUTE 4 – THE WEST COAST OF JURA

After 1km you'll join an ATV track. Follow it northeast, descending to cross Garbh Uisge burn. Climb northeast again, following the ATV track on a winding course to a point (NR 563 832) northwest of Cruib Lodge bothy, which remains out of view. Leave the track, cross a small burn and descend southeast towards deer-fenced woodland. Follow the burn around to the bothy. **Cruib Lodge bothy** is on the Ruantallain Estate and is maintained by the MBA.

DAY 4
Cruib Lodge to Tarbert

Start	Cruib Lodge bothy (NR 567 829)
Distance	6.5km (4 miles)
Total ascent	172m (564ft)
Time	2–2½hr

From the **bothy**, cross the burn and follow an ATV track bearing northeast. Continue along a ridge for 500 metres then turn eastwards down through an obvious gap (NR 570 834) to the mud and sand flats of **Learadail**. Cross the outflow of the burn where it's shallowest and head southeast to cross the neck of the promontory on the eastern side of Learadail. Cross the mud flats of **Sàilean nam Màireach** then climb alongside a tumbling burn – the outflow of **Loch na Pearaich** – for 500 metres to reach the loch, then skirt around to its northern end. Follow an ATV track southeast, up a slight rise then down a slope to cross a very boggy area. Turn northeast following a vague path and continue without losing height for 500 metres. Follow a rough path descending northeastwards to the edge of the mud flats (NR 593 835).

Skirt around the edge of the mud flats to the northeast for 800 metres, making for a weir and dam, beyond which stepping stones ford the river (NR 598 843). Once across, follow the obvious path – marked with white-painted stones – to the point where it divides after 600 metres. Follow the white-painted stones on the left-hand branch of the path, which climbs above the shore, ultimately making for the **A846**, 1.5km further on.

At **Tarbert**, 300 metres southeast of where the path meets the road, you can flag down the Jura Bus. Check times with the bus company, www.garelochheadcoaches.co.uk, tel 01436 810200.

▲ The head of Loch Tarbert at dawn

65

SCOTTISH WILD COUNTRY BACKPACKING

ROUTE 5
Around the coast of Rùm

Start	Dibidil pony path (NM 404 911) or nearby Kinloch Castle (NM 401 995)
Finish	Kinloch Castle (NM 401 995)
Total distance	40km (25 miles)
Total ascent	1295m (4250ft)
Time	3 days
Terrain	The Kinloch–Papadil pony path traverses rough, boggy terrain. Thereafter, faint paths are intermittent. The return to Kinloch follows a metalled track.
Maps	OS Explorer 397 Rùm, Eigg, Muck, Canna & Sanday; OS Landranger 39 Rùm, Eigg, Muck & Canna
Note	During the deer-stalking season on Rùm, which runs from mid August–mid February, notify the head stalker of your intended route, tel 01687 462030.
Warning	After heavy rain several burns can become impassable. Do not attempt to cross rivers in spate.

▲ Ruined croft house at Samhnan Insir

ROUTE 5 – AROUND THE COAST OF RÙM

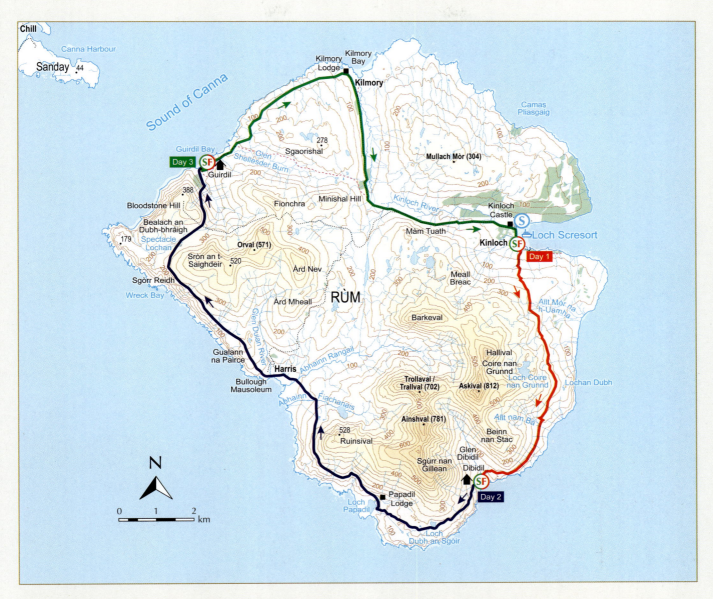

The Isle of Rùm boasts a wild, beautiful coastline, with high cliffs, rugged, rocky shores, magnificent white-sand bays, remarkable geological features and abundant wildlife. Although a strong walker could complete the walk in two days, this challenging route should not be underestimated; the terrain is rough and navigation is difficult in places. The MBA bothies at Dibidil and Guirdil make for obvious overnight stops.

SCOTTISH WILD COUNTRY BACKPACKING

DAY 1
Kinloch to Dibidil

Start	Dibidil pony path (NM 404 911) or nearby Kinloch Castle (NM 401 995)
Distance	8.5km (5¼ miles)
Total ascent	665m (2180ft)
Time	3–3½hr

> The bothy at Dibidil is only a 3–3½hr walk from Kinloch. Other options are to continue to Papadil (4½–5½hr) or Harris Bay (7–8½hr) and bivouac at either of these wonderful spots.

From the **ferry slipway**, follow the track road to a junction where a signpost indicates the castle straight ahead and take the left-hand track road. After 400 metres turn left before a set of white gates, where a small sign indicates that it's 8.5km to Dibidil.

If starting from **Kinloch Castle**, head southeast along the track road keeping straight ahead at the junction; pass through the white gates and join the Dibidil path to your right shortly after.

The Dibidil pony path extends as far as Papadil and is metalled in places with large stones. The path is reasonably distinct, but other than a signpost near the beginning it has no waymarkers and can be easy to lose in places.

The path climbs steadily to 200 metres, contours for a while, crosses **Allt Mòr na h-Uamha** then Allt na h-Uamha. Crossing can be tricky if the burn is in spate. Continue contouring with Hallival and Askival (812m) looming over **Coire nan Grunnd**. As the path passes above **Lochan Dubh**, Eigg comes into view to the southeast. The path soon zigzags down to ford **Allt nam Bà** across a rock slab.

Contouring around the flank of **Beinn nan Stac** the view opens up to Sgùrr nan Gillean and Ainshval towering above Glen Dibidil. The path descends into Glen Dibidil and the **Dibidil bothy** soon comes into view. Cross the Dibidil River at a ford, or higher upstream when in spate – do so with caution.

DAY 2
Dibidil to Guirdil

Start	Dibidil bothy (NM 393 928)
Distance	17km (10½ miles)
Total ascent	940m (3085ft)
Time	7½–9hr

This is the longest, toughest day of the route. There are a number of river crossings, high cliffs to traverse and a steep descent into Glen Guirdil. Much of the route is pathless and it is exposed during rough weather.

To the rear of the **bothy**, regain the pony path, which climbs to 200 metres then contours, passing south of **Loch Dubh an Sgòir** where the path is indistinct. Descend gradually as **Loch Papadil** emerges below to the northwest. The path zigzags on the final stretch down to the loch. Make for the southwest corner of the small woodland and enter by a rusting iron gate. Pass through the woodland and cross a burn to reach the ruins of **Papadil Lodge**. Cross another burn and exit the woods.

▲ Camping by Dibidil bothy

▲ Heading north-east from Guirdil, Bloodstone Hill in the background

The path runs out here and the landscape ahead looks formidable. Cross a burn at the head of the loch and go through an iron gate – there is no fence. Go through a second gate and climb northeast to around 120 metres before contouring around into the broad gully of Allt na Gile. Cross the burn, gain height then contour through rocky terrain at around 150 metres. Climb gradually over the next kilometre to 250 metres. Look for a large cairn marking the start of a path where the flank of **Ruinsival** (528m) is turned. Contour around the hillside before descending gradually. The view opens up across Harris Bay with the whale-backed summits of Àrd Nev and Orval rising to the west of Glen Harris.

Follow the path down to cross **Abhainn Fiachanais** where safe to do so. Continue northwest, soon crossing a bridge over **Abhainn Rangail**. Follow the track, skirt an impressive, raised beach, staying to the right of some cairns. If rivers are in spate continue along the track, cross the bridge over the **Glen Duian River** then follow the track to the **mausoleum**. Otherwise, on passing some dry-stone-walled enclosures, head towards the shore (there is an excellent bivouac site in a rectangular enclosure above the beach) and cross the outflow of the Glen Duian River. Here stands the Bullough Mausoleum – an unlikely Grecian temple perched upon the wild Hebridean shore.

After the Clearance of its native Gaelic-speaking population in the 1820s, Rùm was known as the Forbidden Island for much of the 19th and early 20th centuries. Following the reintroduction of red deer in 1845, the island was treated as a private sporting estate by a succession of owners. In 1888 Rùm was acquired by John Bullough, a cotton machinery manufacturer and self-made millionaire from Accrington in Lancashire. When he died in 1891, his remains were interred in an ostentatious mausoleum at the western extremity of Harris Bay, which included an octagonal stone tower and interior decorated with Italian mosaic tiles. Allegedly, a tactless guest of his son, Sir George Bullough, observed that the mausoleum resembled a public lavatory at Waterloo Station. Sir George had his father's sandstone sarcophagus removed and promptly dynamited the offending structure. John Bullough's remains were finally interred in the neoclassical edifice built nearby, where Sir George and his wife, Lady Monica, would eventually join him.

Follow the dry-stone wall, climbing northwest, then continue towards the rocky summit of **Gualann na Pairce**. Pass between the twin tops (228m and 232m) and continue

SCOTTISH WILD COUNTRY BACKPACKING

northwest, parallel to the clifftop, crossing boggy, hummocky ground. Cross several burns, gain a little height and look for a faint path through the heather. The path runs closer to the cliff edge as it reaches the 250-metre contour, then climbs above **Sgòrr Reidh** with views across the steep slope sliding down to **Wreck Bay**.

Beyond Sgòrr Reidh the path runs dangerously close to the cliff edge, so climb towards a large cairn at around 300 metres and contour north then northeast. Head downhill and pass southeast of **Spectacle Lochan**, continuing northeast towards **Bealach an Dubh-bhràigh**. Cross the *bealach*, passing a *lochan* as the view across Glen Guirdil opens up, with the cliffs of Orval towering above the head of the glen.

Cross the pony path and head north-northwest along the flank of **Bloodstone Hill**. Follow the traces of path that keep above the potentially hazardous scree. Contour at around 240m for 600 metres, then steadily descend a path to cross two burns (140m). Descend a very steep grassy slope heading for the southeast corner of a deer-fenced plantation. Continue along the east side of the plantation then follow the track above the Guirdil River down to the beach, crossing the outflow wherever easiest, to arrive at **Guirdil bothy**.

DAY 3
Guirdil to Kinloch

Start	Guirdil bothy (NM 319 014)
Distance	13.5km (8¼ miles)
Total ascent	405m (1330ft)
Time	5–6hr

From the **bothy**, follow the path zigzagging east on to the clifftops then winding its way for 1km to Glen Shellesder. A ford crosses the **Glen Shellesder Burn** and there is an easier crossing point 75 metres upstream – beware slippery rocks.

Ignore the Glen Shellesder path and climb away from the burn, continuing northeast across country, gaining some height through the boggy terrain. Contour above the clifftops, following vague paths for the next 4km and crossing several burns cascading down to the cliffs along the way.

When **Kilmory Lodge** comes into view, descend towards a small bay. Skirt around the bay, then cut across the open

▲ Guirdil bothy sitting beneath Bloodstone Hill

ROUTE 5 – AROUND THE COAST OF RÙM

ground in front of the lodge. Join the Land Rover track behind the lodge and follow it south for 100 metres before following a vague path east to the **Kilmory River**. If the tide permits, cross the river's outflow, then continue beneath the marram grass-covered dunes onto the beautiful two-tone red and white sand expanse of **Kilmory Bay**.

To Return to **Kinloch Castle**, follow the Land Rover tracks through Kilmory and Kinloch glens.

The incongruous and often maligned Kinloch Castle was built by Rùm's erstwhile owner, Sir George Bullough during the last years of the 19th century. Built from red sandstone quarried at Annan in Dumfriesshire, the castle was finally completed in 1902. Sir George hired 100 stonemasons and craftsmen from Lancashire for the job and purportedly paid them extra to wear kilts. The estate employed around 100 people, including 14 under-gardeners to maintain the extensive grounds, which included a nine-hole golf course, a bowling green, tennis and racquets courts, heated ornamental turtle and alligator ponds and an aviary housing birds of paradise and humming birds. Soil for the grounds was imported from Ayrshire, and grapes, peaches, nectarines and figs were grown in the estate's glasshouses. The castle's interior boasted an orchestrion – a mechanical contrivance that could simulate the sounds of brass, drum and woodwind – an air-conditioned billiards room and an ingenious and elaborate central heating system, which fed piping hot water to the Heath Robinson-esque bathrooms, while also heating the glasshouses and ornamental ponds. Sir George and Lady Monica usually resided at Kinloch Castle during the stalking season and would entertain their wealthy and important guests in some style. A day's stalking would be followed by a lavish evening meal served at the dining suite, which had originally graced the state rooms of Sir George's yacht, *Rhouma*. After dinner the company would repair to the magnificent ballroom, with its highly polished sprung floors and cut-glass chandelier, to dance the night away.

▲ Guirdil Bay and the bothy

SCOTTISH WILD COUNTRY BACKPACKING

ROUTE 6
Isle of Skye: Glen Sligachan, Loch Coruisk and Camasunary

Start	Sligachan (NG 487 298)
Finish	Elgol (NG 520 139)
Total distance	21.25km (13¼ miles); alternative 25km (15½ miles)
Total ascent	775m (2545ft); alternative 1015m (3330ft)
Time	2 days
Terrain	Good path through Glen Sligachan, though rocky and often wet; after heavy rain river crossings may be dangerous.
Maps	OS Explorer 411 Skye – Cuillin Hills; OS Landranger 32 South Skye & Cuillin Hills; Harvey Superwalker Skye: The Cuillin
Public transport	Buses 155 from Portree and Broadford and 52 from Kyleakin – get off at Sligachan Hotel. Bus 55 from Elgol to Broadford.

▲ Heading for Sgùrr na Stri off the Loch Coruisk path, with the northern peaks of the Black Cuillin as a backdrop

ROUTE 6 – ISLE OF SKYE: GLEN SLIGACHAN, LOCH CORUISK AND CAMASUNARY

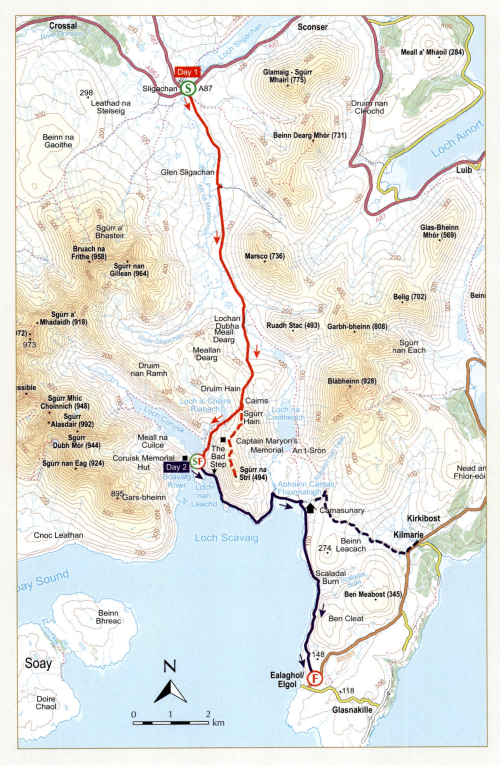

Few paths in the British Isles pass through so much magnificent scenery as the Glen Sligachan path: to the east the elegant sweeping lines of the Red Hills, to the west the saw-toothed ridges of the Black Cuillin. The first day's route follows the path south before climbing over Druim Hain to the mountain-ringed sanctuary of Loch Coruisk. Including an ascent of Sgùrr na Stri (an extra 4.5km and 225m of ascent) is a very worthwhile detour for the magnificent summit panorama of the Black Cuillin.

Day two's route soon leads to the infamous Bad Step, a huge, steeply pitched convex slab of rock that drops directly into Loch nan Leachd, which has to be crossed en route between Coruisk and Camasunary – there is no great difficulty involved, but it requires good nerves.

An additional difficulty may be presented by Abhainn Camas Fhionnairigh, flowing into Camasunary Bay, which can be difficult or impossible to cross at high tide or after heavy rain. A new MBA bothy on the eastern side of the bay was built in 2015 and there is plenty of opportunity for camping; summer can be busy.

From Camasunary the walk out to Elgol along the coast is straightforward if airy in places and benefits from splendid views.

DAY 1
Sligachan to Loch Coruisk/Sgùrr na Stri

Start	Sligachan (NG 487 298)
Distance	11.5km (7¼ miles); variant: 11km (6¾ miles)
Total ascent	390m (1280ft); Sgùrr na Stri variant 600m (1970ft)
Time	7–9hr
Summits	Sgùrr na Stri 494m

Go through a gate by the old bridge over the **Sligachan River** to join the Glen Sligachan path; a signpost for Loch Coruisk and Elgol points along the glen. Pass the Collie and Mackenzie memorial and keep to the main path, crossing several small burns.

> There are fine views of Sgùrr nan Gillean crowning the north-eastern terminus of the Black Cuillin ridge to the right, Glamaig and Beinn Dearg Mhòr to the left and, directly ahead, the elegant form of Marsco standing proud of the other Red Hills.

After 3km the path bends right then left, before reaching **Allt na Measarroch**. Cross the burn on large stones – this can be difficult when it is in spate. Continue along the path beneath **Marsco** then, after a further 3.5km, take the right-hand fork at a large cairn just beyond **Lochan Dubha**.

Cross a burn and the onward route can be seen climbing up towards **Druim Hain**; to the southeast the impressive west face of Blaven (Blàbheinn; 929m) dominates the view. After a boggy section, the path climbs along the right side of the valley. As the path ascends, it becomes compromised by footfall and water erosion. The small pyramidal peak ahead is Sgùrr Hain, with Sgùrr na Stri (494m) lying beyond. The gradient eases before the path reaches a large **cairn** atop the Druim Hain ridge. The views are splendid – Loch Scavaig and the southern end of Loch Coruisk below to the southwest, while the spires and crenellations of the Cuillin dominate the skyline to the west.

The path forks by the cairn. Take the left-hand branch (south) which leads to another **cairn** where the path forks again (see alternative route, below). Take the right-hand fork which descends obliquely south then southwest through Coire Riabhach with Loch a' Choire Riabach to your right. The path is sketchy in places and resembles a burn during wet weather. Continue southwest to reach the outflow of **Loch Coruisk**.

There are various options for pitching a tent; including crossing the stepping stones over the **Scavaig River** (the outflow of Loch Coruisk) and heading west a short way to camp near the **Coruisk Memorial Hut**.

Alternative route: Sgùrr na Stri from Druim Hain

From the second cairn (see above), take the left-hand path contouring along the slopes below Sgùrr Hain.

> After 800 metres the rough path passes above a pyramidal monument known as Captain Maryon's Cairn. Despite its size it can be easy to miss as it is built from the gabbro rock predominant on the mountain. The cairn stands nearly three metres high and marks the place where Staff Captain AJ Maryon's remains were found two years after he disappeared, having set off on a walk from Sligachan in July 1946. Maryon's wartime friend and fellow officer, Myles Morrison, built this fine memorial to his comrade – an endeavour of considerable dedication in such a remote location.

Rejoin the path and continue southwards reaching a small burn flowing down an obvious gully after a further 400 metres. A vague path climbs by the left-hand side of the burn. Follow this up to the *bealach* below and north of the summit of **Sgùrr na Stri** (494m). Turn right (southwest) across the head of the burn and climb a short way up a shallow gully to gain the summit ridge. Bear south and continue climbing, crossing large gabbro slabs on the way. The cairn-marked summit is reached soon after.

> At 494m, the summit of Sgùrr na Stri is half the height of the Cuillin peaks, but it has some of the grandest views in Scotland. The seaward vista takes in Eigg, Rùm, Coll, Ardnamurchan and Mull; to the east there is a tremendous view of Camasunary with Blaven rearing up over Loch na Crèitheach. However, nothing matches the dramatic splendour of the jagged Cuillin Ridge towering above Loch Coruisk to the west.

If you have good weather, then camping near the summit is feasible and has the incentive of sunrise over the Cuillin. Whether you stay or not, you'll need to retrace the route to Druim Hain and follow the route description down to Loch Coruisk.

ROUTE 6 – ISLE OF SKYE: GLEN SLIGACHAN, LOCH CORUISK AND CAMASUNARY

DAY 2
Loch Coruisk/Sgùrr na Stri to Elgol

Start	Loch Coruisk (NG 490 196) or Sgùrr na Stri (NG 500 194)
Distance	9.75km (6 miles); from Sgùrr na Stri 13.5km (8½ miles)
Total ascent	385m (1265ft); from Sgùrr na Stri 415m (1360ft)
Time	5–6hr

▲ Negotiating the Bad Step overhanging Loch nan Leachd

From the stepping stones across the **Scavaig River** follow the path southeast through the gap and emerge at the head of **Loch nan Leachd**. Continue along the rough path for 300 metres to reach the **Bad Step**. Descend along the obvious crack, staying low and keeping three-point contact. Once across, exhale and continue along the obvious path above the shore. The path is rough and boggy in places, but presents no further challenges until **Abhainn Camas Fhionnairigh**, the tidal river flowing into Camasunary Bay, is reached after a further 3km. Find a fordable stretch upriver from the old bridge – do not attempt to cross if the river is deep or fast flowing after heavy rain or when the tide is in. There are plenty of spots for camping and an **MBA bothy** on the eastern side of the bay. It can be busy here during the summer months.

> It's 6km from Camasunary to Elgol along the coast and takes 2–2½hr. The Am Màm path between Camasunary and Kilmarie is shorter (4.2km), easier and quicker (1¼–1¾hr) but lacks the character of the coastal path.

Continue east around the bay for 600 metres towards **Abhainn nan Leac** then head upstream 250 metres to cross the bridge. Follow the initially boggy path south along the shore and, as you begin to climb, the ground improves. Cross a stile over a stock fence and continue along the distinct though intermittently rocky, rough and occasionally exposed path.

The path is easy to follow and makes for an exhilarating walk; an airy clifftop section (care needed) precedes the descent into Glen Scaladal. After crossing the **Scaladal Burn** the climb out of the glen is followed by another exposed clifftop section. The path leaves the cliff edge and continues along the flank of **Beinn Cleat** as you approach Elgol. Go through a gate onto a path between fences then join a lane at the top of **Elgol**, passing a house on your left. Continue past another house to reach the road.

CENTRAL AND EASTERN HIGHLANDS

◂ Bealach Dubh, one of the finest passes in the Central Highlands (Route 7)

SCOTTISH WILD COUNTRY BACKPACKING

ROUTE 7
Ben Alder: Tour of the ridges

Start/finish	Dalwhinnie railway station (NN 634 849)
Total distance	61km (38 miles)
Total ascent	2620m (8595ft)
Time	3 days
Terrain	Road and track, then stalkers' paths. Includes some off-path sections and a Grade One scramble.
Key summits	Càrn Dearg 1034m (M), Geal Chàrn 1132m (M), Aonach Beag 1116m (M), Beinn Eibhinn 1102m (M), Ben Alder 1148m (M), Beinn Bheòil 1019m (M)
Maps	OS Explorer 50 Ben Alder, Loch Ericht & Loch Laggan, OS Landranger 42 Glen Garry & Loch Rannoch
Note	Cycling in on a good track from Dalwhinnie station cuts a long walk in half. If not travelling by train, please park courteously in or near the train station car park and be mindful of residents.

The temptation with a book like this is always to look towards the margins, but the Ben Alder group lies in the very centre of the Central Highlands and shouldn't be overlooked for its more edgy northern cousins.

This is a complex landscape, incorporating both Cairngorm-like plateaux and the airier ridges of the west coast. It was deemed worthy of special mention in WH Murray's *Highland Landscape: A Survey*, commissioned by the National Trust for Scotland in 1962, yet sadly failed to secure NSA (National Scenic Area – the Scottish equivalent of an Area of Outstanding Natural Beauty) status. It's also eminently doable by train from Edinburgh, Glasgow and the Central Belt (if bike storage can be booked in advance, it is a good idea to do so). Most importantly, this route takes you into very remote country, threading a line around three of the finest, easier mountaineering ridges in Scotland via a historic right of way and six Munros.

What price big country, natural architecture, endless skies? What value, wide horizons? Arguably, a mountaineer called Percy Unna knew the cost of these things, and the risk to society of losing our ability or willingness to pay. Unna helped organise (and donated to) the purchase of Glen Coe and other estates in the 1930s, donating the land to what became the National Trust for Scotland. He wrote a letter to the Trust establishing some principles which have helped shape and maintain the character of the Scottish mountains ever since. These included: the protection in perpetuity of public access for all; the ending of deer stalking for sport (but not for grazing control); and strict limits on signage, mechanised transport, new paths and buildings or indeed any artificial means of making the Scottish hills easier or safer to climb.

Unna was passionate about preserving what he termed the 'primitive' state of the mountains, and the experiences and challenges we find there. These principles underlay WH Murray's later survey work for the same organisation. Whatever our own views on his principles, decades later, they helped shaped the landscapes we walk through now.

ROUTE 7 – BEN ALDER: TOUR OF THE RIDGES

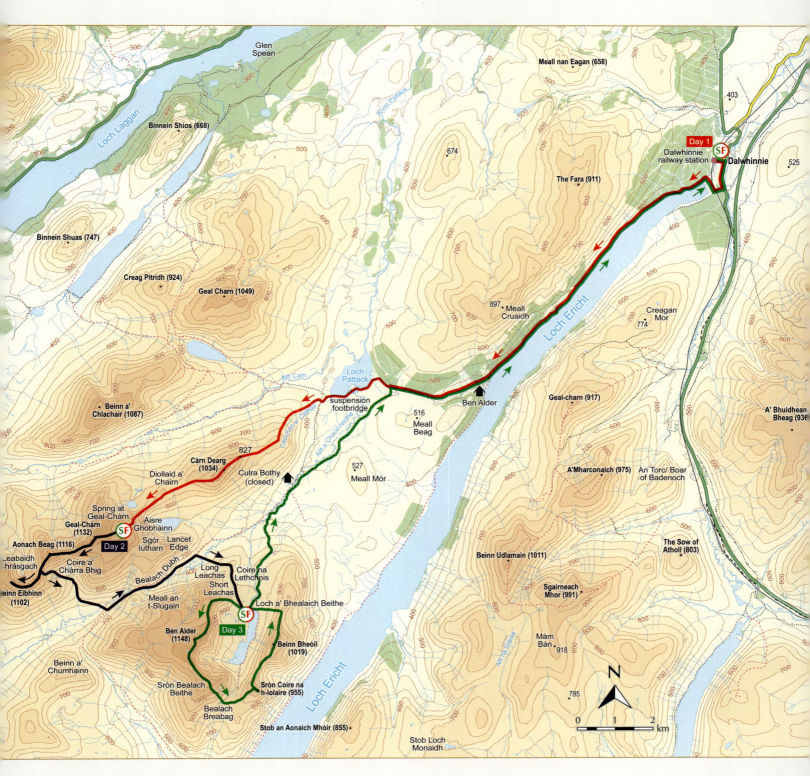

SCOTTISH WILD COUNTRY BACKPACKING

▲ *Top:* Out and back on Ben Alder, overlooking Beinn Bheòil and Loch Ericht
▲ *Middle:* Lancet Edge and the Long Leachas, Beinn Bheòil and a distant Schiehallion
▲ *Bottom:* A camp overlooking Lancet Edge

ROUTE 7 – BEN ALDER: TOUR OF THE RIDGES

DAY 1
Dalwhinnie to Geal-Chàrn

Start	Dalwhinnie railway station (NN 634 849)
Distance	20km (12½ miles)
Total ascent	1075m (3525ft)
Time	6–8hr
Summits	Càrn Dearg 1034m (M), Diollaid a' Chairn 925m

DAY 2
Geal Chàrn to Bealach Beithe

Start	Vicinity of spring at Geal Chàrn (NN 478 749)
Distance	12.5km (7¾ miles)
Total ascent	635m (2085ft)
Time	5–6hr
Summits	Geal Chàrn 1132m (M), Aonach Beag 1116m (M), Beinn Eibhinn 1102m (M)

Sadly the traditional Right of Way, via the level crossing at the end of Ben Alder Road, is obstructed at the time of writing.

If arriving by train, exit the **station** and go straight ahead. After 200m, turn right onto the A889 and head south for around 800m. Just after the petrol station, turn right again and walk to the end of the road. There is a small amount of parking here. Using the underpass, walk or cycle under the railway line and turn right. After around 400 metres, turn left onto Ben Alder Road and follow a well-made track which runs on the north side of **Loch Ericht** for some 7km, passing several modern 'follies' (high-end holiday lets). When you reach the substantial **Ben Alder Lodge**, climb west, cross a cattle grid and head into open country. The hills now swing into view, beyond a vast grassy plain. It can be useful to leave your bike in this vicinity if cycling, perhaps tucked into the forestry on your right.

Take the track (second on the left) towards **Loch Pattack** and cross an old **suspension footbridge**. Turn left at a junction and, shortly after, leave the track for the open hillside on your right, using the burn of **Caochan a' Càthair** as a guide.

Labour up to a spot height of **827m** to be rewarded with a spectacular and rarely seen view of the Ben Alder massif and Lancet Edge, a dramatic spur (and Grade One scramble) of Geal Chàrn. Walk southwest over a broad plateau before ascending the gradually narrowing ridge to the summit of our first Munro, **Càrn Dearg** (1034m).

Leaving the second top of this Munro on its north side, descend over screes to a broad and grassy plateau. It's possible to contour east of the next top, **Diollaid a' Chairn** (925m), to reach the narrowing *bealach* of **Aisre Ghobhainn** under the headwall of Geal Chàrn. It's less intimidating than it looks – there's a clear path to the summit plateau, and plenty of places to camp near the fast-flowing **Geal-Chàrn spring** at the top.

Follow the **Geal Chàrn spring** across the plateau west-south-west, passing the source pool and continuing to the summit of **Geal Chàrn** (1132m). Go southwest down a broad, easy ridge, before climbing around 100m to the third Munro, **Aonach Beag** (1116m). Head south-southwest on a narrowing ridge to the *bealach* of **Leabaidh Chràsgach**; deposit your backpack here if you wish, then climb around the corrie edge for the final Munro in this group, **Beinn Eibhinn** (1102m).

Retrace your steps to the *bealach*. Take a faint path southeast into the **Coire a' Chàrra Bhig** and contour east at first, crossing the burn and then re-joining it at a confluence lower down. Take an intermittent path south that runs on its left (east) side, before again heading east-southeast to ford Uisge Labhair and join a well-made track. Here we join part of the old Thieves Road used in the past by reivers (raiders) to move cattle from Badenoch and Strathspey to market in Fort William.

Continue northeast over **Bealach Dubh** and down under the imposing crags of Ben Alder, a simply fantastic way through the heart of these mountains.

On your right, look for a long ridge running parallel to the path, with a rocky notch at its end. This is the end of the **Long Leachas** (another Grade One scramble). After around 1.5km, leave the path and head across rough, open ground to reach the ridge, to the right of the rocky notch. Contour south into the base of the next corrie (**Coire na Lethchois**) and aim to the left of some glacial erratics on the skyline. Once over the crest, there is plentiful camping and fresh water available in this dramatic hanging corrie.

SCOTTISH WILD COUNTRY BACKPACKING

DAY 3
Bealach Beithe to Dalwhinnie

Start	Camp at Bealach Beithe (NN 510 728)
Distance	28.5km (17¾ miles)
Total ascent	910m (2985ft)
Time	7–8hr
Summits	Ben Alder 1148m (M), Beinn Bheòil 1019m (M)

The route onto Ben Alder – the **Short Leachas** – is the stubby ridge that extends eastwards at the mouth of the *lochan* in this hanging corrie. Once at the base of the ridge, find a gully through boulders and bracken, then join an intermittent path on easier ground. The ridge then narrows markedly, giving one or two exposed steps and a small 'wall' which is a little exposed but offers plenty of holds. The final section is straightforward. Allow about 1hr for this Grade One scramble in wild surroundings.

It's now a simple saunter south across a huge plateau to reach the summit of **Ben Alder** (1148m) for unsurpassed views across the Central Highlands.

> There are a number of stone enclosures north of the summit of Ben Alder. These are remains of 19th-century camps used by teams of Royal Engineers serving under Major General Thomas Colby who were creating the first Ordnance Survey maps.

Follow the corrie edge around to the east (detouring to **Sròn Bealach Beithe** for more wonderful views if you wish) then head off very steeply south to **Bealach Breabag**.

Continue east and then north to **Sròn Coire na h-Iolaire**, and on to last of the six Munros, **Beinn Bheòil** (1019m). It's particularly satisfying here to see the two ridges of Lancet and the Long Leachas from their opposite side. Descend north to around 900m and then drop steeply west on screes to reach the outflow of **Loch a' Bhealaich Beithe** near which you camped. Join the well-kept stalkers' path out to **Culra Bothy** (now closed due to an asbestos roof) and onwards over the grassy plain to return to **Dalwhinnie**.

82 ▶ Camp at the bealach Beithe

ROUTE 8
Blair Atholl to Kingussie

Start	Blair Atholl station (NN 870 653)
Finish	Kingussie station (NH 756 004)
Total distance	52.5km (32½ miles)
Total ascent	2270m (7450ft)
Time	2–3 days
Terrain	Trackless, often boggy terrain for much of the route after an easy initial walk-in on a track up Glen Tilt.
Key summits	Beinn Mheadhonach 901m (C), Beinn Bhreac 912m (C), Leathad an Taobhain 902m (C), Meallach Mhòr 769m (C)
Maps	OS Explorer OL49 Pitlochry & Loch Tummel, OL51 Atholl and OL56 Badenoch & Upper Strathspey; OS Landranger 43 Braemar & Blair Atholl, 42 Glen Garry & Loch Rannoch and 35 Kingussie & Monadhliath Mountains
Note	This is a committing route into remote territory. The central section crosses a high, featureless plateau for several kilometres, offering challenging navigation in poor visibility, and no quick escape routes. There are few river crossings, although the Tarf Water and Allt Bhran may present obstacles in spate. Grassy areas along these rivers provide potential campsites, well placed for the first and second nights of a three-day crossing.

▲ *Left:* Beginning the climb up Beinn Mheadhonach; *Right:* Camping by the Tarf Water

In centuries past, journeying between Atholl and Badenoch was a serious business. It's hard to imagine nowadays: the A9 and the railway via Drumochter Pass render the trip between the settlements of Blair Atholl and Kingussie a trivial one, reducing the great barrier of the Grampian range to a pleasant blur.

For the backpacker, however, the challenge is much as it ever was. People have been crossing this huge massif on foot for hundreds of years. The hills harbour many traces of an extinct way of life, ruined settlements and shielings where people lived through the summer as they grazed their cattle on the high pastures. Ancient through-routes such as the Gaick, Minigaig and the overgrown medieval cart track of Comyn's Road still make for fine journeys. To appreciate fully the blend of wild and lived-in that characterises so much of the Highlands, it's a great area to explore.

That said, it's the scope for off-trail crossings, which the route described here aims to demonstrate, that really marks out this vast area. The nature of the landscape, extensive and rolling rather than steep and rugged, allows the walker to wander far and wide. On these sombre uplands, haunted by the calls of golden plover, imagination is truly the best guide.

Although this route can be completed in two days, the locations of the most obvious potential campsites, by the Tarf Water and Allt Bhran, make a three-day outing more intuitive. This allows for an easier pace and relatively short final day, useful for those planning to catch a train at Kingussie. There is limited parking at Blair Atholl station, and more substantial car parks where the main road through the village crosses the River Tilt (NN 875 655) and near Old Bridge of Tilt (NN 874 663).

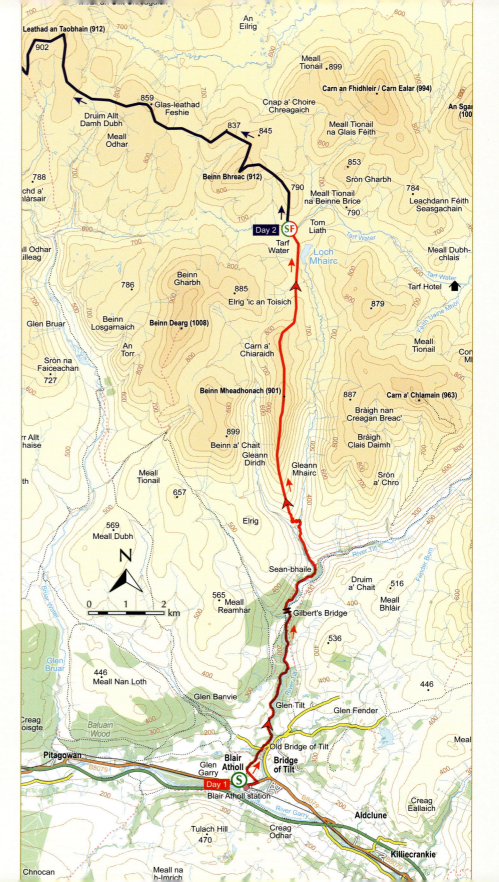

ROUTE 8 – BLAIR ATHOLL TO KINGUSSIE

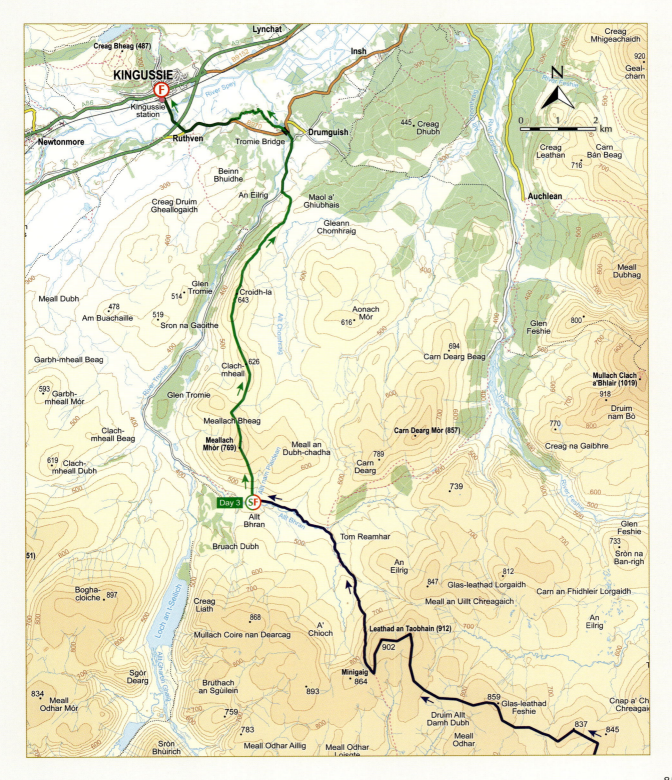

DAY 1
Blair Atholl to the Tarf

Start	Blair Atholl station (NN 870 653)
Distance	17.5km (10¾ miles)
Total ascent	1065m (3495ft)
Time	7–8hr
Summits	Beinn Mheadhonach 901m (C)

Leave **Blair Atholl station** and turn right along the main road. After 250 metres turn left through the imposing entrance to Blair Castle grounds and walk along the drive. After 450 metres turn right on a track that reaches a car park in 750 metres. Bear left and cross a metalled road on to another track. Follow this into **Glen Tilt**.

Ignore a track branching left at NN 878 677 as this leads to a rifle range. Continue close to the **River Tilt**, crossing a bridge to the east bank (NN 881 685). After 1.75km turn left, re-crossing the river via **Gilbert's Bridge** (NN 881 701). Turn almost immediately right on a fainter trail, eventually passing the overgrown remains of **Sean-bhaile**.

Negotiating the rough and overgrown west side of Glen Tilt, it may come as a surprise to find a small but perfectly formed single-arched stone bridge carrying the trail across a narrow gorge. It looks inestimably old and sturdy, as if it had grown out of the rock. A little further back, the route passes overgrown and lichen-crusted mounds of stones, the faint outlines of enclosures and cottages still just visible. More remnants lie further on, beyond another arched bridge across the Allt Mhairc. These are all that remain of the once-thriving settlement of Sean-bhaile, meaning 'old town' in English. Set among open birch woodland, this crofting community comprised 27 buildings and four corn-drying kilns. There were enclosure systems and lazy bed cultivation, and cattle would have been grazed in the woodlands and on the hillsides. By the 1850s, decline and depopulation were underway, and it is well over a century now since cartwheels last rumbled over those redoubtable bridges.

Cross a stone bridge (NN 888 713) then bear left on a path climbing parallel to the burn. In 1.5km cross another bridge and wind uphill past more township remains. **Beinn Mheadhonach** (901m) rises ahead between **Gleann Diridh** and **Gleann Mhairc**. Climb this long whale-backed ridge following paths through the heather. From the cairn the outlook is impressive, across miles of empty, rolling hills.

▲ On the wild north side of Beinn Mheadhonach, heading for the Tarf

ROUTE 8 – BLAIR ATHOLL TO KINGUSSIE

Continue for 1.5km to **Carn a' Chiaraidh**, then keep slightly east of north for 2.25km to **Loch Mhairc**. Bear northwest to the **Tarf**, which has plenty of dry, flat ground for camping along its banks.

DAY 2
Tarf Water to Allt Bhran

Start	Tarf Water (NN 881 804)
Distance	19km (11¾ miles)
Total ascent	643m (2110ft)
Time	7–8hr
Summits	Meall Tionail na Beinne Brice 790m, Beinn Bhreac 912m (C), Leathad an Taobhain 902m (C)

From the **Tarf**, climb north to **Meall Tionail na Beinne Brice** (790m). Bend westwards above a shallow corrie to **Beinn Bhreac** (912m), on the vast watershed that forms the border between Atholl and Badenoch. Descend northeast for 800 metres then bear west, meandering along the watershed for 7km to reach the east summit of Leathad an Taobhain (912m), crowned by a trig point. Navigationally, this is the trickiest part of the route. The featureless landscape and indistinct tops make it hard to stay on track, even in reasonable visibility.

Head west for 750 metres to the lower top (902m) of **Leathad an Taobhain**, then southwest to the summit of the **Minigaig**, an old cattle-droving route.

The Minigaig is a high, exposed route between Badenoch and Atholl. It was favoured by the 19th-century cattle drovers as it enabled them to avoid the tolls on the military road through Drumochter (now the A9).

Follow the track north. Its course is clear as it descends across the hillside but becomes indistinct further down by the burn among deep heather and boggy patches. Keep to the northeast bank. Further on, there are grassy flats for camping by **Allt Bhran**, once grazed by the drovers' cattle.

▲ *A view up Gleann Mhairc showing the New Bridge*

DAY 3
Allt Bhran to Kingussie

Start	Allt Bhran (NN 780 893)
Distance	16km (10 miles)
Total ascent	561m (1840ft)
Time	6–7hr
Summits	Meallach Mhòr 769m (C), Clach-mheall 626m, Croidh-la 643m

Where the path fords **Allt nam Plaidean**, climb north towards **Meallach Mhòr** (769m). The stony summit offers a fine view south towards Loch an t-Seilich and the Gaick Pass. Descend north to the col under **Meallach Bheag**. Bear right across a boggy saddle to **Clach-mheall** (626m). Follow the ridge north to **Croidh-la** (643m). Pause on Croidh-la to enjoy the panoramic view across Strathspey, including the distant buildings of Kingussie, the journey's end, and the great sweep of the Monadh Liath beyond.

After 2.5km bear left, following a path down to the track in **Glen Tromie**. Turn right to reach the B970 at **Tromie Bridge** and follow the road west to **Kingussie**. Some of the road walking can be avoided by detouring via the Badenoch Way. Turn right through a wooden gate just west of Tromie Bridge and follow the waymarked trail through woodland, part of the RSPB Insh Marshes reserve, re-joining the **B970** at Torcroy.

▲ Loch Mhairc at twilight

ROUTE 9
The Mòine Mhòr Munros

Start/finish	Achlean car park, Glen Feshie (NN 850 983)
Total distance	49km (30½ miles)
Total ascent	2250m (7380ft)
Time	2–3 days
Terrain	High mountain, moorland, bog, heather and bracken bashing, pine forest.
Key summits	Càrn Bàn Mòr 1052m (M), Sgòr Gaoith 1118m (M), Braeriach 1296m (M), Sgòr an Lochain Uaine 1258m (M), Càirn Toul 1291m (M), Devil's Point 1004m (M), Mullach Clach a' Bhlàir 1019m (M)
Maps	OS Landranger 43 Braemar & Blair Atholl
Note	This walk could be done over 2 longer days, but is described over 3, primarily to allow an overnight in Glen Feshie.

▲ Dawn above Loch Eanaich

SCOTTISH WILD COUNTRY BACKPACKING

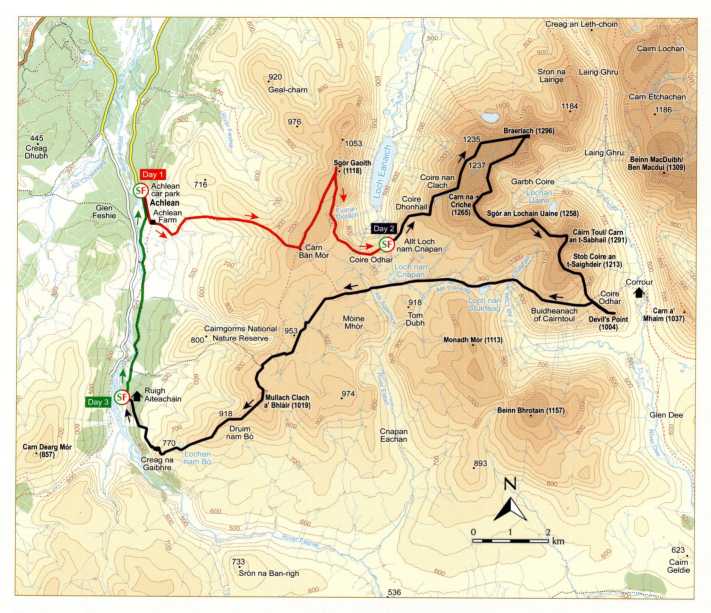

The Cairngorm massif is made up of three distinct plateaux, and this route explores the lesser-visited western plateau – the Mòine Mhòr (Great Moss). It includes seven Munros arranged around the edge of a bewildering high moor of lichen and crag, like the pinched edge of a gigantic pie – some of the highest and most remote ground in the UK.

This walk also introduces the wonder and magic of Glen Feshie, a place once heavily overgrazed but now repopulated with wildlife, young trees and local people. It contains some of the finest old-growth forest to be found in the UK. The forests of the Cairngorms provide the landscape grammar to the mountains' punctuation: relief and shelter from the austere grandeur of the high ground. Because of the distance from help, and the altitude, you are advised to choose a good weather window.

DAY 1
Achlean to Allt Loch Nan Cnapan

Start	Achlean car park (NN 850 983)
Distance	11.5km (7¼ miles)
Total ascent	820m (2690ft)
Time	4–5hr
Summits	Càrn Bàn Mòr 1052m (M), Sgòr Gaoith 1118m (M)

From the car park at **Achlean**, walk south into the glen for around 10 minutes, before turning left at a large farm gate, next to a stone marked for Càrn Bàn Mòr, the first Munro in the circuit. Proceed along the path through flat heather for a few minutes more, ignoring two paths to the right, until you meet the tree line and begin a gradual climb into the woods. After a short while, go through a green gate. There are glimpses of Glen Feshie through the trees as you ascend.

The path swings around to the north before leaving the tree line and contouring up towards the plateau onto **Mòine Mhòr**. Around 40 minutes from the start, you will pass a burn, the last source of reliable water until the plateau. The climb steepens at the end. Expect to take around 2hr from the start of the walk. Crest the plateau and marvel at Scotland's only subalpine environment. Scale and distance are deceptive here – the summits may be huge but they are dwarfed by the headwalls, coires (corries) and lochans which stretch out in front of you.

Càrn Bàn Mòr (1052m), around 300 metres to the north of the path, has a blunt top marked with a low-lying shelter cairn. From here, head north to **Sgòr Gaoith** (1118m), whose sail-like peak marks it out from the bulky tops elsewhere. A delightful single-track loses height before becoming eroded and slowly rising to the top, around 2km from Càrn Bàn Mòr.

Rather than rejoin the main track, make the most of the views and descend east to find a thin path that shadows the cliff edge, making for swift progress. Pass the natural spring at **Fuaran Diotach** and continue around the vast bowl of **Coire Odhar**. The ground underfoot now becomes much rougher and rockier as you descend, but the views straight down the glen are worth the slower pace.

There's good camping on the banks of **Allt Loch nan Cnapan** or at its source, the **Loch nan Cnapan**.

DAY 2
Allt Loch Nan Cnapan to Glen Feshie

Start	Allt Loch nan Cnapan or vicinity (NN 917 963)
Distance	32km (20 miles)
Total ascent	1380m (4525ft)
Time	8–10hr
Summits	Braeriach 1296m (M), Carn na Criche 1265m, Sgòr an Lochain Uaine 1258m (M), Càirn Toul 1291m (M), Devil's Point 1004m (M), Mullach Clach a' Bhlàir 1019m (M)

Continue over rough glacial ground before the climb north, following the edge of the **Coire Dhonhail**. The views are expansive as you climb onto a broader and grassy upper shoulder above **Coire nan Clach**.

Avoid the temptation to be drawn onto the high ground to the southeast; instead, keep to the north edge of the plateau. Follow a series of cairns across the high ground, first northwest and then east over gravelly tundra to the spectacular lookout of **Braeriach** (1296m), the UK's third highest mountain.

From the summit descend gradually southwest to follow the edge of the plateau again – this time around the immense **Garbh Coire**. Cross the burn (the source of the River Dee, the highest river in the UK) and contour around **Carn na Criche** (1265m), taking care of cornices which can persist late into the season. Descend on an intermittent path before the straightforward easterly climb to **Sgòr an Lochain Uaine** (1258m), also named 'Angel's Peak' (probably to match the 'Devil's Point', see below). This is a beautiful viewpoint for the UK's second highest point, Ben Macdui, across the ancient pass of the Lairig Ghru.

The route to the UK's fourth highest point, **Càirn Toul** (1291m), continues in much the same vein, with an easy descent to a pink sandy *bealach* followed by a climb over mixed ground to the summit. As you climb there are good views down into the 'green lochan' which gives Sgòr an Lochain Uaine it's Gaelic name.

Descending south from the summit on blocky talus requires more concentration, before the ridge narrows and gently rises again to Stob Coire an t-Saighdeir. The path heads

SCOTTISH WILD COUNTRY BACKPACKING

▲ Cairn Toul

▲ The Falls of Dee

▲ The 'green lochan' under Sgòr an Lochain Uaine, with Ben Macdui opposite

east, descending over grass before becoming more defined and regaining about 100m to reach the final summit on this side of the plateau – the **Devil's Point** (1004m). Rumour suggests the Devil's Point was renamed from the Gaelic for something much ruder! Its priapic nature is less obvious from the summit, but the views once again are breathtaking.

Descend the way you came and contour easily around the back of Stob Coire an t-Saighdeir, across the lonely **Buidheanach of Cairntoul**. Go west, then around the hill to the north. Avoid losing too much height and aim to cross **Allt Clais ant-Sabhail** and meet **Loch nan Stuirteag**. In the right conditions, this is a heavenly spot and a good option for camping.

From the loch, head west keeping **Allt Luineag** on your left, which can be tricky as the river braids. After 1km or so, cross the river but continue west, past the south end of Loch nan Cnapan (again, good camping) aiming to meet the track that terminates by **Allt Sgairnich**. Cross the burn and join this ugly intrusion into the wilds, climbing gradually.

Continue on this track as it swings southwest, ignoring the quartz-topped cairn and a smaller path to your right. Ford two small rivers and ignore another path to your right. Head south and then leave the main track for a smaller dirt track continuing south to the final Munro of **Mullach Clach a' Bhlàir** (1019m). Follow this straight over and continue southwest, descending to the seldom-visited **Druim nam Bò**.

Pass **Lochan Nam Bò** on your right and descend on heather and boggy ground to the magnificent cairn at **Craig na Gaibhre**. The view of Feshie's fertile plains, trees and the river's braids are compensation for the ugly track!

Go south to find the start of an old stalkers' path which zigzags down the hill. The track is very overgrown, disappears and reappears on the hillside, before becoming more apparent at its foot, running northwest, parallel with the tree line. Cross the burn via a tiny, beautiful old footbridge, following the burn for short while, before peeling off right and into the trees, juniper and blaeberry. It's hard going; the ancient track is barely discernible, but it gives an unparalleled aspect on Glen Feshie.

In the early 2000s a new landowner and management regime brought the deer grazing under control in Glen Feshie. As a result, the old pine trees are now self-seeding and there is widespread regeneration. The area has been transformed almost beyond recognition and has become one of the jewels of the Highlands and an exemplar of the principles of 'rewilding'.

For its final few hundred metres the path widens and then heads steeply downhill. Turn right for a short walk to the **Ruigh Aiteachain bothy**, recently renovated by the estate, and with plentiful camping, spring water and even basic toilets nearby.

The newly refurbished Ruigh Aiteachain bothy, in Glen Feshie, is now the sole building standing in the vicinity of a collection of small follies built by a 19th-century aristocrat. The writer Patrick Baker describes it as a series of 'faux rustic refuges', by cruel irony freshly constructed at a time where generations of highlanders were being forcibly removed from their crofts.

Georgina Russell and her guests created a retreat from the prying eyes of high society, which included her husband and patron of the arts, the Duke of Bedford. Her friend, the artist Edwin Landseer had his cake and ate it, painting frescoes and making studies for some of his best-known works there, while consorting with the good lady herself. The chimney stack of a building he decorated, and most probably worked in, still stands a short distance away from the bothy itself.

There's a lack of historical clarity about whether Ruigh Aiteachain is the exact site of Russell's commune, but in the 1850s it was certainly home to her favourite servant, the gamekeeper John Fraser, his wife Mary and their two daughters. It sits under slopes of gnarled juniper trees that give the place its name, and the prefix 'Ruigh' shows that it was inhabited as a shieling long before the arrival of modern romantics, past or present.

DAY 3
Ruigh Aiteachain bothy to Achlean car park

Start	Ruigh Aiteachain bothy or vicinity (NN 846 927)
Distance	6km (3¾ miles)
Total ascent	50m (165ft)
Time	2hr

From the bothy, head north on an obvious track, through the forest and clearings. You may spot eagle, merlin and other birds of prey among the statuesque pines. Follow the main track which mostly stays away from the River Feshie, which is free flowing and has many fast-changing braids. Continue through old plantation, to ford **Allt Garbhlach**, which again is very untamed and can be difficult to cross in spate. The trees thin and the glen opens out to moorland. Pass the refurbished **Achlean Farm** on your left and turn left to rejoin the track and then the road to the car park.

▲ Camping under the tall Caledonian pines of Glen Feshie
▶ Looking back to Glen Feshie from the climb onto the plateau

ROUTE 10
Ben Avon and Beinn a' Bhuird

Start/finish	Car park for Queen's Cairn and Delnabo, just outside Tomintoul (NJ 164 176)
Total distance	50km (31 miles)
Total ascent	1625m (5330ft)
Time	2 days
Terrain	Single-track road, moorland, high mountain tundra, off-path heather bashing, this route has it all!
Key summits	Ben Avon 1171m (M), Beinn a' Bhuird 1197m (M)
Maps	OS Explorer 58, Braemar, Tomintoul & Glen Avon; OS Landranger 36, Grantown & Aviemore
Note	This is a perfect route to access by bike – it complements the trip as well as making it more accessible. Tomintoul itself is a charming place to finish up (the Glen Avon Hotel has an open fire, a good bar and food).

▲ Hiking towards Beinn a' Bhuird's north top, with Glen Sluggan in the far distance

Ben Avon is massive. It's less a single mountain and more a whole flank of the entire Cairngorm range itself, and the long way in via Tomintoul and Glen Avon is the perfect way to pay it the respect it's due. Crucially, it sets us up for a full east–west traverse and a visit to many of the large, pink granite tors that characterise this mountain.

Along the way, you may see owls, eagles, dippers and other birds using the wild and beautiful River Avon as a thoroughfare, and visit the remains of a World War II training aircraft on a northern spur of the route's second mountain, Beinn a' Bhuird.

SCOTTISH WILD COUNTRY BACKPACKING

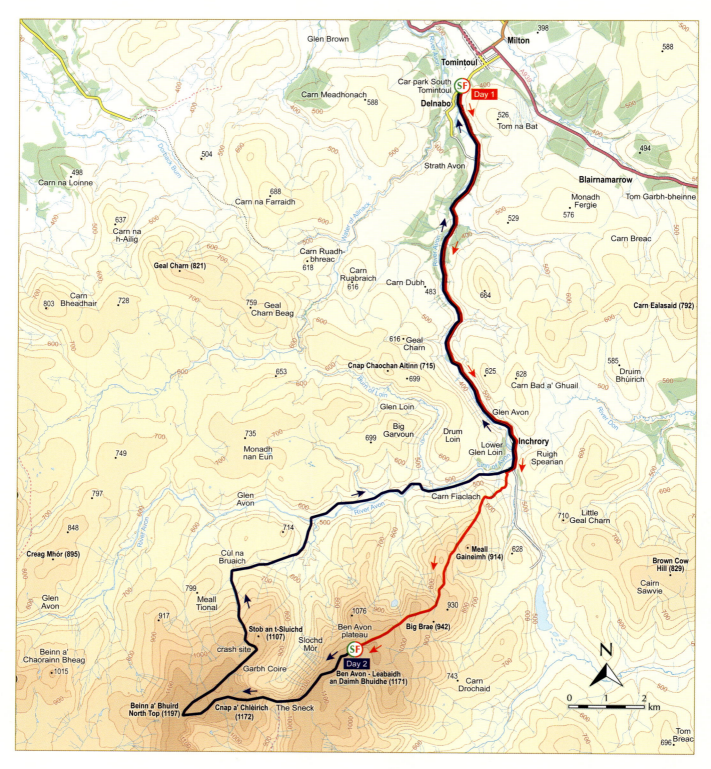

96

ROUTE 10 – BEN AVON AND BEINN A' BHUIRD

DAY 1
Tomintoul to Ben Avon Plateau

Start	Car park for Queen's Cairn and Delnabo, just outside Tomintoul (NJ 164 176)
Distance	20km (12½ miles)
Total ascent	1005m (3300ft)
Time	5–6hr (using bike) or 8–9hr (on foot only)
Summits	Meall Gaineimh 914m, Ben Avon 1171m (M)

From the **car park** on Delnabo road, just south of Tomintoul, simply follow the track south along the **River Avon** for around 10km. This alternates between tarmac and gravel and will take 1–2hr by bike, somewhat longer on foot. Pass several homesteads before reaching **Inchrory**, where the track descends to the river flats and then splits; straight ahead to Glen Builg, and right to the **Linn of Avon**. The Linn of Avon sports a fine series of cascading waterfalls and beautiful regenerating woodland.

Leave your bike here and take the footpath that climbs steadily south onto the heathery mass of **Carn Fiaclach**. Continue on intermittent paths uphill towards **Meall Gaineimh** (914m). Meall Gaineimh was re-surveyed in 2015 to see if it might qualify for Munro status, but fell less than a metre short of the 914.4m needed.

The path continues west of this top, through a cleft between house-sized, mushroom-like granite tors that hang either side of the path. Slowly the character of the Avon plateau begins to reveal itself, a miniature Monument Valley.

Continue on a clear path with the ground sloping away to your left to reach **Big Brae**, where a good spring can often provide drinking water. Follow the higher ground west and then southwest, visiting as many of the tors as you like, which, given their size at close quarters, loom surprisingly small on the horizon at first glance. It's all about scale and space on Ben Avon.

Ground for camping on the plateau is extensive but shelter is almost non-existent, so check the weather forecast carefully before the off!

▲ Looking north to Slochd Mòr from The Sneck

SCOTTISH WILD COUNTRY BACKPACKING

DAY 2
Ben Avon plateau to Tomintoul

Start	Vicinity of Ben Avon plateau (NJ 139 024)
Distance	31km (19¼ miles)
Total ascent	620m (2035ft)
Time	7–9hr (using bike) or 10–12hr (on foot only)
Summits	Ben Avon 1171m, Cnap a' Chlèirich 1172m, Beinn a' Bhuird 1197m (M), Stob an t-Sluichd 1107m

Be sure to visit the official summit tor of **Ben Avon** – **Leabaidh an Daimh Bhuidhe** (1171m) – but note that climbing to the very top is slippery under wet or icy conditions. Continue southwest and descend to **The Sneck**, a *bealach* overhanging the remote and dramatic **Slochd Mòr**. Marvel at your situation among a jumble of smooth red granite as the ground falls away to the north; a vast stage in a natural amphitheatre. Once you've finished marvelling, water can be collected a short distance to the south.

Now climb west following the corrie edge before departing for the summit of **Cnap a' Chlèirich** (1172m), a useful staging post before heading west across gently undulating ground to the North (and highest) Top of our second Munro, **Beinn a' Bhuird**, which is very easy to miss in poor visibility.

From the summit cairn, head northeast for the rim of **Garbh Coire**, and then north for the first of the summit tors of **Stob an t-Sluichd** (1107m). The Oxford PH404 crash site and memorial are situated between the first and second rock outcrops to the south of the main summit. It's a moving place to pay your respects. If you do visit, please treat it as a war grave and don't remove or disturb anything from the crash site.

There are several aircraft crash sites across the Cairngorms, and two on Ben a' Bhuird. The site of the Oxford plane (registered as PH404), which crashed in January 1945, was discovered later that year by two local hillwalkers. They were alarmed to find not only the wreck, but also the bodies of the crew. One man had apparently survived the initial impact and had retrieved clothing from his companions in an attempt to bandage a wound and keep himself warm, but had later perished.

Locals, mountain rescue and the RAF collaborated in a rescue and clear-up operation, and the men were brought down off the hill and put to rest. Most of the plane was destroyed on site to prevent it from being mistaken for any future incidents. The engines were (and still are) intact, probably because the aircraft had crashed into snow.

The deceased crew members were Czech air cadets of 311 Squadron: Squadron Leader Karel Kvapil (pilot), Flying Officer Leo Linhart (pilot), Flying Officer Jan Vella (pilot), Flying Officer Valter Kauders (wireless operator/air gunner) and Warrant Officer Rudolph Jelen (pilot).

A memorial organised by members of the RAF was placed on site in 2005.

Descend west and then north, following the burn that bears the same hill's name – Allt Stob an t-Sluichd. Reach a stalkers' track and bear right over the peaty shoulder of the same hill before descending to the watershed of **Cùl na Bruaich**. The path disappears for a while but follow the burn east and then north over challenging and boggy terrain. You are rewarded by superlative views back up to the Sneck. Meet a rickety footbridge, cross the **River Avon** and turn right at the small hut.

Now head east on the main track. Note that the route splits around 2km from the hut. The higher track is simpler but steeper, the low path follows the river and is very eroded in places. The paths converge at a large bridge. Cross the bridge and continue south of the river again to reach the **Linn of Avon**, to return by way of **Glen Avon** to **Tomintoul**.

▲ The remains of the Oxford PH404, with Cairn Gorm and Bynack More in the background

ROUTE 11
Northeast Cairngorms

Start/finish	Car park (free), Tomintoul village centre (NJ 169 186)
Total distance	93.5km (58 miles)
Total ascent	2230m (7315ft)
Time	3–4 days
Terrain	Mostly a mix of Landrover tracks and footpaths. Deep heather and intermittent sheep tracks along the Ailnack Gorge, precarious and exposed in places.
Maps	OS Explorer 57 Cairn Gorm & Aviemore and 58 Braemar, Tomintoul & Glen Avon; OS Landranger 36 Grantown & Aviemore and 43 Braemar & Blair Atholl
Note	Although the route mostly follows paths and tracks, the cumulative ascent is significant. It's therefore best to allow 4 days. If attempting the route over 3 days, consider camping around Loch Builg or Glen Gairn on the first night and the Fords of Avon on the second night.

▲ Walking through the pass between Glen Gairn and Glen Quoich

The Cairngorms are big by Scottish standards. These venerable mountains bear the imprint of ice ages on a grand scale, offering a powerful glimpse into deep time. No public roads cross them, and there are few other places where you can walk for miles through unbroken native woodland or spend a day following a trail through wild glens and passes. It's a landscape made for long treks of a type more associated with the mountains of continental Europe or North America.

This route is a classic Scots 'stravaig' or wander, threading together lesser-known landscapes and paths, while keeping away from the region's fleshpots and ski slopes. Instead of the Lairig Ghru, the route follows the longer but lesser-known trans-Cairngorm route, the Lairig an Laoigh. The busier parts of Abernethy Forest are avoided and its remote eastern fringes are explored instead. Best of all, this route is a journey of discovery along the Ailnack Gorge, Scotland's finest glacial meltwater channel.

There are many river crossings to consider, several of which may be impossible in spate. This route is therefore best saved for a prolonged spell of settled weather.

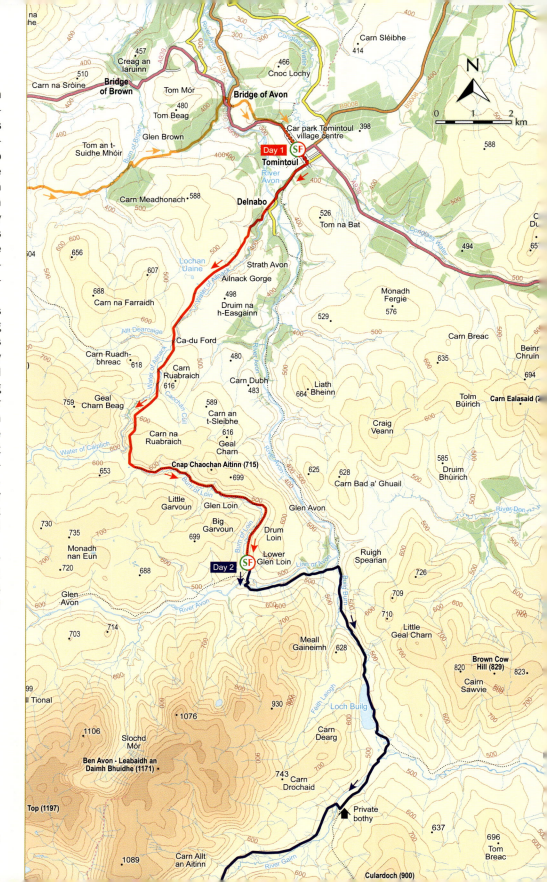

100 ▶ Map continues on page 102

ROUTE 11 – NORTHEAST CAIRNGORMS

DAY 1
Tomintoul to Glen Loin

Start	Car park, Tomintoul (NJ 169 186)
Distance	16.2km (10 miles)
Total ascent	552m (1810ft)
Time	5–6hr

Head south along Main Street, **Tomintoul**, then right on the road signposted for Delnabo. In 1.25km, cross the **River Avon**. Immediately leave the tarmac road and go straight on for 400 metres past the lodge and farm buildings. Beyond a final cottage, the track fords a burn and climbs steeply above the wooded lower reach of Ailnack Gorge to the moorland beyond.

The track ends near **Lochan Uaine** (3km). Boggy vehicle tracks continue for 200 metres to a fence with a tiny tarn just beyond. Bear slightly left, cross the fence, and pick up a sheep path just east of the tarn. Follow this as it contours around the steep slopes above the **Water of Ailnack**, slightly exposed in one place.

Descend steeply alongside the birch-filled ravine of **Allt Dearcaige** to reach **Ca-du Ford** (NJ 136 135), a historic crossing on the Ailnack. Across the river bear immediately right, slanting uphill on a faint path. Continue for 500 metres until a path descends to the river again. This is the most open section of the Ailnack. Follow it upstream for 600 metres, crossing back briefly to the west bank to avoid where the river cuts into the eroded slopes of **Carn Ruabraich** (616m).

Back on the east bank, climb a shoulder between the Ailnack and a tributary (**Caochan Cùil**). After 1km, the steepest, most dramatic section of the **Ailnack Gorge** begins. Paths are sketchy and care needed to avoid straying too far down. At one point (NJ 124 107) the path is especially precarious with a serious run-out over crags.

On the hillside above the entrance to the gorge it's worth stopping to admire a classic example of river capture. The Water of Caiplich comes in from the huge, empty moors to the west. It's clear to see that the river once continued into what is now Glen Loin. That was before a build-up of glacial ice and meltwater forced a new channel northwards, creating the Ailnack Gorge.

Beyond the gorge, descend gradually south into austere **Glen Loin** with its uniformly steep, scree-patched sides. After 650 metres a good track starts. Camping is straightforward, with flat, grassy areas throughout the glen.

DAY 2
Glen Loin to Glen Quoich

Start	Lower Glen Loin (NJ 155 073)
Distance	24km (15 miles)
Total ascent	424m (1390ft)
Time	8–10hr

At a junction at NJ 156 072 bear right across the **Burn of Loin**. In 200 metres, another track joins from the right. Continue downhill to cross the **River Avon** by a bridge. Head east for 2.5km past the **Linn of Avon**, where the river charges through a tree-fringed gorge, and across the **Builg Burn** by a bridge. Turn right up Glen Builg, criss-crossing the burn several times.

After 3km the track becomes a path and hugs the eastern shore of **Loch Builg**. Beyond, reach a track and turn left, winding between *lochans* for 400 metres to another junction. Turn right down to the River Gairn and

▲ The Ailnack Gorge with Ben Avon beyond

SCOTTISH WILD COUNTRY BACKPACKING

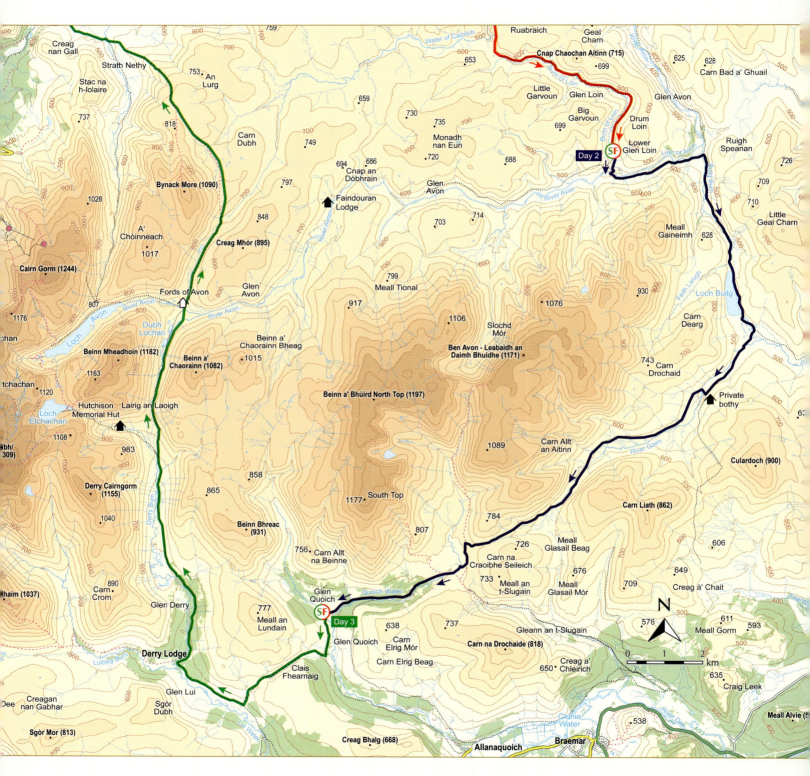

ROUTE 11 – NORTHEAST CAIRNGORMS

over a bridge. Bear right and head upstream. After 1.25km reach a **private bothy** and turn right down to the river. The footbridge marked on OS maps is gone, so the Gairn must be forded (alternatively there is a bridge just over 1km upstream, reached via the trackless south bank).

Walk southwest following faint Landrover tracks across a grassy area. Beyond, find the beginning of the path that leads eventually through a steep-sided pass to **Glen Quoich** (8.5km).

At the junction of paths above the **Quoich** (NO 117 967) turn left and continue for 800 metres, then right. Ford the river (NO 111 959) and follow a path, not marked on OS maps, west into the pinewoods, where careful prospecting is needed to find a campsite.

> When you leave Glen Gairn behind and descend into Glen Quoich, the change in the landscape is dramatic. Glen Gairn is rather bleak, an area managed for driven grouse shooting and deer stalking, bereft of tree cover. Glen Quoich, on the other hand, boasts a vibrant and growing Caledonian pine woodland. It lies within the Mar Lodge Estate, an area of great conservation significance from the relict pinewoods of the glens to the subarctic plateaux of the high Cairngorms. Since 1995 the estate has been managed by the National Trust for Scotland, primarily in the interests of conservation and landscape restoration. Once part of the ancient Earldom of Mar, the land was forfeited after the Jacobite rebellion of 1715. After that, for nearly 300 years it followed a course common to many areas of the Highlands, through depopulation, recreational shooting and fishing, and more recently a succession of owners including a property company and a Swiss family, the Panchauds, who planned to build a ski resort on Beinn a' Bhuird. That such a culturally and ecologically rich area could be made a hostage to fortune in this way must seem strange to many non-Scots. For now, however, the future of Mar Lodge Estate and its burgeoning forest seems secure.

DAY 3
Glen Quoich to Ryvoan bothy

Start	Glen Quoich (NO 080 948)
Distance	28.5km (17½ miles)
Total ascent	755m (2475ft)
Time	9–11hr

Bear south across Allt an Dubh-ghlinne. After 1km turn right onto a well-made path that climbs to the **Clais Fhearnaig**. Continue west through this delightful little defile complete with shallow, rush-fringed *lochans*. Beyond, the path descends to the Glen Lui track.

> Clais Fhearnaig is another glacial meltwater channel driven across the watershed thousands of years ago, but the largest *lochan* in it is much more recent, created when the eastern outflow was deliberately dammed. This may have been to create a pond for fishing, although its date and origins are unclear.

▲ The Linn of Avon

SCOTTISH WILD COUNTRY BACKPACKING

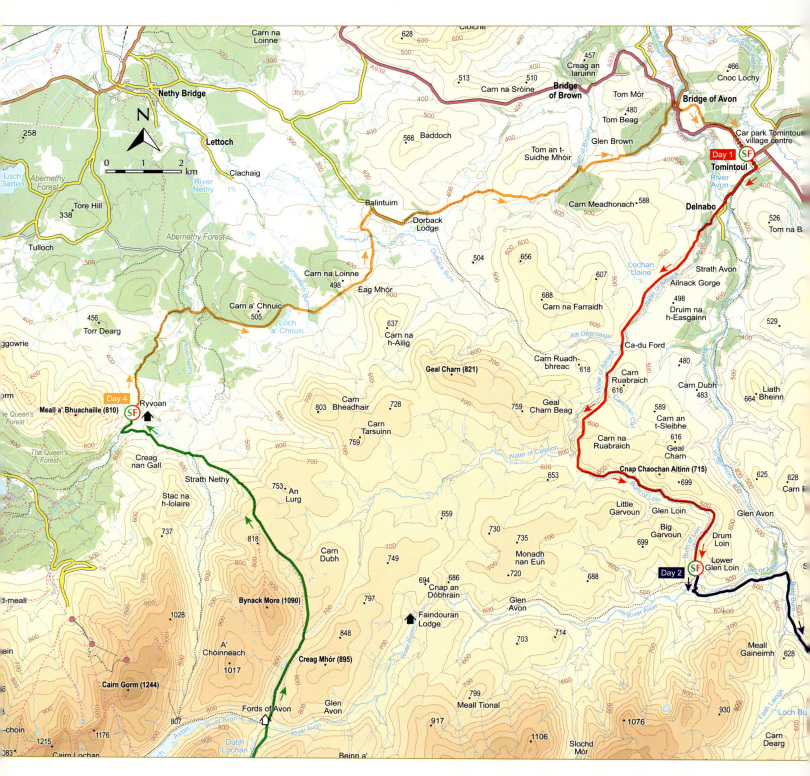

104

ROUTE 11 – NORTHEAST CAIRNGORMS

Turn right towards **Derry Lodge**. About 100 metres beyond the boarded-up building, bear right on the signposted path and climb gradually through pinewoods on the eastern side of **Glen Derry**. After 6km the path forks, with the left fork leading to the Hutchison Memorial Hut, an open bothy. Take the right fork over the **Lairig an Laoigh** to the **Fords of Avon**, another serious river crossing. On the north bank there is an emergency shelter.

The path continues north for 9km over high, exposed uplands and down to a footbridge over the **River Nethy**. At a junction of tracks 2km further on, turn right to reach **Ryvoan bothy** in 500 metres.

DAY 4
Ryvoan bothy to Tomintoul

Start	Ryvoan bothy (NJ 006 115)
Distance	25km (15½ miles)
Total ascent	500m (1640ft)
Time	8–10hr

Continue north into **Abernethy Forest**. After 3.75km (NJ 018 144) turn right onto a path that descends to the **Nethy** in 275 metres. Ford the substantial river; the far bank is heavily overgrown so pick your spot carefully. Rejoin the path, climbing away from the river to reach a crossroads after 325 metres (NJ 025 145). Continue straight ahead for 3.25km, past **Loch a' Chnuic** to the **Faesheallach Burn**. Just before the burn the track bends right. Follow instead the path that goes straight on across the burn and climbs eventually to **Eag Mhòr**, a notch in the hills that has been intermittently visible for a while.

Walk through the old glacial breach, ford the **Dorback Burn** and reach the public road just beyond the modern house at **Balintuim**. Turn right; after 1km the tarmac ends at the entrance to **Dorback Lodge**. Bear left following a track signposted to Tomintoul, bypassing the lodge grounds. Continue west for 4.5km towards **Glen Brown**. At NJ 115 176 ford a burn and turn immediately left onto a grassy track, again signposted for Tomintoul. After 1km, following the track as it criss-crosses the **Burn of Brown** several times, bear right at the end of a conifer plantation to pick up a track that leads in 3.5km to **Bridge of Avon**. Follow the green Scotways signage for **Tomintoul** that directs you over the old bridge, steeply up to Campdalemore farm, then down into the village.

▲ Looking across Abernethy Forest to the mountains

NORTHWEST HIGHLANDS

◀ Topping out on Sgùrr a' Chaorachain (Route 15)

SCOTTISH WILD COUNTRY BACKPACKING

ROUTE 12
Inverinate Forest and the Gates of Affric

Start/finish	Large roadside parking area for Clachan Duich burial ground on minor road to Morvich just off A87 (NG 947 212)
Total distance	39km (24¼ miles)
Total ascent	3110m (10,205ft)
Time	3–4 days
Terrain	Mostly off trail over rough, sometimes boggy, mountainous terrain. Some stretches on well-graded deer stalkers' paths.
Key summits	Sgùrr an Airgid 841m (C), Sgùrr Gaorsaic 839m (C), Beinn Fhada 1032m (M), A' Ghlas-bheinn 918m (M)
Maps	OS Explorer 414 Glen Shiel & Kintail Forest; OS Landranger 33 Loch Alsh, Glen Shiel & Loch Hourn
Note	This route requires much stamina as there are long climbs and much off-trail travel. There is one serious river crossing – Abhainn Gaorsaic – which is substantial even in dry conditions and may be impassable in spate.

Tucked beyond the high ridges of Affric and Kintail with their long chains of Munros is an obscure and fascinating hinterland filled with hidden interest. This route charts a course over a disparate and rugged collection of peaks, some little visited. There is much more to this route than the summits, however. The Falls of Glomach, one of the highest waterfalls in Britain, is well worth the short detour. Arduous travel by Abhainn Gaorsaic is livened by small trout darting in the shallows and the lonely calls of moorland birds. The traverse of sprawling Beinn Fhada, high above the fastnesses of its northern corries, offers classic mountain travel, and Bealach an Sgàirne – also known as the Gates of Affric – is one of the finest passes in the country. This tough, varied route will provide the backpacker with a wealth of memories and reflections.

▲ Camping near the summit of Beinn Fhada

ROUTE 12 – INVERINATE FOREST AND THE GATES OF AFFRIC

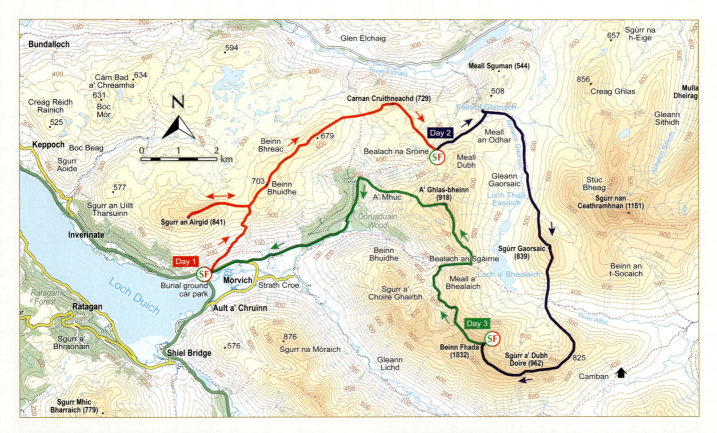

▲ By Abhainn Gaorsaic

109

DAY 1
Clachan Duich to Bealach na Sròine

Start	Large roadside parking area for Clachan Duich burial ground (NG 947 212)
Distance	12.5km (8 miles)
Total ascent	1320m (4330ft)
Time	7–9hr
Summits	Sgùrr an Airgid 841m (C), Beinn Bhuidhe 703m, Carnan Cruithneachd 729m

Opposite the **Clachan Duich burial ground parking area** go through a gate and follow a path climbing northeast across the hillside. After 1.25km the path emerges east of a wide *bealach* at a small cairn, a good spot to leave rucksacks for an out-and-back trip to **Sgùrr an Airgid** (841m; 3.5km return). Follow the path west towards the hill. The steep east ridge is divided by a shallow gully; the path straggles up the right-hand spur to the summit, crowned by a trig pillar and commanding fine views west to Skye.

Return to the cairn. Climb northeast to **Beinn Bhuidhe** (703m). Continue northeast for 1.75km along the rough crest to reach **Beinn Bhreac** (649m) and another unnamed top beyond (679m).

Bold, rocky **Carnan Cruithneachd** (729m) lies 2km to the northeast. Descend to Bealach Con and climb a wide, heathery gully flanked by crags (gully entrance NG 988 256). At the top climb left to the summit ridge. Head east past a large pool below the lower west top before climbing to the summit cairn. Enjoy the vertigo-inducing view into **Glen Elchaig** before continuing west for around 100 metres until it is safe to descend steeply right to reach flat moorland. Continue southeast towards **Bealach na Sròine**, scouring Allt na Laoidhre and surrounding moorland for a campsite.

DAY 2
Bealach na Sròine to Beinn Fhada

Start	Bealach na Sròine (NH 005 245)
Distance	13km (8 miles)
Total ascent	1235m (4050ft)
Time	7–9hr
Summits	Sgùrr Gaorsaic 839m (C), Sgùrr a' Dubh Doire 962m, Beinn Fhada 1032m (M)

From **Bealach na Sròine**, follow the path northeast for 1.5km to the top of the **Falls of Glomach**, where there is a National Trust for Scotland (NTS) sign.

> One of the tallest waterfalls in Britain, with a drop of 113 metres into a deep wooded gorge, the Falls of Glomach are well worth the detour. To view the upper falls, leave your rucksack at the National Trust for Scotland sign and go left down the path above the gorge for around 100 metres to reach a vertiginous viewpoint.

Return to the sign and follow **Abhainn Gaorsaic** upstream, taking advantage of deer trods where possible. The lively river becomes sluggish and meandering in the wide upper glen, with deep pools linked by occasional shallow runs. Use one of these to cross to the east bank and continue south to reach Allt Thuill Easaich which tumbles down the hillside towards **Loch Thuill Easaich**.

Cross the burn and follow it uphill, passing many attractive waterfalls. Reaching the lip of Coire Thuill Easaich, where the burn braids over three parallel waterfalls, bear right towards **Sgùrr Gaorsaic** (839m). The climb steepens considerably before emerging onto a little plateau. A short walk southeast leads to the summit – just a shoulder of **Sgùrr nan Ceathramhnan** (1151m) to the east, but a great vantage point for the surrounding mountains.

◀ Upper section of the Falls of Glomach

ROUTE 12 – INVERINATE FOREST AND THE GATES OF AFFRIC

Continue south and descend steeply. Stay a little left of a line of rusty metal fenceposts and keep a close eye on the ground ahead for outcrops and hollows. Reaching the glen floor, cross a path and Allt Cnoc na Cuaille and climb southeast up a long spur for 1.5km to reach the **unnamed 825m point** where another spur merges from the east. Bear west, climbing to **Sgùrr a' Dubh Doire** (962m). Follow the ridge above the north-facing corries to **Beinn Fhada** (1032m). Finding a campsite on the grassy plateau west of the summit is straightforward.

DAY 3
Beinn Fhada to Clachan Duich

Start	Beinn Fhada (NH 018 192)
Distance	13.5km (8½ miles)
Total ascent	560m (1840ft)
Time	6–7hr
Summits	A' Ghlas-bheinn 918m (M)

Head northwest then north onto the ridge towards **Meall a' Bhealaich**. On reaching a cairn (NH 011 203), take the path left into the corrie then north above Allt Coire an Sgàirne, gradually bearing east into the narrow approach to **Bealach an Sgàirne**. At the top of the pass (large cairn) a hillwalkers' path climbs steeply left. Follow it north-northwest for 1.75km to **A' Ghlas-bheinn** (918m).

Undoubtedly the finest portal between Affric and Kintail is the Bealach an Sgàirne – the 'pass of the murmuring stones'. The common interpretation of the name suggests the wind sighing through the boulders in this narrow, remote-feeling gap in the hills, and perhaps the occasional falling rock. However, on a quiet day in midweek when the pass is empty, the lone backpacker could be forgiven for nursing a curious feeling of being watched. Strange meetings and apparitions have been reported in the past. Certainly there's history here – the Bealach an Sgàirne has seen traffic for at least 1000 years and probably many more. It's the highest point of St Duthac's Way, a historic route of great antiquity between the settlements of Tomich in the east and Morvich in the west. Duthac was a Bishop of Ross-shire in the 11th century, patron saint of the Royal Burgh of Tain in Easter Ross, and a favourite of Scottish kings and warriors. It's likely that he used this route to travel between his parishes in Easter Ross and Kintail, and maybe even on to Ireland, where he was educated. Whatever your views on the supernatural, the echoes of centuries past seem almost within hearing in this secluded and awe-inspiring place.

Descend west-southwest for 800 metres then bear northwest to **A' Mhuc spur**. The descent to Allt an Leoid Ghaineamhaich is steep and requires concentration. Head west, avoiding being drawn into stream gullies to the north and south. The final stretch to the glen floor is the steepest; there is a rough path around 50 metres out from the forest fence which takes a good line.

At the foot of the slope, bear left to reach a track. Follow it south through the forest. After 1km the track forks: take the left branch downhill. In 200 metres, where the track bends sharply left, turn right through a metal gate and continue south through a rough grazing area and eventually onto a metalled road. Follow this west-southwest out of the forest and through sheep-grazing land. At NG 959 216 the road forks; bear right for a short distance until you come to another junction. Turn right to reach the **Clachan Duich burial ground car park** in 1km.

▲ View west from Bealach an Sgàirne

SCOTTISH WILD COUNTRY BACKPACKING

ROUTE 13
Affric Haute Route

Start/finish	Car park signposted Loch Beinn a' Mheadhain (marked Coille Ruigh na Cuileige on the OS map), NH 243 262
Total distance	50km (31 miles)
Total ascent	3860m (12,665ft)
Time	3 days
Terrain	Remote ridges, some simple scrambling.
Key summits	Toll Creagach 1054m (M), Tom a' Chòinnich 1112m (M), Càrn Eige 1183m (M), Beinn Fhionnliadh 1005m (M), Mullach na Dheiragain 982m (M), Sgùrr na Ceathramhnan 1151m (M), Màm Sodhail 1181m (M), Sgùrr na Lapaich 1036m (M)
Maps	OS Landranger 25 Glen Carron & Glen Affric and 33 Loch Alsh, Glen Shiel & Loch Hourn
Note	The first day can be shortened by camping at Loch a' Gharbh-bhealaich. For Day 3 it's useful to leave a bike at the River Affric car park, NH 200 233.

Taking in eight Munros, our 'Haute Route' is a spectacular, remote journey over some of the highest and wildest ground in Scotland, but with straightforward navigation and entry level scrambling. Airy ridges roll and pitch between the deep fjords of lochs Affric and Mullardoch like Viking long ships. Linking them are short but dramatic arêtes, towering spires, lonely buttresses and vast hanging corries that ring with the sound of waterfalls and wildlife.

This classic ridge traverse begins and ends by way of another of Scotland's 'rewilding' jewels. Glen Affric is a National Nature Reserve, its magical loch sheltered by regenerating forests of birch and Caledonian pine.

Glen Affric was purchased by the Forestry Commission in 1951 and is without doubt one of Scotland's, perhaps even Europe's, most spectacular landscapes. In the past, Clan Chisholm cut trees for the bridges of Inverness and later evicted their tenants to make way for sheep farming and deer stalking. The huge post-war hydroelectric expansion bought 'power to the glens' and also a dam to Loch Beinn a' Mheadhain. The middle of the glen is now a National Nature Reserve, chock full of Scots pine and associated wildlife, while charity Trees for Life and the National Trust for Scotland are working on broadleaf regeneration further west. The glen is cradled on three sides by some of Scotland's finest and most rugged mountains.

In 2021 a new, 30-year plan called Affric Highlands was announced, with the idea of expanding the existing natural regeneration into a much larger area, stretching from Inverness to the west coast. This ambitious 'rewilding' project stands to improve wildlife habitat, providing that enough landowners within the catchment can be convinced of its efficacy.

ROUTE 13 – AFFRIC HAUTE ROUTE

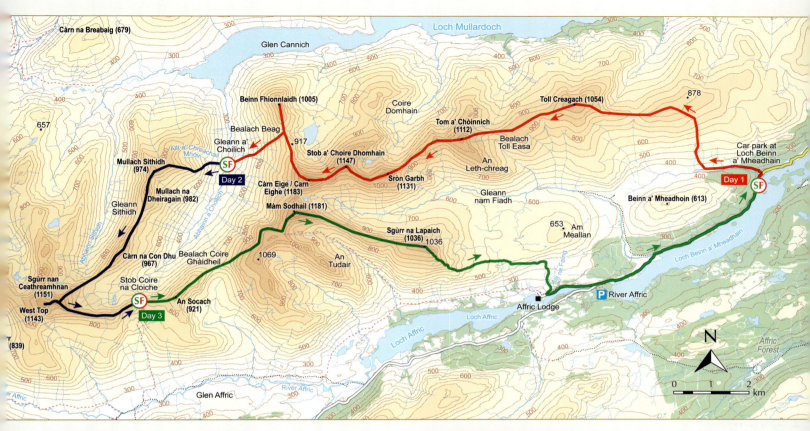

▲ Approaching the first Munro, Toll Creagach

DAY 1
Loch Beinn a' Mheadhain to Gleann a' Choilich

Start	Car park at Loch Beinn a' Mheadhain (NH 243 262)
Distance	19.5km (12 miles)
Total ascent	1720m (5645ft)
Time	10–12hr
Summits	Toll Creagach 1054m (M), Tom a' Chòinnich 1112m (M), An Leth Chreag 1051m, Sròn Garbh 1131m (M), Càrn Eige 1183m (M), Beinn Fhionnliadh 1005m (M)

Turn right out of the car park signposted **Loch Beinn a' Mheadhain** (on the OS map – Coille Ruigh na Cuileige), go over a stone bridge, then a cattle grid. Take a track immediately on your left, go through a gate and zigzag uphill on a beautiful old track, following Allt na h-Imirch among birch and pine. There are some good camping spots where the trees thin out.

Where a fence begins climbing the hill on the other side of the glen, look for a small cairn on your right marking a faint path running parallel to a burn. Follow a series of intermittent grassy 'rides' to meet another small cairn on a rock at 500m. Toil upwards past a few false summits before gaining the ridge, with a big shelter cairn to the northeast.

Descend west-southwest easily on grass before labouring 265 metres up to your first Munro, **Toll Creagach** (1054m). Note the rusting fence posts which can be used as a guide in poorer weather. Descend again west-southwest on a clearer path before reaching a grassy plateau. At its western end, descend to characterful **Bealach Toll Easa** (water and camping to the south), before climbing the dramatic east ridge of **Tom a' Chòinnich** (1112m). The path winds left and right of the crest.

Descend west on a broad grassy slope which narrows and rises before turning southwest, climbing briefly to the beautiful **An Leth Chreag** (1051m). Descend its knobbly back to a stony *bealach* with breathtaking views into **Coire Domhain**. Water and good camping can be found by dropping southeast 100m to the Loch a' Gharbh-bhealaich. A short, steep but simple climb to the summit of **Sròn Garbh** (1131m) awaits.

Now traverse the rim of the corrie. Initially broad and undulating, the ridge narrows to a dramatic arête. A thin path hangs to the right of the crest, before winding through a series of rocky pinnacles with a couple of airy steps on the way. Turn left (southwest) as the ridge flattens for **Stob a' Choire Dhomhain** before descending on a grassy plateau. The climb to **Càrn Eige** (1183m) is brief, its trig point and shelter offering superlative views over Applecross, Torridon and Skye.

Descend north on a path following the corrie edge. At **Bealach Beag**, drop your pack and continue north for the outlier of **Beinn Fhionnliadh** (1005m). Returning to your pack, descend

▲ One of many vast, wild corries that line the ridge

ROUTE 13 – AFFRIC HAUTE ROUTE

steeply southwest, contouring beneath crags. Cross two or three burns cutting into the hillside. Descend to the glen floor.

DAY 2
Gleann a' Choilich to Stob Coire na Cloiche

Start	Gleann a' Choilich or vicinity (NN 102 268)
Distance	10km (6¼ miles)
Total ascent	1200m (3935ft)
Time	8hr
Summits	Mullach na Dheiragain 982m (M), Càrn na Con Dhu 967m, Sgùrr na Ceathramhnan 1151m (M), Stob Coire na Cloiche 915m

Ford the **Abhain a' Choilich** and begin the climb back out of the glen, using **Allt a' Chreachail Mhòir** as a guide. Continue steeply above the first crags on your left and join the east ridge of Mullach Sithidh. The gradient now eases a little, but there's a lot of height to regain.

At the top of the ridge, go left (southwest) for **Mullach Sithidh**, with superb views over Killilan Forest (see Route 14). The route now follows the ridge south-southwest for around 4km. The north-facing crag of the next Munro – **Mullach na Dheiragain** (982m) – appears to bar the way, but there's an easy path to the left. Pass the cairn and descend gently to a broad *bealach* (good camping). An easy climb of **Càrn na Con Dhu** (967m) follows. Take the path on its west side before a short traverse over a fantastic jumble of rocks. Traverse a long, characterful ridge on a path that winds between outcrops, savouring the all-encompassing silence.

The northeast ridge of one of Scotland's most remote hills, **Sgùrr na Ceathramhnan** (1151m) dominates the view ahead. This steepens at the end but there is a loose path which mostly stays left of the crest. The summit itself is an airy and magnificent star shape perched at the head of Glen Affric. Sgùrr na

▲ The start of 'the pinnacles' above Coire Domhain

SCOTTISH WILD COUNTRY BACKPACKING

Ceathramhnan's Gaelic name, meaning Peak of the Quarters, refers to how it seems to divide the land.

Go west along a grassy arête, before a brief descent and briefer climb to the **West Top** (although it's the lower of the two summits, it benefits from uninterrupted sea views.)

Retrace your steps and descend steeply southeast on an obvious ridge. Small burns and good camping spots can be found either side of **Stob Coire na Cloiche** (915m).

DAY 3
Stob Coire na Cloiche to Loch Beinn a' Mheadhain

Start	Stob Coire na Cloiche or vicinity (NH 067 224)
Distance	20.5km (12¾ miles)
Total ascent	950m (3115ft)
Time	7–9hr
Summits	An Socach 921m (M), Màm Sodhail 1181m (M), Sgùrr na Lapaich 1036m (M)

Continue on a clear path to the next Munro – **An Socach** (921m) – as the ridge broadens. Descend easily from a spot height of 906m, sometimes zigzagging, to **Bealach Coire Ghàidheil** (good camping).

Climb northeast gradually on a beautifully graded, *garron* (Highland pony) path. At 984m it seems to disappear but continues shortly after on the same, level contour, becoming a 'balcony' walk with spacious views of yesterday's glen as you round the corner. Where the path disappears again head east, cross a burn and then climb east-southeast to the level ground south of **Màm Sodhail** (1181m). Turn north on a path to the summit. The enormous summit cairn was built by Ordnance Survey in 1848, and the old hut (now ruined) passed on the way up was probably built by them too.

From the summit, turn east-southeast on an obvious path, descending steeply on a narrow ridge before it levels out, offering superb views over the outward leg. The climb to our final Munro of **Sgùrr na Lapaich** (1036m) on a broad stony shelf is a little unforgiving. Continue beyond the cairn for a short distance to find a shelter bivi, before turning southeast to join a thin stalkers' path which descends to the right of steep crags before cutting ingeniously between outcrops for nearly 400 metres, then disappearing.

Cut across country due east, crossing **Allt na Faing** to meet the track for **Affric Lodge** at a U-shaped bend. Join the track, descend to the lodge and turn left, continuing on the lochside road back to **Loch Beinn a Mheadhain** car park.

▲ Camping near Stob Coire na Cloiche

ROUTE 14
Killilan Forest: Sgùman Còinntich, Faochaig and Aonach Buidhe

Start/finish	Parking area at end of public road at Killilan (NG 941 303)
Total distance	39.5km (24½ miles)
Total ascent	2010m (6595ft)
Time	2–3 days
Terrain	Good path for first 2.5km. Rough paths from Faochaig to Maol-buidhe, boggy in places. Good track throughout Glen Elchaig for the return. Elsewhere trackless, rocky mountain and moorland terrain.
Key summits	Sgùman Còinntich 879m (C), Faochaig 868m (C), Aonach Buidhe 899m (C)
Maps	OS Explorer 414 Glen Shiel & Kintail Forest and 429 Glen Carron & West Monar; OS Landranger 25 Glen Carron & Glen Affric
Note	The MBA bothy at Maol-buidhe is close to the halfway point of the route. It can get busy as it is on the Cape Wrath Trail, so a tent or other shelter should be carried. It is also closed to visitors during the stag-stalking season (1 July–20 October), and permission should be sought from the estate during the hind-stalking season (21 October–15 February). Contact Killilan Estate on 01599 530055. Glen Elchaig is a working landscape with sheep and free-ranging Highland cattle. Care should be taken in spring and early summer when cows with young calves can occasionally be aggressive.

From the populous environs of Loch Long, this route pitches the backpacker into remote and lightly trodden mountain country. The outlook from the three summits en route is almost overwhelming – rugged peaks as far as the eye can see in most directions, like an ocean frozen mid-storm. The summits themselves fall just short of Munro height so receive far fewer visitors than they otherwise would. As a result, they offer great solitude. The high-level walk between the first two summits is long and exhilarating, and the final peak, Aonach Buidhe, boasts two spectacular, deeply carved corries. Maol-buidhe bothy is a dry and comfortable billet in the wide wilderness and well placed for this walk if completing it over two days. For those taking three days, good camping in fair weather can be found on the high country between Sgùman Còinntich and Faochaig for the first night, and by the An Crom-allt for the second night.

The walk can be completed in two days by strong walkers. However, given the rugged nature of much of the route, it may be preferable to allow 2½–3 days. Allt a'Choire Mhòir is crossed early in the outward journey and An Crom-allt on the return. The path to Maol-buidhe crosses Allt na Sean-lùibhe a couple of times. None should present problems, though all river crossings should be approached with caution.

SCOTTISH WILD COUNTRY BACKPACKING

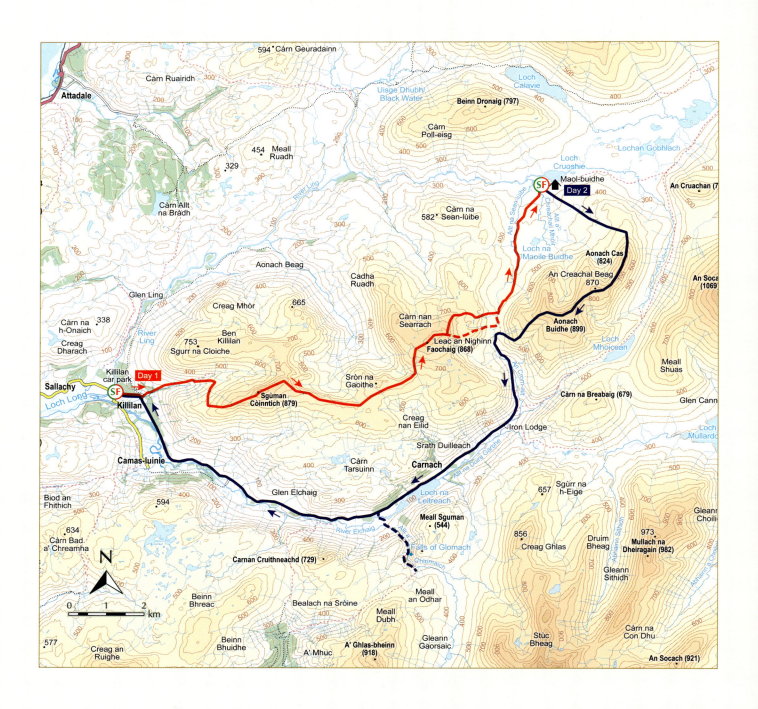

ROUTE 14 – KILLILAN FOREST: SGÙMAN CÒINNTICH, FAOCHAIG AND AONACH BUIDHE

DAY 1
Killilan to Maol-buidhe bothy

Start	Parking area at end of public road at Killilan (NG 941 303)
Distance	16.5km (10¼ miles)
Total ascent	1138m (3735ft)
Time	7–8hr
Summits	Sgùman Còinntich 879m (C), Faochaig 868m (C)

> Maol-buidhe bothy is the obvious overnight destination if completing the walk over two days. For those taking longer, there are substantial areas of flat, grassy, well-drained ground on the high ground between Sgùman Còinntich and Faochaig, allowing for a shorter and more relaxed first day and a fine high camp. Thought should be given to weather conditions, however, as this area is exposed.

From the parking area follow the road towards **Killilan hamlet**. Just before the bridge over Allt a'Choire Mhòir, turn left past a community hall. Follow a path climbing into the trees by the lively burn which cascades over moss-covered rocks. Higher up, a track comes in from the left. Follow it east into Coire Mòr. Ahead, a wedge of land divides the main burn from a tributary rising on the upper slopes of Sgùman Còinntich. Around 200 metres east of the junction of streams, leave the track, cross Allt a'Choire Mhòir and climb up to the crest of this wedge. Head east for around 350 metres then bear south, turning a few crags and outcrops to reach the west ridge of **Sgùman Còinntich** (879m). Climb east to reach the summit trig point. The views take in an enormous mountainous hinterland with few signs of human presence.

Descend east, following the high ground towards Faochaig's distant dome. On the left, crags plunge to the massive bowl of Coire Caol and Coire Shlat. The top of **Sròn na Gaoithe** (725m) can be bypassed to the south. After a further 1km, turn north and climb steadily to the summit of **Faochaig** (868m), marked by a cairn on an outcrop.

Cross the plateau to a second outcrop at its east end, then northeast to pick up a stalkers' path that winds down to meet the path between **Srath Duilleach** and Maol-buidhe. Alternatively, there's a more adventurous descent via the **Leac an Nighinn**

▲ Looking back to Loch Long from the Coire Mòr path

119

spur southeast of the second outcrop. This is straightforward if steep, requiring care in wet or wintry conditions, and offers a fine view of the great sweep of **Coire a'Chadha Ruaidh Mòr**. Where the spur merges suddenly into flatter ground, head northeast for 300 metres and shadow a deep gorge downhill on its south side. Keep well back as the slopes above it are steep. At its foot, where the stream emerges, peer back into the dark recesses before continuing down to the path. Follow it north for 4km to **Maol-buidhe bothy**.

As you descend north on the rough path from Glen Elchaig over the pass between Faochaig and Aonach Buidhe, the distant whitewashed walls of Maol-buidhe bothy are a welcome sight even on a clear summer day. This small but solid redoubt is one of the most remote habitable buildings in Scotland. It's a dry, comfortable billet with thick stone walls and a good fireplace. In the 19th century Maol-buidhe housed estate workers and their families. The last resident was a gamekeeper and shepherd. It was abandoned in 1916 and gradually fell into grave disrepair. Enter the Mountain Bothies Association who took the building into their care in the late 1960s. With a mix of love, dedication and many hours of hard physical work (not least the manhandling of a staircase over the bealach in a car trailer), the building was made weatherproof and comfortable once more. In the decades since, Maol-buidhe has enjoyed a second life as a fabled and much-loved mountain bothy open to all. With the Cape Wrath Trail now passing the front door, it can expect a steady stream of visitors for years to come.

DAY 2
Maol-buidhe bothy to Killilan

Start	Maol-buidhe bothy (NH 052 359)
Distance	23km (14¼ miles)
Total ascent	770m (2525ft)
Time	8–9hr
Summits	An Creachal Beag 870m, Aonach Buidhe 899m (C)

From the **bothy**, climb gradually southeast across trackless moors. To the south looms Aonach Buidhe. After 2.5km the foot of its most easterly spur is reached. Climb south up the spur then continue along **Aonach Cas**, a fine, rough ridge above a deep corrie. Bear west onto broader ground to gain the top of **An Creachal Beag** (870m). A short descent past a tarn is followed by a sharp climb and brief walk along the rim of another deep corrie to reach the well-made summit cairn of **Aonach Buidhe** (899m).

The descent west requires navigation as the lower slopes are uncomfortably steep and outcropped in places. From the summit, continue along the corrie rim for 400 metres to another top at around 890m. Head southwest down open slopes for 1km. Avoid veering left towards the burn recessed into the hillside. Bear west more steeply, keeping just south of the small streams trickling off the flank, to meet the path between **Srath Duilleach** and Maol-buidhe.

Follow the path south to the head of Srath Duilleach. The deserted shepherd's house of **Iron Lodge** stands across **Allt na Doire Gairbhe**. Stay on the north side of the river, following the track down the length of Srath Duilleach and **Glen Elchaig** for 14km to Killilan, a long but enjoyable walk through spectacular scenery.

If time allows, the walk down Glen Elchaig can be broken with a side-trip to view the **Falls of Glomach**. Around 300 metres west of **Loch na Leitreach**, turn left onto a path, across the **River Elchaig** by a footbridge, and steeply up by **Allt a' Ghlomaich** for around 1.5km to view the spectacular 113m-high waterfall. Return to Glen Elchaig by the same route.

▲ The northern ridges of Aonach Buidhe, from Aonach Cas

ROUTE 15

The Applecross Peninsula: Sgùrr a' Chaorachain and Beinn Bhàn

Start/finish	Roadside parking just west of the bridge over the River Kishorn on the single-track road to Bealach na Bà and Applecross village (NG 836 423). Please don't park in the adjacent passing place.
Total distance	27.5 km (17 miles)
Total ascent	1420m (4660ft)
Time	2–3 days
Terrain	Mostly off trail over rough, mountainous terrain with much exposed rock and a little Grade One scrambling on the high ground. Trackless moorland on the return.
Maps	OS Explorer 428 Kyle of Lochalsh, Plockton & Applecross; OS Landranger 24 Raasay & Applecross
Note	Very careful navigation is needed in poor visibility as much of the route passes above deep corries and huge cliffs which may carry big cornices in winter. It is important to keep a good sense of general direction while micro-navigating the many small crags and terraces on parts of the route to avoid straying on to more dangerous ground.

The mountains of the Applecross Peninsula pack a hugely varied array of landscapes into a small area. There are soaring cliffs and deep corries, massive barrel-shaped buttresses and rocky terraces, secretive lochs and an upland plateau haunted by ptarmigan and golden plover. Set right on the western seaboard, the views stretch easily to the mountains of Harris on a clear day. This route explores all that in depth, but also leaves the visitor in no doubt that this is and always has been a peopled, working environment.

It's highly advisable to tackle this circular route clockwise as described here. The climb up to the first summit, Sgùrr a' Chaorachain, is a straightforward but very steep scramble which cannot be recommended as a descent route. Walking north over Beinn Bhàn's plateau towards the Minch and distant Outer Hebrides is magical, and the trackless walk below the buttresses and corries of Beinn Bhàn's east face is easier to tackle on the return as it tends gently downhill.

Although the first stage described here looks short on paper, it can easily take the best part of a day. The overall ascent is considerable. There's a sustained steep scramble to reach the first summit, Sgùrr a' Chaorachain, followed by further scrambling and intricate route-finding over rocky terraces to reach Bealach nan Arr. The terrain on Beinn Bhàn will be a welcome relief; there are many places to pitch a tent on the extensive grassy plateau.

For those tackling the route over three days, careful searching around the tiny *lochans* to the north of the 773m top, crowned with a mobile phone mast, beyond Sgùrr a' Chaorachain or around the Bealach nan Arr may turn up some suitable patches among the rocks to pitch a tent on the first night. For the second night, search for dry grassy patches by the burns flowing out of Beinn Bhàn's eastern corries.

SCOTTISH WILD COUNTRY BACKPACKING

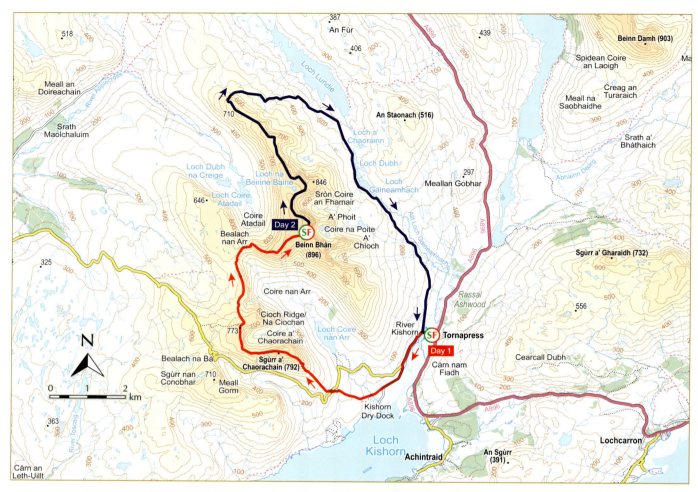

▲ Sublime views to Skye from the summit of Sgùrr a' Chaorachain

ROUTE 15 – THE APPLECROSS PENINSULA: SGÙRR A' CHAORACHAIN AND BEINN BHÀN

DAY 1
Loch Kishorn to Beinn Bhàn

Start	Roadside parking just west of bridge over River Kishorn (NG 836 423)
Distance	11.5km (7¼ miles)
Total ascent	1260m (4135ft)
Time	7–8hr
Summits	Sgùrr a' Chaorachain 792m (C), Beinn Bhàn 896m (C)

From the parking area follow the Bealach na Bà road over the river and left alongside the saltmarsh at the head of **Loch Kishorn**. In 1km bear left onto a road signposted for Kishorn dry dock. After approximately 850 metres leave the road as it bends left and go straight ahead on a track. After 350 metres cross a bridge over the Russel Burn. Ahead, follow a tarmacked drive for a short distance. As it bears sharply left, take to the open hillside, following a line of pylons to meet an old, overgrown cart track. Turn right and follow this uphill to the Bealach na Bà road.

Cross the road and climb towards the imposing prow of Sgùrr a' Chaorachain. Around the 350m contour the route steepens significantly. Concentration and a head for heights are required but nowhere is the route especially difficult or exposed. Climb northwest, keeping to the crest as much as possible, ensuring you maintain your overall direction as you turn crags and outcrops to find the easiest lines uphill. Take care not to drift too far left or right onto steeper ground. The crux of the climb is around the 550m contour. Traverse right below a crag for around 40 metres, keeping good balance as tough heather stalks try to 'push' you outwards, to find a way up over heather and rocks. There is some respite around the 600m contour where the gradient eases, before a final steep push then an easy walk for the final 400 metres to the summit cairn of **Sgùrr a' Chaorachain** (792m).

As you reach the summit of Sgùrr a' Chaorachain after a relentlessly steep scramble, the scale and architecture of the Applecross *massif* becomes very apparent. The great tableland is deeply bitten by huge corries and buttressed by burly ridges. Unsurprisingly, this is a climber's and scrambler's domain as much as a walker's. Perhaps the most famous climbing route is the Cioch Nose or Na Ciochan, well seen across Coire a' Chaorachain from Sgùrr a' Chaorachain. The eye is drawn inexorably up a soaring, stepped ridge that climbs from the moorland over a succession of barrel-shaped buttresses, each higher than the last, to merge finally with the plateau. The route was first climbed in 1960 when the legendary Ullapool-based climber and GP Tom Patey persuaded Chris Bonington to join him in an attempt. The story goes that the climb, while scenically magnificent, proved technically less tricky than Patey anticipated. Referencing the route's 'Difficult' rock-climbing grade, he later quipped that it was 'the Diff to end all Diffs' and gave 'the best value for Difficult' in Scotland. For the non-climbing backpacker gazing across at the mighty and intimidating Na Ciochan, Patey's breezy assessment may be 'difficult' to credit!

Continue west along a narrow ridge with the gulf of Coire na Bà on the left. A craggy tower (NG 792 417) is bypassed to the north by a path along a terrace. Bear north around the head of Coire a' Chaorachain to reach **Sgùrr a' Chaorachain's subsidiary summit** (773m) crowned with a mobile phone mast.

Ignore the track and descend north, negotiating a series of rocky terraces with occasional scrambling and downclimbing. Keep a sense of your overall direction as you twist and turn; avoid being led too far right along ledges onto more hazardous ground. Around 1.5km onwards, two broad terraces curve right to **Bealach nan Arr**. Take the lower terrace, then climb broadly east for 1.75km to reach the

▲ Camp overlooked by the Sròn Coire an Fhamair

summit of **Beinn Bhàn** (896m), where the void of **Coire na Poite** opens suddenly at your feet. The terrain north of the summit is largely grassy and easy-angled, so finding a place to pitch camp should be easy.

DAY 2
Beinn Bhàn to Loch Kishorn

Start	Beinn Bhàn
	(NG 804 450)
Distance	15.5km (9¾ miles)
Total ascent	160m (525ft)
Time	5–6hr

Continue north then northwest over the plateau, keeping close to the corrie edges for the best views, for 4.75km to the **final high point of the ridge** (710m; NG 784 483). Drop northwest for 350 metres then turn northeast to descend a steep, grassy slope between a craggy rib to the right and broken crags to the left. On more level ground below, bear east to traverse the moors beneath Beinn Bhàn's long east face, gradually bending southwards. Look for deer paths to ease your passage. Stay well above **Loch Lundie**, descending gradually across the hillsides to reach **Loch a' Chaorainn**. Head south along the west shore of Loch a' Chaorainn, then **Loch Gaineamhach**. Pick up a good path by the loch's outflow and follow it around the foot of Beinn Bhàn's south ridge to the head of **Loch Kishorn**.

▶ Views over Being Bhàn from high above the Coire nan Arr

ROUTE 16
Achnashellach, Bendronaig and West Monar

Start/finish	Parking area just off A890 at Craig (NH 038 493)
Total distance	41km (25½ miles)
Total ascent	2785m (9140ft)
Time	2–3 days
Terrain	Useful tracks and stalkers' paths speed progress in some places, but there is also much steep, rocky, trackless terrain, and some rough, boggy ground by Loch an Laoigh.
Key summits	Sgùrr na Feartaig 862m (C), Beinn Dronaig 797m (C), Lurg Mhòr 987m (M), Bidein a' Choire Sheasgaich 945m (M), Beinn Tharsuinn 863m (C)
Maps	OS Explorer 429 Glen Carron & West Monar; OS Landranger 25 Glen Carron & Glen Affric
Note	The MBA bothy at Bearnais is a welcome refuge in the wilds beyond Sgùrr na Feartaig and is perfectly placed as a first night's stop for those completing the route over 3 days. There is another bothy further south at Bendronaig Lodge (NH 014 389). Although not maintained by the MBA, it is left open for visitors. Check availability with the landowner during the deer-stalking season (Attadale Estate, tel 01520 722308). There are few river crossings, but Allt a' Chonais may be impassable in spate.

South of Glen Carron is a rugged hinterland straddling the watershed between Loch Carron and Loch Monar. Although recent run-of-river hydro schemes have impinged on the area, these mountains still feel isolated and remote. Indeed, the two Munros on the route, Lurg Mhòr and Bidein a' Choire Sheasgaich (known affectionately as 'Cheesecake' to Scottish hill-goers) rank among the most awkward to reach in Scotland, accessible from Glen Carron only by traversing the Corbett of Beinn Tharsuinn.

This is a disparate, characterful clutch of hills. 'Cheesecake' is the finest: sharp, bold, and unmistakeable from a distance, with a narrow summit ridge verging on Alpine in the right conditions, and requiring care on the descent. Beinn Dronaig, by contrast, lacks definition but climbing this craggy lump is an adventurous joy. There is serpentine Beinn Tharsuinn, requiring a little unexpected scrambling; commanding Lurg Mhòr, where you may be lucky enough to witness a fiery sunset beyond the jagged crown of the Skye Cuillin; and the effortless grace of Sgùrr na Feartaig's long ridge, swooping above the inky depths of its north-facing corries. Together, they comprise a varied, challenging and memorable expedition.

SCOTTISH WILD COUNTRY BACKPACKING

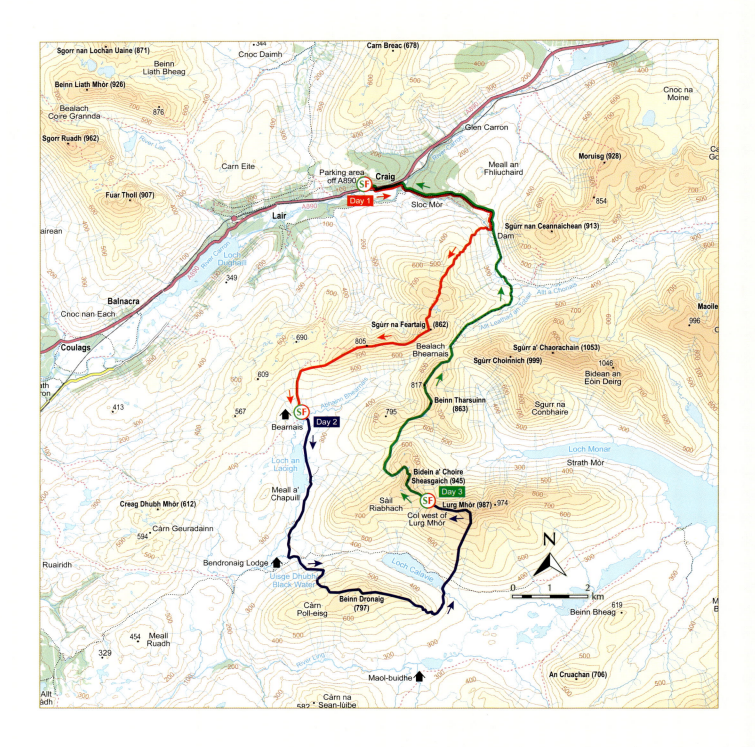

ROUTE 16 – ACHNASHELLACH, BENDRONAIG AND WEST MONAR

DAY 1
Craig to Bearnais bothy

Start	Parking area a short distance along a track off A890 at Craig (NH 038 493)
Distance	13km (8 miles)
Total ascent	935m (3070ft)
Time	5–6hr
Summits	Sgùrr na Feartaig 862m (C)

Cross the **A890**, then a level crossing. Bear sharp left and follow a track that parallels the railway for 700 metres then bears right to cross the **River Carron** by a bridge. Cross the bridge and head straight on, ignoring a track to the left, then one to the right. Just beyond the second junction, the track forks again. Bear left, climbing uphill above the hidden gorge of Sloc Mòr. Keep on the main track, ignoring a couple of other tracks that branch off to the right. As height is gained, the imposing west face of Sgùrr nan Ceannaichean comes into view.

Descend gradually into the upper glen. Look for a path on the right (NH 071 481) that leads down to the burn near a small hydropower dam. Cross a bridge and follow a stalkers' path that eases the long climb southwest towards **Sgùrr na Feartaig** (862m). After 3.25km you'll reach the summit.

Continue for 2km along the ridge to the **west summit** (805m). Descend the crest for a further 1.25km to meet a stalkers' path from Achnashellach. Turn left and follow it downhill for 2.25km to **Bearnais bothy**.

A plaque inside Bearnais bothy dedicates the shelter to Eric Beard, a renowned hill runner who set a number of notable records in the 1960s, including the Welsh 3000ft and Cairngorm 4000ft summits. He became the only person ever to run from Ben Nevis to Snowdon via Scafell Pike. He died aged only 38.

▲ Above: Sgùrr na Feartaig with the Coulin Forest peaks on the horizon

Crossing a frozen loch Sgùrr na Feartaig

SCOTTISH WILD COUNTRY BACKPACKING

DAY 2
Bearnais bothy to col west of Lurg Mhòr

Start	Bearnais bothy (NH 021 430)
Distance	13.5km (8½ miles)
Total ascent	1235m (4050ft)
Time	7–8hr
Summits	Beinn Dronaig 797m (C), Lurg Mhòr 987m (M)

Cross **Abhainn Bhearnais** (care needed in spate) and head south to **Loch an Laoigh**. Follow the rough, trackless east shore to meet a good track near its southern end. The track crosses a bridge and swings right towards Bendronaig Lodge; instead bear left, following Allt Coire na Sorna. Follow its second tributary on the right up to an obvious cleft, then a flatter area. Bear right uphill to avoid some crags, then bear gradually southeast, picking a line through outcrops to reach the summit of **Beinn Dronaig** (797m), crowned by a cylindrical, concrete trig point (known as Vanessas), and admire the fine views south to the peaks of Killilan Forest.

Descend the east ridge, picking up an overgrown stalkers' path after 1.5km. Follow the path down the steepening slope then north to the outflow of **Loch Calavie**, which is bridged.

Next, tackle the long climb north to **Lurg Mhòr** (987m). Peer over dark, north-facing precipices, contrasting with the relentless grassy slopes just ascended.

Progress and modernism were all the rage after World War II, for better and sometimes for worse. Few places in Britain were unchanged by the white heat of the post-war boom, not even the seemingly wild and remote landscape this journey takes you through. As you climb the shoulder of Bidein a' Choire Sheasgaich and look down to your right, you'll see a body of water extending far up the glen known as Strath Mòr (anglicised to Strathmore). This is Loch Monar, dammed and artificially extended as part of the Affric-Beauly hydro-power scheme in the 1950s. The last tenants of Strathmore house were Iain R Thomson and his family. His powerful memoir *Isolation Shepherd* captures their year-round life of rugged and austere self-sufficiency in a beautiful but perilously indifferent landscape. Where now there is open water was then a wide strath and river teeming with birdlife. All the hills round about were well known to Thompson, who would have tramped prodigious distances to tend to his landlord's sheep. It's now getting on for 70 years since a light shone in Strathmore, a place that can now only be reached through the pages of Thompson's evocative book.

Descend west to the **col between Lurg Mhòr and Bidein a' Choire Sheasgaich**. There are flat, grassy areas and running water a short distance southwest.

▲ Descending from Lurg Mhòr with Skye on the skyline

ROUTE 16 – ACHNASHELLACH, BENDRONAIG AND WEST MONAR

DAY 3
Col west of Lurg Mhòr to Craig

Start	Col west of Lurg Mhòr (NH 054 406)
Distance	15km (9¼ miles)
Total ascent	615m (2020ft)
Time	6–7hr
Summits	Bidein a' Choire Sheasgaich 945m (M), Beinn Tharsuinn 863m (C)

Climb northwest to reach the summit ridge of **Bidein a' Choire Sheasgaich** (945m). Turn north to reach the summit, marked by a small cairn. Continue along the sharp crest for 150 metres. Where the ridge starts to drop more steeply, look for a gully to the left which can be descended easily to a *lochan* at NH 049 416. Descend southwest into Coire Seasgach, keeping to the north side of the burn.

Continue shadowing the burn as it turns northwest and cascades into a gorge. Take care on the slope above in wet or wintry conditions as the run-out into the gorge is unprotected. When the steepest ground on the right is passed, bear right away from the burn, contouring under the mountain's northwest crags. Head for the col between Bidein a' Choire Sheasgaich and Beinn Tharsuinn, crossed by a wall. Angle northeast uphill to reach the ridge west of the summit of **Beinn Tharsuinn** (863m). A brief scramble leads to a tarn commanding a fabulous view back to Bidein a' Choire Sheasgaich. The summit cairn is a further 350 metres northeast.

Continue north along the ridge to its end above **Bealach Bhearnais**. Descend to the *bealach* and head northeast into Coire an Tobair. Pick up a stalkers' path and follow it down to **Allt a' Chonais**. Ford the river to reach a good track. Turn left and follow it back to **Craig**.

▲ *Top:* Pinewoods old and new, following Allt a' Chonais; *Bottom:* Bearnais bothy, rebuilt in memory of Eric Beard

SCOTTISH WILD COUNTRY BACKPACKING

ROUTE 17
Coulin Forest

Start/finish	Achnashellach Station (NH 002 484) or verge-side car park on the A890
Total distance	36km (22½ miles)
Total ascent	2990m (9810ft)
Time	3 days
Terrain	Tracks, excellent stalkers' paths, a little off-path navigation and easy scrambling on very steep and often loose rock.
Key summits	Beinn Liath Mhòr 926m (M), Sgorr Ruadh 962m (M), Fuar Tholl 907m (C), An Ruadh Stac 892m (C), Maol Chean-dearg 933m (M)
Maps	OS Explorer 429 Glen Carron & West Monar; OS Landranger 25 Glen Carron & Glen Affric
Note	A bike left at Coulags before you begin will save a road walk on the A890. The excellent Coire Fionnaraich bothy is also en route and could be used as a base at the end of Day 2.

▲ Sunrise over the ridge, Beinn Liath Mhòr

ROUTE 17 – COULIN FOREST

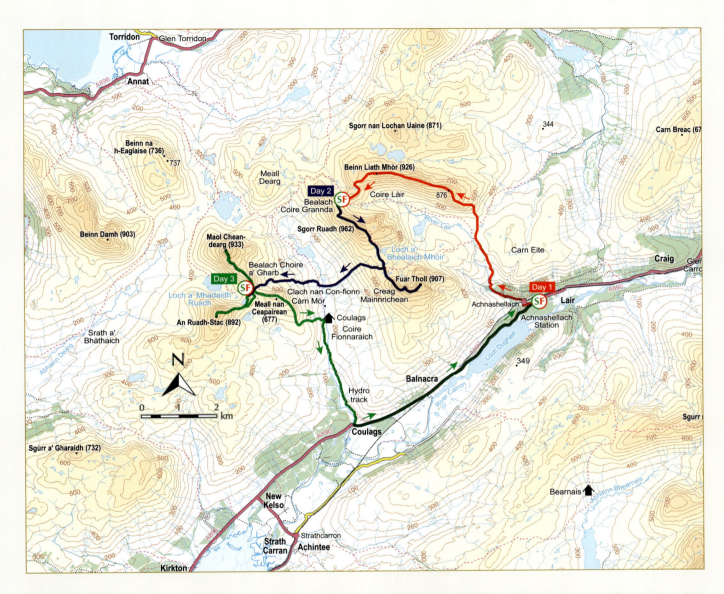

While neighbouring Torridon becomes ever busier with bikers and boulderers, the Coulin has so far managed to avoid most of the limelight. This route encompasses three Munros and two Corbetts and offers relative solitude, grandeur and genuinely world class scenery in all directions.

The route climbs through a remnant of Caledonian pinewood (quite rare for the west coast), tours fine quartzite ridges that glow red and gold at sunrise and sunset, traverses improbable crags, and crosses *lochan*-dotted passes on some of the finest stalkers' paths in the country. The Coulin Forest is a Highland Shangri-la, but with straightforward access by train from Inverness.

SCOTTISH WILD COUNTRY BACKPACKING

DAY 1
Achnashellach to Bealach Coire Grannda

Start	Achnashellach Station (NH 002 484) or verge-side car park on the A890
Distance	8.5km (5¼ miles)
Total ascent	1045m (3430ft)
Time	6–8hr
Summits	Beinn Liath Mhòr 926m (M)

From the verge-side car park by **Achnashellach station**, walk up the track signposted for walkers, which switchbacks past some buildings to reach the station. From the station, go over the level crossing and continue to a junction. Turn left, go through a deer fence and into an area of recently felled forestry. Fuar Tholl (see Day 2, below) is straight ahead. After a few hundred metres turn left at the signpost and small cairn marked Coire Làir. A charming footpath follows the line of the burn before emerging from the trees and veering north to the low point on the skyline. It's a steady climb with some switchbacks on a superbly made stalkers' path.

Once in **Coire Làir**, ignore the first cairn and a path to your left. A second junction marked with a larger cairn lies a short distance ahead. Take the right fork, then a left fork; the path winds around some knolls and then climbs steeply up the east side of **Beinn Liath Mhòr** (926m). It's eroded in places and grows very faint near the top.

Once on the ridge, the way ahead is both spectacular and straightforward. Pass a dramatic quartzite crag on your right, descend to a col, regain around 100m and then descend again before reaching the rocky summit itself, marked with a large cairn. Drop west to a flatter area of '*cnoc* and *lochan*' terrain, contour over terraces and pick up a path, descending steeply via a short gully to a larger *lochan*. Contour south around a spot height of 769m and descend to the main path connecting Coire Làir with **Coire Grannda**. There is ample camping and water nearby.

DAY 2
Bealach Coire Grannda to Loch a' Mhadaidh Ruadh

Start	Bealach Coire Grannda or vicinity (NG 954 512)
Distance	10km (6¼ miles)
Total ascent	1020m (3345ft)
Time	7–9hr
Summits	Sgorr Ruadh 962m (M), Creag Mainnrichean 857m, Fuar Tholl 907m (C)

Join a path heading west to gain the ridge for the Munro of **Sgorr Ruadh** (962m), swinging south over broken quartzite and climbing steadily. Keep right of the broad ridge until it narrows and steepens. The path swings around towards the head of the ridge for the final section.

From the summit, descend southeast on a broad slope before descending steeply between rocky terraces, burns and grass. Aim to the right (west) of **Loch a' Bhealaich Mhòir** and then cross a path to the south of Bealach Mòr (which comes up from the station). Leave your pack if you wish and

▲ Fuar Tholl on the walk in

head south to meet a cairn and a faint path on the northwest side of **Creag Mainnrichean** (857m) – it's easier to see from a distance than when underfoot! From the cairn, make your way steeply up very loose, quartzite screes. Note a red rock *gendarme* (rocky pinnacle), and take a steep, stony rake just beyond. Pick your way over mixed ground to top out for breathtaking views on this complex mountain.

Follow the obvious path around the two tops, the second (and highest) of which has a stone shelter, marking the summit of Corbett **Fuar Tholl** (907m). It's possible to return via the main gully immediately west of the summit (a scree chute), or else return the way you came and retrieve your pack.

Now head west, following the track over the *bealach* then descending to meet a burn where the track ends. Contour west-northwest before turning west and descending alongside the second of two burns on its right-hand side. Reach the boggy glen floor, cross a burn and then the river before joining the main path for Coulags. The bothy lies a short way to the south.

Between Coulags bothy and the switchback path for the Bealach a' Choire Ghairbh, you'll find the Clach nan Con Fionn – allegedly the place where the giant Fionn would tie his hunting dogs, Bran and Sceolan, while hunting for deer and boar. It's worth a small detour if you have the time.

The Fionn in question is Fionn mac Cumhail, anglicised to Finn MacCool. The story of Finn and his landless tribe of warrior hunters (the Fianna) is told in the *Fenian Cycle*, one of four mythological sagas, a mix of poetry, prose and song. Fionn pops up all over, from Ireland and Scotland to Newfoundland and the Isle of Man, variously appearing as seer, poet, martial artist and giant. He carries a spear that never misses, and a sword called Mac an Luin, 'the son of the waves'. Every type of bold claim is made for this handsome fellow, from creating the Giant's Causeway as a means of joining Ireland and Scotland, to defeating a fire-breathing entity called Åillen and catching a salmon that, when he tried to cook it and burned his thumb, imbued him with divine knowledge. What a cool guy!

▲ Looking towards Beinn Damh and An Ruadh Stac

Despite these outlandish fables, he is thought to have been based, at least in small measure, on a real-life nobleman. The Fianna also have basis in fact – they were loose bands of young aristocrats in early medieval Ireland who had yet to come into their inheritance.

Walk north on the footpath and then turn left at a cairn, to climb a loose quartzite switchback path, which then contours alongside another burn.

Climb to **Bealach Choire a' Gharb** for heart-stopping views of the Corbett An Ruadh Stac. Camping pitches and fresh water abound.

DAY 3
Loch a' Mhadaidh Ruadh to Achnashellach

Start	Loch a' Mhadaidh Ruadh or vicinity (NG 929 486)
Distance	17.5km (10¾ miles)
Total ascent	925m (3035ft)
Time	5–6hr
Summits	An Ruadh-Stac 892m (C), Maol Chean-dearg 933m (M), Meall nan Ceapairean 677m

Take the path west of and below the *bealach*. It first heads south and then southwest over a smashed quartzite ridge to the smooth slabs at the foot of **An Ruadh Stac** (892m). Climb west over the slabs to a loose, intermittent path above. Continue very steeply, a little to the left of the ridge, until you reach a broad summit with superb views towards Torridon and the sea beyond. Descend the way you came, perhaps detouring around **Loch a' Mhadaidh Ruadh** on your return.

Return to **Bealach Choire a' Gharb** before heading north-northwest steeply on very loose quartzite for the ridge of Munro, **Maol Chean-dearg**. It's worth avoiding the path braids to the west and opting for a more central line, for better footing. Follow the ridge as it rises and falls, before a very steep final pull over small boulders for the summit plateau, once again offering superlative views. Return the way you came.

From Bealach Choire a' Gharb, head simply east-southeast for the top of **Meall nan Ceapairean** (677m), before descending easily on grass above the crags of **Càrn Mòr**. As the crags end and the ground begins to level off, turn sharp left and descend on grass, sometimes steeply, to meet the path and **bothy**. From here, walk south to reach the main road at **Coulags** bridge. There's a minor detour (signposted for walkers) which offers a shortcut away from the **Hydropower track**.

▲ Sunrise over the Fannichs from a camp on Beinn Liath Mhòr

ROUTE 18
The Fannichs

Start/finish	Layby and car park on A832, just east of Grudie power station (NH 313 626)
Total distance	57km or 35½ miles
Total ascent	3275m (10,745ft)
Time	2 days in summer, 3 days or more in winter
Terrain	Tarmac and gravel tracks, mountain paths and some pathless terrain. The hills alternate between gentle and rolling to vertiginous following along corrie edges that drop very steeply to the north.
Key summits	An Coileachan 923m (M), Meall Gorm 949m (M), Beinn Liath Mhòr Fannaich 954m (M), Sgùrr Mòr 1108m (M), Meall a'Chrasgaidh 934m (M), Sgùrr nan Clach Geala 1093m (M), Sgùrr nan Each 923m (M) Sgùrr Breac 999m (M), A' Chailleach 997m (M)
Maps	OS Explorer 435 An Teallach & Slioch and 436 Beinn Dearg & Loch Fannich; OS Landranger 19 Gairloch & Ullapool and 20 Beinn Dearg and Loch Broom
Note	A bike is useful to save a tiring road march at the start and end. It can be tucked away at the foot of the range, near the reservoir or in the disused stone quarry.

▲ Breathtaking scale under Sgùrr Mòr

SCOTTISH WILD COUNTRY BACKPACKING

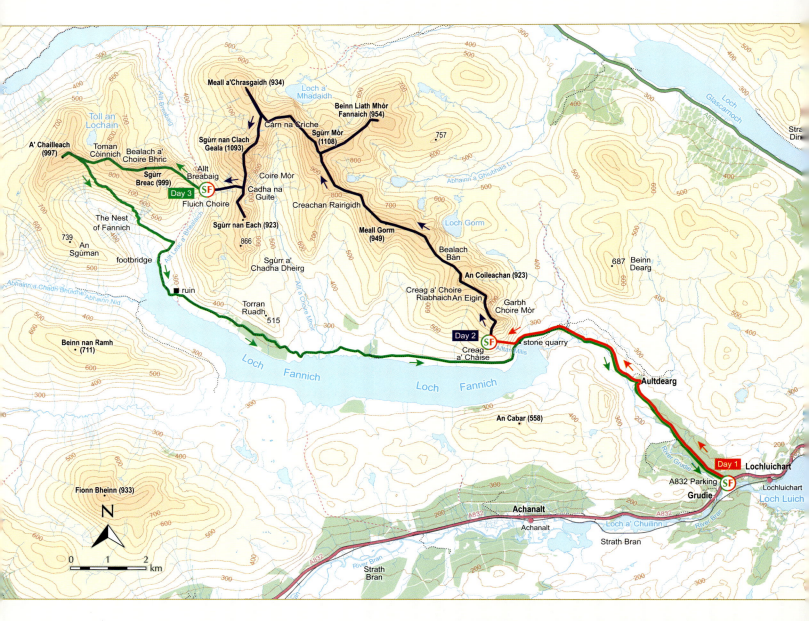

Occupying a huge swathe of land between Inverness and Ullapool, the Fannichs range is relatively under-visited. This may be due to its distance from the road, or the fact that the approach is somewhat marred by deer overgrazing and large-scale hydroelectric works. Forgive these initial impressions and you'll be rewarded with a superb ridge traverse with unrivalled views of the Highlands in all directions.

This route makes the most of the Fannichs' central position by including the entire ridge from the eastern end, beginning above dramatic Garbh Choire Mòr. It takes in nine Munros, including the two highlights of Sgùrr Mòr and Sgùrr nan Clach Geala, where the terrain becomes increasingly dramatic. Time your trip for late winter (February–April) and the full traverse becomes a challenging and remote outing well worthy of the term 'expedition'.

ROUTE 18 – THE FANNICHS

DAY 1
Car park on A832 to Creag a' Chàise

Start	Car park on A832 (NH 313 626)
Distance	8km (5 miles)
Total ascent	445m (1460ft)
Time	3hr

A short first day allows for road travel to the start of the route, but it can easily be extended. From the layby car park just west of **Lochluichart**, take the road signposted for Fannich Estates, through the forestry. Ignore a turning to the left as views open out to the river, passing through a stand of old pine trees. Continue over a bridge near the estate cottages at **Aultdearg**, then across meadows until you meet a crossroads. Continue over this, noting the old **quarry** on your right. Ascend steeply with no path between the quarry and **Alltan Milis**, keeping the burn on your left. **Creag a' Chàise** provides a wonderful vantage point over **Loch Fannich**.

▲ Sgùrr nan Clach Geala

DAY 2
Creag a' Chàise to bealach under Sgùrr nan Clach Geala

Start	Creag a' Chàise, the east end of the ridge (around NH 248 663)
Distance	20km (12½ miles)
Total ascent	1690m (5545ft)
Time	9–12hr
Summits	An Coileachan 923m (M), Meall Gorm 949m (M), Beinn Liath Mhòr Fannaich 954m (M), Sgùrr Mòr 1108m (M), Meall a'Chrasgaidh 934m (M), Sgùrr nan Clach Geala 1093m (M), Sgùrr nan Each 923m (M)

Pick your way steeply north through boulders, until the incline eases. Meet a 797m spot height and the vertiginous drop into dramatic **Garbh Choire Mòr**. Now head northwest to reach **An Eigin** and then over easier ground to the first Munro summit of **An Coileachan** (923m) before dropping to **Bealach Bàn**. Your eye will no doubt be drawn to Loch Gorm and the mountains of Assynt to the north. Another gradual climb follows to a spot height of 922m before the ridge widens, leading to the Munro summit of **Meall Gorm** (949m), beyond. Follow a small spine of rock until you veer right for the descent, to traverse under **Creagchan Rairigidh**.

Ahead lies the distinctive crescent moon of Meall nam Peithirean and the wizard's hat of Sgùrr Mòr, the scale of the range now truly impressive. If snow cover and weather allow, the outlier of **Beinn Liath Mhòr Fannaich** (954m) is best tackled without the burden of a pack and by using the contouring path to the northeast. The distance there and back is not to be underestimated. Ascend this Munro on its northwest flank and then return the way you came to collect your pack and climb the final metres to the highest peak for miles around, **Sgùrr Mòr** (1108m).

It's easy to be distracted by the rocky fortifications of Sgùrr nan Clach Geala as you descend towards Càrn na Crìche, but our second outlier of **Meall a'Chrasgaidh** (934m) lies another kilometre or so to the northwest. Thankfully it's a straightforward out-and-back and there is good, if exposed, camping in the *bealach* beforehand if needed. Water is also available nearby.

Rejoin the edge of **Coire Mòr** for the steep climb to **Sgùrr nan Clach Geala** (1093m), which provides plenty of mountaineering atmosphere, whether in summer or winter. Descend south on expansive slopes, before the short climb to **Sgùrr nan Each** (923m). Return to the *bealach* at **Cadha na Guite** and descend west, with a very brief downclimb over a small crag, to the lower ground at the foot of the northeast ridge of the next Munro, Sgùrr Breac. There is good camping and water here, if you haven't succumbed to fatigue beforehand!

DAY 3
Bealach under Sgùrr nan Clach Geala to car park on A832

Start	Fluich Choire, the *bealach* southwest of Sgùrr nan Clach Geala (NH 174 706)
Distance	28.5km (17¾ miles)
Total ascent	1085m (3560ft)
Time	12–14hr
Summits	Sgùrr Breac 999m (M), A' Chailleach 997m (M)

From the *bealach* the route crosses to the western Fannichs and the final two Munros. The ridge leading to **Sgùrr Breac** (999m) pitches and rolls, retaining interest all the way to the summit. Glimpse An Teallach and Ben Mòr Coigach to the north. Descend west to **Bealach a' Choire Bhric**, with the first of a series of breathtaking corries at your feet. It's possible to bypass **Toman Còinnich** but you won't regret a brief visit. Climb simply to its summit before descending steeply, passing a rocky *howff* (rough rocky shelter) halfway down as the imposing presence of of **A' Chailleach** (997m) makes itself fully known. Sticking as close to the corrie edge as you dare, the climb from *bealach* **Toll an Lochain** is increasingly dramatic, passing *gendarmes* (rocky pinnacles) and outcrops and then finishing very simply on a platform with a small cairn, offering a unique perspective over Fisherfield and Torridon to the west and south. Depending on the weather, it's possible to leave your pack at this bealach to be collected after the Munro summit visit.

WISE WOMEN, BRIDES AND CELTIC LIFE CYCLES

The summit furthest to the west on this route, A' Cailleach (or A' Chailleach), is one of Scotland's many places named after the Celtic 'old woman', elder or mystic.

The Cailleach was responsible for the creation and protection of landscape and wild nature for the pre-Christian clans, who migrated with their cattle twice a year in sync with those same seasonal shifts marked by our current Halloween and May Day. She is born on All Hallows' Eve when the summer shielings are shut down for the coming winter.

The Cailleach was primarily a mountain-maker and weather-creator, a destructive Shiva-like deity linked with the coming of storms and snow. She is often depicted as a terrifying one-eyed witch or hag, blue-faced from the cold and wrapped in a ragged shawl, sometimes leading a coven of crones on giant goats across stormy, cloud-streaked skies. Occasionally, she carries a hammer which brings frost wherever it strikes, knocking the peaks and corries into shape. The boulders and screes we associate with glaciation instead tumble from her basket as she works. This elemental dervish must be placated with tributes and offerings, often in the form of venison from the hunt.

In other stories, the old woman of winter becomes a bride in the spring and is cast as benign, a keeper of deer as cattle, a milkmaid of hinds, or a Francis of Assisi-like figure who befriends all wild creatures. In our case, it's worth noting that the Nest of Fannich that provides our exit route from the hill provides food and shelter to plentiful deer who enjoy the snowmelt-fed meadow grass.

For the people of the time, the Cailleach was divine explanation for the fortunes of hunting, weather and the physical geography that surrounded them. The stories come from the land itself, each piece jigsawed to its neighbour.

Return to the *bealach* Toll an Lochain, before peeling off south on grassier ground to meet an escarpment at around the 650m contour. You are now in a massive cirque-like glen called the **Nest of Fannich**. Follow deer trods in an easterly direction for around 1km, descending through boulders only as the gradient eases. Don't be tempted to descend too early. Cross several burns feeding Abhainn Nid, some tussocky ground and a few peat hags, finally joining the old stalkers' path which follows **Allt Leac a' Bhealaich**. Head towards **Loch Fannich**, meeting a **footbridge** and a **ruined house**. The walk back along the foot of the range you have just visited is as simple as it is long.

ROUTE 19
Fisherfield and Letterewe

Start/finish	Layby on A832 at Corrie Hallie (NH 114 850)
Total distance	39.75km (24¾ miles)
Total ascent	2865m (9400ft)
Time	2–3 days
Terrain	Tracks and paths for much of the route, although the path in Gleann na Muice is poor and wet in many places. Elsewhere, high-level walking on stony ridges and some stretches of rough, boggy moorland.
Key summits	Beinn a' Chlaidheimh 914m (C), Sgùrr Bàn 989m (M), Mullach Coire Mhic Fhearchair 1019m (M), Beinn Tarsuinn 937m (M), A' Mhaighdean 967m (M), Ruadh Stac Mòr 918m (M)
Maps	OS Explorer 433 Torridon – Beinn Eighe & Liathach and 435 An Teallach & Slioch; OS Landranger 19 Gairloch & Ullapool
Note	A round of the Fisherfield Six can be bookended by nights at Shenavall bothy, with a long day over all the summits in between. However, the bothy is popular in summer as it is on the Cape Wrath Trail, so the route is described here as a 2-day expedition with a remote wild camp.

The round of the Fisherfield Six is a great prize of Scottish hill-walking. Although there are now only five Munros since Beinn a' Chlaidheimh's demotion to sub-3000ft status following a resurvey, the logic and allure of the route remain undimmed, and the name has stuck. The route heads deep into a huge, roadless tract of lochs, cliffs, corries and rugged mountains. A' Mhaighdean and Ruadh Stac Mòr are probably the most remote Munros in Scotland. Fitness, stamina, sensible planning and skills are essential to provide a margin of safety and ensure enjoyment. There are serious river crossings, with Abhainn Loch an Nid, Abhainn Srath na Sealga and Abhainn Gleann na Muice usually impassable in spate.

It's tempting to call this a wilderness, and many do. However, there are few places that exemplify more clearly the tensions around how we think about wild land in Scotland. A key reason why it's so empty and undeveloped is that for decades it was maintained thus by the landowners for their deer stalking. Famously, in the 1960s the English brewing magnate Colonel WH Whitbread, owner of adjacent Letterewe Forest, successfully opposed plans for a hydropower scheme that would have altered this area significantly while, its supporters argued, bringing electricity for the first time to many Highland homes. It's an uncomfortable irony that this wild, unspoiled landscape has been bequeathed to us partly by a system that allows a tiny number of often absentee landowners to monopolise land use over huge areas of the Highlands.

SCOTTISH WILD COUNTRY BACKPACKING

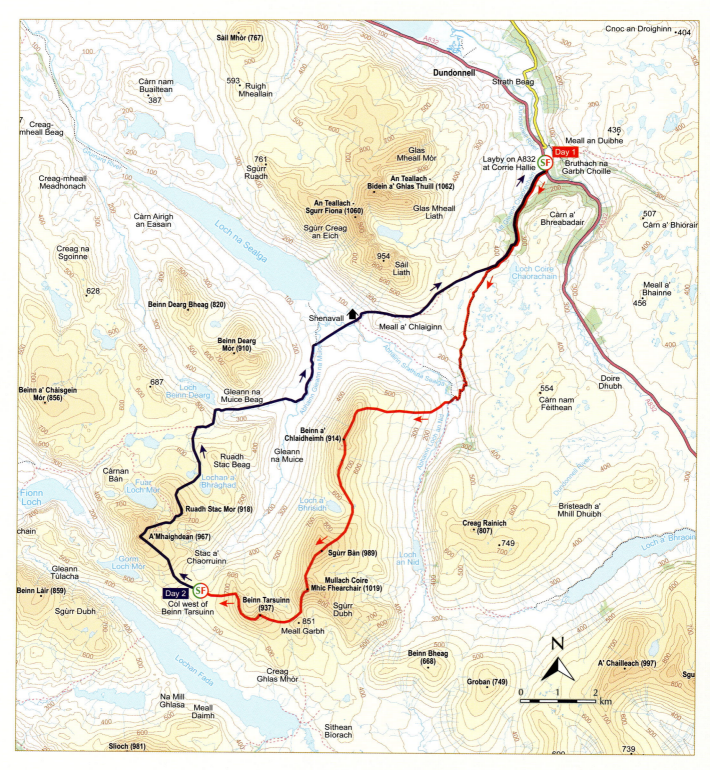

142

ROUTE 19 – FISHERFIELD AND LETTEREWE

DAY 1
Corrie Hallie to col west of Beinn Tarsuinn

Start	Layby on A832 (NH 114 850)
Distance	19.75km (12¼ miles)
Total ascent	1920m (6300ft)
Time	9–11hr
Summits	Beinn a' Chlaidheimh 914m (C), Sgùrr Bàn 989m (M), Mullach Coire Mhic Fhearchair 1019m (M), Beinn Tarsuinn 937m (M)

As the first day is especially strenuous, with nearly 2000m of ascent, it demands an early start. A signposted right of way to Kinlochewe begins opposite the roadside layby at **Corrie Hallie**. Follow this track steadily uphill by **Allt Gleann Chaorachain**. Initial birch woods give way after a couple of kilometres, and the track climbs steeply away from the river, which cascades down a waterfall from **Loch Coire Chaorachain** above. The climb levels out on a high moorland, with An Teallach's ridges and deep corries coming into view on the right.

An Teallach, not on the routes in this book, is arguably the finest mountain on the Scottish mainland, an enormous and complex sandstone bastion of razor-sharp ridges and deep corries. Before you've even set foot on the Fisherfield Six, the tantalising glimpses of this mountain as you pass by will quite possibly seal your next visit to the area.

At NH 101 823 the path to Shenavall branches right. Ignore this and continue south, with the sharp profile of Beinn a' Chlaidheimh now rising ahead, eventually winding down to **Abhainn Loch an Nid** near a patch of alder woodland. Fill your bottles, as water is in short supply on the long ridge walk ahead. Ford the river and climb towards Beinn a' Chlaidheimh over boggy moorland with much exposed rock. Higher up there are some excessively steep and craggy slopes. To avoid the worst, aim to reach the summit ridge to the right of the 900m north top, then approach it from the north. Continue south along a narrow but easy ridge for 500 metres to the summit of **Beinn a' Chlaidheimh** (914m).

Descend south for 1.5km to a col at 650m. Continue up boulder-covered slopes to the plateau-like summit of **Sgùrr Bàn** (989m). Make a straightforward descent to another col followed by a steep, zigzagging climb up a loose path ground into the stony mountainside opposite to reach **Mullach Coire Mhic Fhearchair** (1019m), the highest point on the route.

▲ Looking south from the summit of Mullach Coire Mhic Fhearchair

Descend south and follow a path cutting across the northwest-facing slopes of **Meall Garbh** (851m) to Bealach Odhar. Climb west up broad slopes to **Beinn Tarsuinn** (937m). The ridge beyond becomes sharper and more difficult. Keep to the left of the crest in places where it proves too tricky. At one point a strange, flat table of rock, about the size of a tennis court, is crossed.

Continue north along the ridge for 200 metres until the slopes on the left relent enough to allow a steep descent west to a wide saddle. Much of this area is boggy but careful searching should reveal a suitable place to pitch with running water not far away.

DAY 2
Col west of Beinn Tarsuinn to Corrie Hallie

Start	Col west of Beinn Tarsuinn (NH 021 736)
Distance	20km (12½ miles)
Total ascent	945m (3100ft)
Time	8–9hr
Summits	A' Mhaighdean 967m (M), Ruadh Stac Mòr 918m (M)

Climb west, quite steeply at first then up broad, easy slopes. On the left, the cliffs of Beinn Làir form a 4km-long rampart above Lochan Fada and **Gleann Tùlacha**. Beinn Làir boasts the longest line of inland cliffs in the UK. Reaching the summit of **A' Mhaighdean** (967m), savour the unforgettable view northwest over **Fionn Loch** and the moorlands beyond to the sea. A' Mhaighdean has perhaps the best summit view of any mountain in the country.

Head north for 200 metres to the shallow saddle between the summit and the 948m north top. Follow the hillwalkers' path that descends westwards to the jumbled col below **Ruadh Stac Mòr** (918m).

What's the furthest you can get from a public road on mainland Britain? Not surprisingly, the point most distant from a tarmacked road is deep inside the Fisherfield Forest. As you start the descent on the stalkers' path into Gleann na Muice Beag you'll pass within less than 2km of this momentous spot – as it happens, a nondescript bit of hillside above Loch Beinn Dearg, seen on your left as you scamper down the switchbacks. Although it feels very far from anywhere around here, the nearest road, the A832, is actually only 11.25km east-northeast as the crow flies. In the absence of wings, however, the journey back to the starting point from here will feel far more significant.

Scramble up a path through a gap in the lower crags. Above, bear right, climbing steeply over scree to the summit. Descend north to a flat shoulder then right. Aim between the two lochans on the moor below, then head north for 1.25km to meet a good path. Follow it east down to **Gleann na Muice**, then northwards to the private bothy at Larachantivore. Ford **Abhainn Gleann na Muice**. Bear northeast for 1km over flat, boggy ground. Ford **Abhainn Srath na Sealga** to reach **Shenavall bothy** (NH 066 810).

Behind the bothy, a path climbs east up a steep slot in the hillside, keeping to the north of the little burn. Follow this out onto the open moor to meet the outward route back to the A832 at **Corrie Hallie**.

▲ Shenavall bothy and the Corbett of Beinn Dearg Mòr

ROUTE 20
Flowerdale Three: Beinn an Eòin, Beinn Dearg and Baosbheinn

Start/finish	Car park on the A832 called 'Red Stable' (the hut is green) (NG 856 720)
Total distance	35km (21¾ miles)
Total ascent	2375m (7795ft)
Time	2–3 days
Terrain	Rough track to begin, otherwise rocky, boggy and often pathless. The crux is 'the castle' on Beinn Dearg, an airy scramble when bypassed, or a moderate climb if taken direct. Steep downclimbs from Beinn Dearg and Baosbheinn.
Key summits	Beinn an Eòin 855m (C), Beinn Dearg 913m (C), Baosbheinn 875m (C)
Maps	OS Explorer 433 Torridon – Beinn Eighe & Liathach; OS Landranger 19, Gairloch & Ullapool
Note	After Baosbheinn, it's possible to simply rejoin the main stalkers' track at the stepping stones and avoid Loch Bad an Sgalaig. The final section as described is stunning but requires stamina and good navigation. Both options work well if you choose to reverse the route direction.

▲ Sunset over Loch a' Bhealaich

SCOTTISH WILD COUNTRY BACKPACKING

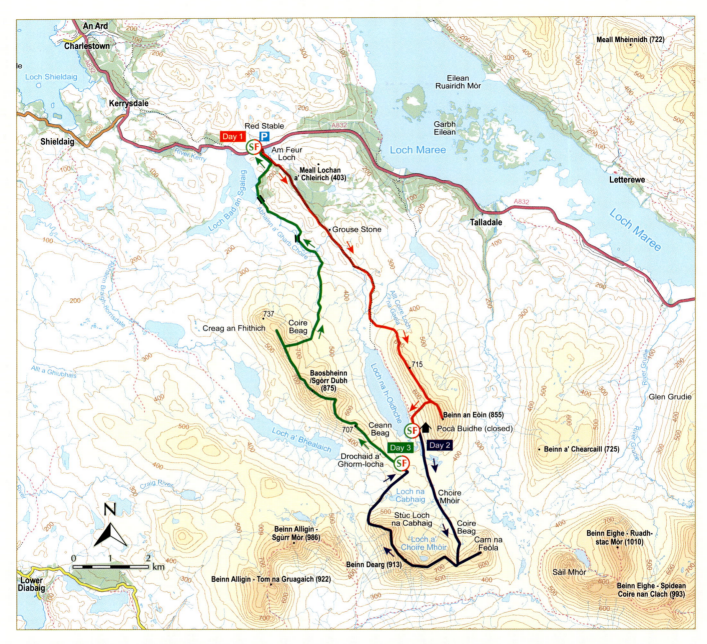

This is a challenging tour of the quieter, northern end of the Torridon range, taking in three Corbetts and the hinterland between them. The lack of Munros means that you can enjoy a profound sense of solitude.

The route passes through new native woodland (over a million trees were planted by Gairloch Estate in the late 1990s) and ancient Celtic settlements; traverses gneiss tabletops littered with glacial erratics; scrambles past sandstone tors; and finishes in a tussock-filled meadow. The distances and ascent may not be great, but don't let that deceive you – this is a short but muscular adventure in a world-class mountain landscape.

ROUTE 20 – FLOWERDALE THREE: BEINN AN EÒIN, BEINN DEARG AND BAOSBHEINN

DAY 1
Red Stable to Pocà Bhuide bothy

Start	Red Stable car park, A832 just east of Loch Bad an Sgalaig (NG 856 720)
Distance	11.5 km (7¼ miles)
Total ascent	790m (2590ft)
Time	6–8hr
Summits	Beinn an Eòin 855m (C), Beinn Dearg 913m (C), Baosbheinn 875m (C)

Cross the road and a bridge and enter **Loch Bad an Sgalaig native pinewood**, taking time to read the fascinating interpretation panels both at the entrance and further along the track. Head southeast through an almost alpine landscape, with the **Lochan a' Chleirich** (Loch of the Cleric) on your left. Drop down to a junction and continue on to the **'Grouse Stone'**, which forms part of the shooting estate history here.

Enter open moorland and continue south, over the stepping stones. Follow the track for around 300 metres until it levels out, then head east over heather and peat to meet a spur protecting **Allt Coire Loch na Gaela**. Using a small burn as a guide, until you reach a sloping platform dotted with erratics, then climb south up a series of easy, mixed terraces to gain the ridge of **Beinn an Eòin** (855m). After nearly 2km of straightforward walking the summit is reached, providing grandstand views of the journey ahead, as well as Liathach beyond. Double back to the saddle and descend over heather-covered rocks, to the left of a small burn. Turn left to join the path and reach the **Pocà Bhuide bothy**, which is now closed to the public. Camping ground is scarce but can be found nearby.

DAY 2
Pocà Bhuide bothy to camp under Baosbheinn

Start	Environs of Pocà Bhuide bothy (the bothy is closed to the public) (NG 898 643)
Distance	10.5km (6½ miles)
Total ascent	830m (2725ft)
Time	7–10hr
Summits	Beinn Dearg 913m (C) and its subsidiaries (Carn na Feòla, Stùc Loch na Cabhaig)

Continue south over rough moorland scattered with lochans and bog; this requires good micro-navigation. The ground rises slowly to meet Beinn Dearg. Skirt the headwaters of **Choire Mhòir** and proceed carefully over large boulders, refilling your bottle once

WILDERNESS OR POST-INDUSTRIAL LANDSCAPE?

Walking up through the native pinewood of Bad an Sgalaig looks and feels as close to an idea of wilderness as it's possible to get in the UK, but it is, in fact, closer to a post-industrial landscape in the early stages of managed rebirth. As the excellent estate interpretation boards explain, the land was stripped bare of its woodland for grazing and fuel for over 5000 years. And during the first half of the 17th century, many trees were plundered to fuel the iron-smelting furnaces dotted around nearby Loch Maree. Even the crooked, twisted branches we associate with pine woodland is a legacy of this period, as tall, straight-trunked trees were in high demand for shipbuilding during the Napoleonic Wars. Large-scale sheep farming followed and, as the UK wool market collapsed, deer stalking and then grouse shooting took over. These animals helped to consolidate a new peaty, acidic moorland landscape devoid of much of its native wildlife.

The suffix 'forest' attached to the Flowerdale area, as well as many other areas now considered wild, derives from the Latin *foris*, meaning places 'outside of' common law rights to farm, graze and hunt. These places were set aside for royalty to hunt. After the Union of 1750 this practice became more widespread in Scotland and a century later Scottish commoners were forcibly removed in the Clearances. As hunting became more fashionable in Victorian Britain, upper-class tourists travelled by train and then car to stalk deer and shoot grouse.

In his polemic *The Book of Trespass* (2020), Nick Hayes refers to this gradual enclosure as a 'cult of exclusion'. In Flowerdale, the estate has begun to reverse centuries of social and environmental inequity.

inside beautiful **Coire Beag**, ready for the ridge to come. There's a fairly benign, grassy climb at the back of the corrie followed by an impressive, erratic-strewn platform once at the saddle.

For the full traverse, leave your bag and head east for breathtaking views of Beinn Eighe at the summit of **Carn na Feòla** (761m) then return west to the saddle. From here, either climb steeply to a spot height of 750m or contour (equally steep!) to the next saddle, which hovers above **Loch a' Choire Mhòir**.

The crux of 'the castle' now stands guard, straight ahead. Stowing poles and camera, it can be bypassed to the left via a series of thin trods and grassy banks. This is an exposed, somewhat intimidating position and not a place to slip. Thereafter, the summit of **Beinn Dearg** (which, at 913m, narrowly misses the height needed to be classified as a Munro) is simple enough on a gravel path, which is easily followed to the final peak of **Stùc Loch na Cabhaig**.

Descend on an increasingly steep, braided and eroded path to the west of the summit. Turn right and head downhill over rough, heathery slopes to the westerly outflow of **Loch na Cabhaig**. Camping can be found to the northeast.

▲ Looking back along Beinn Dearg to Beinn Eighe, with 'the castle' on the right

ROUTE 20 – FLOWERDALE THREE: BEINN AN EÒIN, BEINN DEARG AND BAOSBHEINN

DAY 3
Camp under Baosbheinn to Red Stable

Start	Baosbheinn ridgeline (NG 896 630)
Distance	13.5km (8¼ miles)
Total ascent	760m (2495ft)
Time	6–9hr
Summits	Baosbheinn 875m (C) and its subsidiaries (Ceann Beag, Sgòrr Dubh)

Gain the ridge of **Drochaid a' Ghorm-locha**, and ascend simply northwest to **Ceann Beag**. Water can be found just east of the next *bealach* if needed, before you reach a wonderful viewpoint over **Loch na h-Oidhche**. There's a stony descent to another saddle, and then a shaly switchback path to the miniature plateau of **Sgòrr Dubh**, which marks the summit of **Baosbheinn** (875m) itself. From here, the ridge narrows dramatically while sea views open out to the north. After a couple of promontories, either climbed or bypassed, there is a short, steep and eroded downclimb. It's not quite a scramble but care is needed.

Should you wish to visit it, the grand cairn at the northern end of the hill commands fantastic views. Double back and descend east on an obvious spur that shelters **Coire Beag**. At its foot, turn north across the moorland plateau towards the erratic-strewn terraces overhanging the meadows of Abhainn a' Gharb Choire. This becomes both steep and rough, requiring good navigation. Cross a deer fence via the stile, then wade and tussock hop across the meadows, keeping the meandering river on your right if possible. Find a bridge (unmarked, at around NG 866 695), but continue on the left-hand bank, ignoring a path on the other side. Rejoin a path (below the area marked 'No Ford' on the OS), pass through a small gorge, and cross a **footbridge** over the river where it meets **Loch Bad an Sgalaig**. Follow this path to rejoin the main track and turn left to return to **Red Stable**.

▲ The tussock meadows of Abhainn a' Gharb Choire

149

THE FAR NORTH

◀ Looking west to Creag an Lochain (Ben Klibreck) from the shores of Loch Choire (Route 23)

SCOTTISH WILD COUNTRY BACKPACKING

ROUTE 21
The Postie's Path and the Coigach group

Start/finish	Car park at road end, Blughasary, off the A835, Strath Canaird (NC 134 014)
Total distance	33km (20½ miles)
Total ascent	2610m (8565ft)
Time	3 days
Terrain	Rough path with occasional waymarks, some mountain paths but mostly pathless, some low-grade scrambling on Ben Mòr Coigach, easily bypassed.
Maps	OS Explorer 439 Coigach & Summer Isles; Landranger 15 Loch Assynt
Note	Don't park at the cottages, but continue on a rough track until it ends at a gate. This route is best done (as described) in a clockwise direction – the rough ascent out of Cadh' a' Mhoraire to Beinn Tarsuinn is unpleasant as a downclimb. Expect the coastal section to be tough going in places.

▲ Lochan Tuath from the bealach under Sgùrr an Fhìdhleir

ROUTE 21 – THE POSTIE'S PATH AND THE COIGACH GROUP

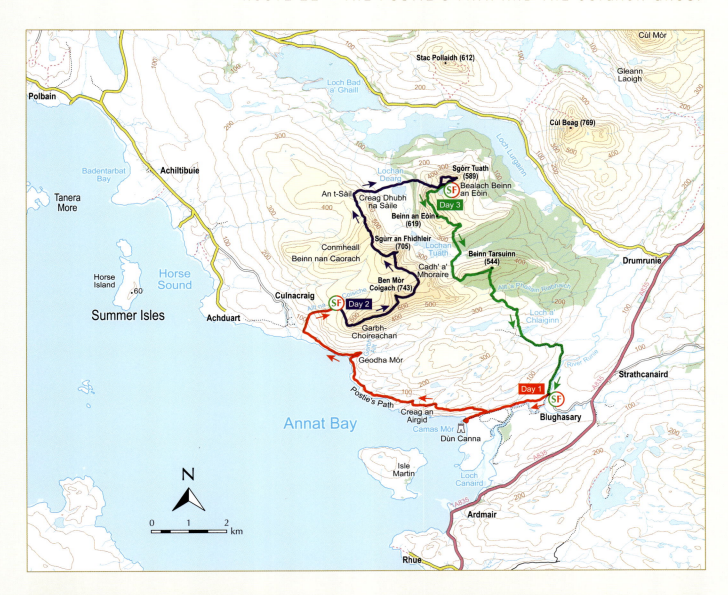

Height isn't everything, and this route shows why. It combines sea and summit, natural and cultural history in a compact circuit that also includes some of the least frequented hills in the area.

This route embarks on a rugged, historic coastal path before indulging mountaineering dreams on Ben Mòr Coigach – squeezing maximum adventure from minimum jeopardy. Unparalleled views unfold, across the Viking long ship silhouettes of Assynt. The area is the Scottish Wildlife Trust's largest reserve, and it's likely the only company you'll have will be red deer, frogs and golden eagles.

DAY 1
Blughasary to camp under Ben Mòr Coigach

Start	Car park at road end, Blughasary (NC 134 014)
Distance	11.5km (7¼ miles)
Total ascent	890m (2920ft)
Time	4–7hr

From the car park at **Blughasary**, go through a gate, over a new bridge, and turn left (west) taking a rough, peaty path alongside a deer fence. Follow this until you join a wider track, to visit the remains of **Dùn Canna**, an Iron Age hill fort above a striking beach. Return a short distance and head steeply uphill at the sign for the **Postie's Path**, to gain flatter, boggy ground above. This was once the twice-weekly route for the postman between Ullapool and Achiltibuie, but it was used by generations of churchgoers and cattle drovers before that.

With occasional waymarks and still undergoing renovation, the terrain is both spectacular and challenging. You will meet an outwardly facing sandstone slab as you round the first headland. Continue northwest along the coast, climbing down terraces and crossing bogs and small burns. After **Creag an Airgid** there is another exposed section and from here, the approach to **Geodha Mòr** can be very overgrown and tricky to navigate, especially in late summer. The postman would have been very fit indeed!

Once past the secluded ravine of **Garbh Allt**, the path becomes more established. Continue west high above the sea before dropping down to grass to meet the deeply cut Allt nan Coisiche. Follow faint braids to the right of this small river up onto the moorland to the north of the main ridge of **Ben Mòr Coigach**, where camping and water can be found if needed.

After a postal service was established in the 1860s, Kenneth McLennan of Blairbuie would walk this way twice a week with the mail. It was called a *Gabhail na Creige* – 'taking the rock'. Until World War II, when the circular road around to the north was put in, this was the only way to travel on land from Achiltibuie to Ullapool. Before that, churchgoers and cattle drovers would gather at the meeting stone above Achiltibuie and 'take the rock', heading for the church at the head of Loch Broom or the markets further south.

The Postie's Path runs for about 11km and is slowly being restored. Both ends of the path are of easier grade and, while the longest, middle section has some nice new stone markers to show the way, it's surprisingly challenging. However, it's a perfect route on which to enjoy bird and marine wildlife, especially in the spring and equipped with a pair of binoculars.

▲ Garbh Choireachan, the start of the Ben Mòr Coigach ridge

DAY 2
Camp under Ben Mòr Coigach to Sgòrr Tuath

Start	Moorland under Ben Mòr Coigach (around NC 078 038)
Distance	11.5km (7 miles)
Total ascent	1175m (3855ft)
Time	6–8hr
Summits	Garbh-Choireachan 716m, Ben Mòr Coigach 743m, Sgùrr an Fhìdhleir 705m, Sgòrr Tuath 589m

Make for the prow of the Ben Mòr Coigach massif – **Garbh-Choireachan** – which rises improbably on your right. It is easily climbed via a series of broken sandstone terraces, giving superlative views along the coastline, An Teallach and the Beinn Dearg group, beyond Ullapool. The ridgeline itself is over a kilometre of easy, slabby sandstone scrambling, with a bypass path mostly on the north side, in the most fantastic position imaginable. It drops down before a final pull to the much flatter summit of **Ben Mòr Coigach** (743m) and a cairn.

Continue east and then gradually contour north for gentler ground, to meet a spring and the saddle under **Sgùrr an Fhìdhleir** (705m). Climb steeply to the very prominent summit overlooking Coigach and Assynt. Now descend southwest and then northwest, following the ridge above the watershed of **Lochan Tuath**. Pass sandstone tors to the next cairn at 648m, a dizzyingly thin-feeling place, poised between heaven and earth. Continue north until you reach a break in the crags on your right after **Creag Dhubh na Sàile**. Descend steeply east on grass and cross to the outflow of **Lochan Dearg**.

Continue east over deer fence remains and head up between Beinn an Eòin (see Day 3, below) and Sgòrr Tuath, over very rough, heather-covered boulders, which cover a submerged burn. There is water and camping at the saddle, the **Bealach Beinn an Eòin**. **Sgòrr Tuath** (589m) can be climbed by its south ridge, immediately to your left, which becomes very steep at the top, or by heading northeast up roughly vegetated slopes. The views of Assynt from its summit ridge are unrivalled.

DAY 3
Sgòrr Tuath to Blughasary

Start	Camp at Bealach Beinn an Eòin (NC 104 073)
Distance	11km (6¾ miles)
Total ascent	550m (1805ft)
Time	4–6hr
Summits	Beinn an Eòin 619m, Beinn Tarsuinn 544m

The ridge of **Beinn an Eòin** is soon reached via broad grassy slopes at its northeastern end, once again providing unusual perspectives on Stac Pollaidh, Cùl Beag and beyond, over the shoulders of Sgòrr Tuath. Head south on grass and more sandstone slabs to the summit (619m), before descending on its easterly shoulder towards Cioch Beinn an Eòin. At around the 450m contour, where the incline eases, cut southwest to find a broad, heathery terrace and descend steeply south, picking your way past small crags to meet the deer fence. Go through a gate and follow the fence around, crossing a delightful burn, to a very steep gully tucked away at the back of **Cadh' a' Mhoraire**. The climb here is hands on, quite wet and eroded, but is not technical and is mercifully short.

Head east to the easily won summit of **Beinn Tarsuinn** (544m), before doubling back from the small summit crag. Descend steeply south to meet the gentle waterfall slabs of **Allt 'a Phollain Riabhaich**, a wonderful place to rest. Continue south, crossing a deer fence at a stile, before descending more gently along a small ridgeline, to meet the track to the south and west of **Loch a' Chlaiginn**. Now head southeast for a while, following the track as it turns south to return to the road end at **Blughasary**.

SCOTTISH WILD COUNTRY BACKPACKING

ROUTE 22
Glencoul, Gleann Dubh and Beinn Leòid

Start/finish	Parking area by A894 (NC 240 292)
Total distance	41.5km (25¾ miles)
Total ascent	2170m (7120ft)
Time	2–3 days
Terrain	Rocky mountain and moorland terrain. Some ATV tracks and footpaths; boggy and tussocky in places.
Key summits	Beinn Leòid 792m (C)
Maps	OS Explorer 442 Assynt & Lochinver; OS Landranger 15 Loch Assynt
Note	Though it is a manageable distance, at nearly 25km, the second day's route may be best walked over two days with an overnight at Glencoul bothy. The MBA bothies at Glendhu and Glencoul are obvious places to overnight, but carry a tent or shelter as they can get busy.

Deep in the heart of Sutherland, lying to the east of the whale-backed summit ridges of Quinag, the elegant form of lonely Beinn Leòid is the fulcrum around which this fine walk turns. Although the route follows a number of established tracks and paths, it nonetheless retains a 'wilderness' feel; the expansive views across glens, ridges, summits, lochs and coastline play a significant part. However, there are also a couple of off-piste sections where the terrain is rough and navigational acumen comes into play.

The terrain is engagingly varied and the route also benefits from ever-changing perspectives on the landscapes traversed. As well as spectacular views there are good chances of spotting some wildlife, including mountain hares, red deer and golden eagles. The lochside MBA bothies at Glencoul and Glendhu are beautifully situated, with plenty of camping ground close by, and are the obvious choice for overnighting. Abhainn an Loch Bhig is crossed on the outward and return legs and, while this should present few problems, all river crossings should be approached with caution.

▲ Abhainn an Loch Bhig flowing into Loch Beag

ROUTE 22 – GLENCOUL, GLEANN DUBH AND BEINN LEÒID

THE BOTHY AT THE BACK OF BEYOND

Cùl or cùil is the Gaelic word for 'back' and the name 'Glencoul' is most often translated as 'the glen at the back of beyond', which has a certain romantic appeal. It has also been translated as 'narrow glen'; *caol* being the Gaelic word for 'narrow', usually in the sense of a body of water – a sound or strait. Both work as descriptions of Glencoul and its environs.

Glencoul bothy sits above the shore at the head of tidal Loch Glencoul some 14km from the coast. The bothy itself is a small house somewhat bizarrely appended to the gable end of a larger house, which was built as an estate keeper's residence by the Duke of Westminster in the early 19th century. The bothy was formerly used as a schoolroom attached to the home of the Elliot family who lived in the house for many decades. The bothy has a copy of a journal written by John Elliot who grew up in the house and worked as a deer stalker on the estate. He describes the freedom of growing up here – '[w]e did more or less as we liked out of school hours' – and a life of improvisation and self-sufficiency.

'School was in a bedroom in the house. Teachers were whoever we could get, my eldest brother, Will, as often as not. He ruled with firmness, but must have had some quality as a teacher, because he taught me to love books. [...] We had a cousin, for one year, and he was tough. When he joined the Seaforths in the 1914 war we thought the German Army might as well give up. They didn't. Norman was killed in action.' John's older brothers, Alastair and Will were also killed during World War I.

'We were self-supporting in some things. We had a venison allowance from the Estate. We had our own mutton, lamb, pork, hams, fowls, eggs, butter, cream, and cheese. My mother made soft cottage cheese and she had a huge stone cheese press for making harder cheese, which would keep for months. We salted venison in the shooting season and stored it in barrels.'

157

SCOTTISH WILD COUNTRY BACKPACKING

DAY 1
Loch na Gainmhich to Glendhu Bothy

Start	Parking area by A894 (NC 240 292)
Distance	17km (10½ miles)
Total ascent	645m (2115ft)
Time	6–7hr

From the parking area follow the track east, parallel to the road, bear left where the road bends and follow an often-boggy path to cross the outflow of **Loch na Gainmhich** on stepping stones. To the left Allt Chranaidh drops precipitously into a fine gorge. Ignore the lochside path and head up an eroded path which soon climbs steadily above the east side of the loch. Leaving the loch behind, the path becomes firmer as it climbs towards **Bealach a' Bhuirich**, becoming steeper before easing then levelling where the *bealach* is gained. As the high point (450m) is reached just beyond **Loch Bealach a' Bhuirich**, there are splendid views back to Quinag and east to the wild hinterland ahead. Continue descending roughly eastwards. Soon you'll reach the burn feeding Eas a' Chùal Aluinn waterfall; the highest in the UK with a 200-metre drop. Ignore the boggy path on the left and descend alongside the stream to the top of the falls as there are better views from below; cross the burn where the path meets it and ignore the vague path descending along the far side. Continue along the sinuous path for 1km then, after passing a v-shaped *lochan*, take a vague path branching left off the main path, descending initially alongside the burn flowing down from the *lochan*. The grassy path winds steeply down through the crags to the floor of the glen where **Abhainn an Loch Bhig** can be crossed with care – unless it is in spate, in which case you'll need to head upstream and find a safe crossing point.

Once over, turn northwards (left) and head down the glen towards Loch Beag below.

The spectacular view of **Eas a' Chùal Aluinn** cascading into the glen is some compensation for the ensuing 2km trudge through boggy, heathery, tussocky ground to the head of the loch.

Try to follow vague paths through the rough, boulder-strewn terrain around the edge of the loch and, after 1.5km, turn right along a track by a jetty. Follow this around to the **Glencoul bothy** standing by the shore of **Loch Glencoul**.

▲ Descending from Bealach a' Bhuirich

ROUTE 22 – GLENCOUL, GLEANN DUBH AND BEINN LEÒID

Cross a footbridge, pass around a sheep fank (pen) and continue by the shore to cross another footbridge over the outflow of the Glencoul River. Bear right along the path for 100 metres then turn sharply left along a track that soon climbs steadily up above the eastern shore of Loch Glencoul. After 2.5km you'll reach a high point (210m) above the **Àird da Loch**, which juts out between Loch Glencoul and Loch Glendhu. Continue along the path as it turns north then east, steadily descending towards the south shore of **Loch Glendhu**. The path peters out, but continue to the head of the loch and cross the footbridge over the Amhainn a' Ghlinne Dhuibh. Pick up the glen track and turn left, soon to arrive at **Glendhu bothy**.

DAY 2
Glendhu bothy to Loch na Gainmhich

Start	Glendhu bothy (NC 284 337)
Distance	24.5km (15¼ miles)
Total ascent	1525m (5000ft)
Time	8–9hr
Summits	Beinn Leòid 792m (C)

From the **Glendhu bothy** head southeast up through Gleann Dubh on the ATV track with very little gradient for the first 2km. A steep climb follows before the gradient eases then levels. Cross a footbridge over the **Amhainn a' Ghlinne Dhuibh**, with picturesque **Eas Creag an Luchda** waterfall upstream, and continue climbing quite steeply for 1.5km until the metalled track runs out. Just beyond a brief zigzag section of path, strike out southwards across open, boggy moorland for the north ridge of **Beinn Leòid**. The ridge is grassy in its lower reaches, giving way to awkward bouldery slopes higher up. The summit, with a trig point and low shelter wall, is gained at 792m. The views really are magnificently expansive: a tumult of moorland, lochs, mountains and sea with Ben More Assynt to the south, Quinag to the east, Arkle and Foinaven to the north.

From the summit, head southwest, soon descending bouldery slopes that give way to grass on Bealach Beinn Leòid between the summit and the lower southwest top (729m). Contour southwestwards around the top and continue descending the grassy southwest ridge, making for a narrow *bealach* at 560 metres. Now descend northwestwards following the course of a stream flowing into an unnamed *lochan*. Continue descending alongside the burn flowing down from the *lochan* as it winds its way eventually down to join the **Glencoul River** at the outflow of **Loch an Eircill**. Turn right and follow the Land Rover track down **Glen Coul**, passing beneath the craggy eminence of the **Stack of Glencoul**. After 4km keep left on the main track where a path forks right and soon cross a footbridge over the river. Continue along the shore to **Glencoul bothy**. Retrace your outward route to return to the start of the walk.

▲ Glendhu bothy

SCOTTISH WILD COUNTRY BACKPACKING

ROUTE 23
Ben Klibreck and the Ben Armine Forest

Start/finish	The Crask Inn (NC 524 247)
Total distance	56.5km (35 miles)
Total ascent	2360m (7745ft)
Time	3 days
Terrain	Rugged mountain and moorland terrain, some boggy sections.
Key summits	Ben Klibreck 962m (M)
Maps	OS Explorer 443 Ben Klibreck & Ben Armine; OS Landranger 16 Lairg & Loch Shin

▲ Looking northwest from Bealach Easach with Loch a' Bhealaich ahead and Loch Choire beyond

ROUTE 23 – BEN KLIBRECK AND THE BEN ARMINE FOREST

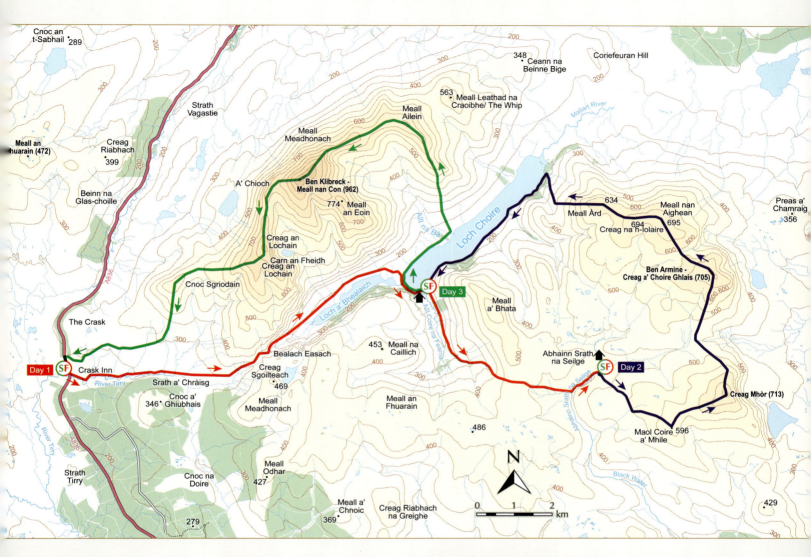

Situated in the heart of Sutherland, the isolated massifs of Ben Klibreck and Ben Armine form natural ramparts rising to the west of the Flow Country – a vast waterlogged expanse that is Europe's largest blanket bog. This seemingly empty area provides rich botanical and ornithological habitat that has survived the depredations of commercial forestry and proposed wind farm developments, and is now being considered as a potential UNESCO World Heritage Site.

Expansive views across the Flow Country are a feature of the second and third days of the route described here, when the ridges of Ben Armine and Ben Klibreck are traversed; the first day is essentially a long walk into the heart of this wild country. This is a fairly demanding route, but the walking is never exceptionally tough. The route traverses some challengingly boggy ground in places, but the terrain is varied and there are fine grassy ridges and firm tracks to enjoy as well. Two simple estate bothies provide an option for shelter on each of the nights out.

DAY 1
Crask Inn to Abhainn Srath na Seilge bothy

Start	The Crask Inn (NC 524 247)
Distance	17.5km (10¾ miles),
Total ascent	490m (1610ft)
Time	7–8hr

From the **Crask Inn** head south down the road until level with the nearby house. Turn left through a gate then follow an ATV track roughly eastwards alongside the River Tirry for around 4km. The track can be hellishly boggy in places, but the going becomes firmer as it narrows to a path and climbs northeastwards to the narrow pass of **Bealach Easach**. Once atop the bealach the view opens out over a magnificent U-shaped glacial valley that cradles two connected lochs.

A firm track descends steadily into the glen, soon passing alongside **Loch a' Bhealaich** and eventually reaching the shore of the larger **Loch Choire** with its sandy beaches and wooded crags rising above the head of the loch. Bear right by the shore and cross the outflow of Loch a' Bhealaich to the left of the footbridge unless it has been repaired in the meantime. Continue around the loch edge to cross another footbridge – cross the Allt Coire na Feàrna upstream if the bridge is not safe. Head towards the Loch Choire bothy perched above the shore, but before reaching it turn right and head south, following an ATV track up the glen, alongside the burn. After a gentle 2km (ignore the path forking right) follow the path through a metal gate then through a deer gate (ignore the ATV track climbing to the left) and climb steadily along the wooded river bank before exiting the fenced enclosure and continuing up to a bealach at around 460m.

The path descends gently for 1.5km before reaching **Abhainn Srath na Seilge**; turn left and follow the river upstream on an intermittent boggy path for 1km to reach the **estate bothy** at a bend in the river.

DAY 2
Abhainn Srath na Seilge bothy to Loch Choire bothy

Start	Abhainn Srath na Seilge (NC 665 246)
Distance	19km (11¾ miles)
Total ascent	815m (2675ft)
Time	7–8hr
Summits	Creag Mhòr 713m, Creag a' Choire Ghlais (Ben Armine) 705m, Meall nan Aighean 695m, Creag na h-Iolaire 694m

From the **bothy**, **Abhainn Srath na Seilge** must be crossed to follow an ATV track heading southeast. Depending on the level of the river it may be possible to cross close to the bothy, otherwise head upstream until you can find a safe crossing point. Once over, follow the ATV track heading southeast, climbing steadily alongside Allt an Inne Bheag. The track levels at a peatland plateau after 1km. Where it begins descending again, head southeastwards away from the track, climbing steadily up through peat hags along the western flank of **Maol Coire a' Mhile** to the cairn-marked summit (598m). Descend northeastwards to the *bealach* beneath the southwest ridge of Creag Mhòr. Keep to the south side of the *bealach* to avoid the worst of the peat hags. From the *bealach* climb (150m) northeast for 1km to reach the exposed, mossy summit of **Creag Mhòr** (713m), which is furnished with a trig point and shelter wall.

▲ Approaching the Allt na Seilich bothy

Creag Mhòr is the higher of Ben Armine's two summits with Creag a' Choire Ghlais lying 3.5km to the north across the Coir an Eas. The eastern flank of Ben Armine drops away in a steep-sided escarpment with fine views across the empty country to east and north.

Descend north then northwest and keep to the eastern edge of the *bealach* to avoid the worst of the boggy ground and peat hags. Head north, crossing the ATV track then climbing steeply up the south ridge of **Creag a' Choire Ghlais** (705m).

From the summit descend northwest to a *bealach* at 595m – keep to the east side to avoid the worst of the peat hags – before climbing northwest to the flat summit of **Meall nan Aighean** (695m). Continue along the ridge, bearing west to the summit of **Creag na h-Iolaire** (694m) before descending northwest again to **Meall Àrd** (634m). Descend steadily westwards from the summit then more steeply into the glen, picking up the ATV track that continues northwards down towards the shore of Loch Choire. Go through deer gates either side of a woodland enclosure then turn left after another deer gate to follow the track southwest along the wooded shore of **Loch Choire**. Continue for 5km – forking right along the shore after 1.2km – to arrive at the **estate bothy** perched above the shore. If the bothy is fully occupied, continue a short way around the shore of the loch to find a good camping pitch.

DAY 3
Loch Choire bothy to the Crask Inn

Start	Loch Choire bothy (NC 619 270)
Distance	19.5km (12¼ miles)
Total ascent	1055m (3460ft)
Time	7–8hr
Summits	Ben Klibreck (Meall Ailein, Meall Meadhonach, Meall nan Con, Creag an Lochain) 962m (M)

From the **bothy** continue around to the head of the loch recrossing the rivers crossed on the first day. Where the path forks, bear right to follow it northeast along the shore of **Loch Choire**. Continue past a woodland plantation, cross a wooden bridge over **Allt na Bà** and bear left off the track. Climb roughly north up a seemingly interminable grassy slope; there is no path but the going underfoot is good. Pass a small cairn and gain the broad, rocky ridge. Head northwest along the ridge, soon reaching a stone memorial commemorating the victims of an air crash. Continue climbing steadily for 1km to the rocky summit of **Meall Ailein** (724m). Loch Naver lies a short way north and the mountains of Assynt can be seen far to the west, while the vast expanse of the Flow Country stretches away to the east.

Continue westwards along the ridge. The going is easy at first but becomes hard work negotiating a way up through peat hags over the top of **Meall Meadhonach**. Once over, the ridge is restored to grass once again; ahead the elegant northeast ridge narrows and rises steeply to **Meall nan Con** (962m), Ben Klibreck's highest point. Descend steeply westwards (take care in poor visibility) to **A' Chioch** then swing south along the narrow crest to a broad col at 688m. Continue southwards, climbing steadily along the ridge to gain the summit of **Creag an Lochain**.

From here descend southwards a short way before bearing southwest then west, steadily descending on an intermittent path through peat hags to arrive at a broad col. A relatively short climb southwestwards then leads to the summit of **Cnoc Sgriodain** (544m). From here descend the south spur then bear right across the lower slopes to pick up a wide ATV track. Follow this often-boggy track to arrive back at the A836 a little north of the **Crask Inn**.

The Crask Inn is very much out on its own in the wild heart of Sutherland, 20km north of the village of Lairg and 13km south of the small hamlet of Altnaharra. Built as a coaching inn in the early 19th century, the homely inn is something of an institution for hill walkers, anglers and 'end-to-end' cyclists riding from John O'Groats to Land's End. The Crask was run for years by the legendary Mike and Kai Geldard before they donated it to the Scottish Episcopal Church in 2017. It is still run as an inn on behalf of the Church and has four rooms for guests, a dining area and a small bar with a peat-burning stove. An added dimension to the Crask experience is the availability of morning and evening prayer and an informal church service is held on the third Thursday of every month.

Heading east into the Ben Armine Forest with Ben Klibreck behind

SCOTTISH WILD COUNTRY BACKPACKING

ROUTE 24
Around Strath Dionard

Start/finish	Roadside parking area on A838, 200 metres west of Carbreck house (NC 330 591)
Total distance	37.5km (23¼ miles)
Total ascent	2250m (7380ft)
Time	2 days
Terrain	Challenging, rocky mountain terrain with large areas of scree and boulders; some rough moorland between summits. A few miles on a good track eases the initial walk-in.
Key summits	Foinaven: Ganu Mòr 911m (C), Cranstackie 801m (C), Beinn Spionnaidh 773m (C)
Maps	OS Explorer 445 Foinaven, Arkle, Kylesku & Scourie and 446 Durness & Cape Wrath; OS Landranger 9 Cape Wrath
Note	Magnificent ridge walking on Foinaven is tempered by tricky loose scree in places. Extensive boulder fields on Cranstackie require stamina and concentration. The only river crossing of note is Allt an Easain Ghil which may require care in spate conditions. It is best to tackle the route anticlockwise – as described here – as the scramble up from Cadha na Beucaich is difficult in reverse. Strath Dionard is on a working estate where deer stalking and salmon fishing take place in season.

▲ Camp on the east side of Strath Dionard, Foinaven opposite

ROUTE 24 – AROUND STRATH DIONARD

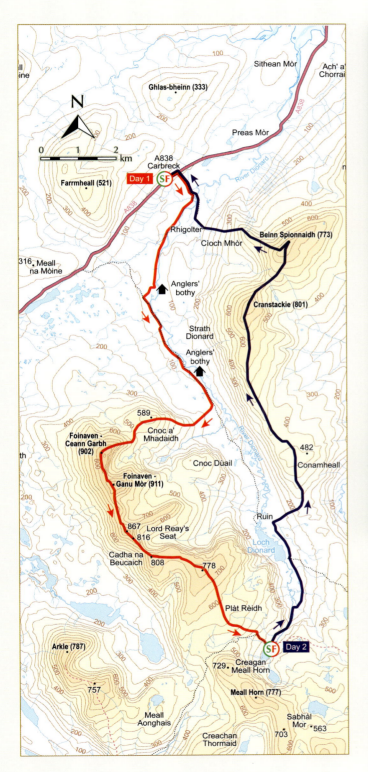

▶ The brief but steep scramble to spot height 808m on Foinaven

You would expect the closest high ground to Cape Wrath to be especially wild, rugged and uncompromising, and indeed the mountains around Strath Dionard are all these things. Foinaven especially is one of the finest massifs anywhere in Scotland. Its backbone runs north–south and offers spectacular travel above corries filled with acres of smashed talus, and subsidiary ridges draped with vast grey mantles of scree. Across the strath, Cranstackie and Beinn Spionnaidh form the most northerly high ground above 2500ft (760m) in Scotland. While lacking the high drama of Foinaven, these are burly, boulder-clad beasts with airy summits overlooking the long moorland miles to the Cape.

167

DAY 1
Carbreck to Coir' an Dubh-loch

Start	Roadside parking area west of Carbreck (NC 330 591)
Distance	19.5km (12 miles)
Total ascent	1265m (4150ft)
Time	9–11hr
Summits	Foinaven (Ceann Garbh 902m, Ganu Mòr 911m) (C), Lord Reay's Seat 816m

Follow the road east to **Carbreck cottage**. Turn right on a track towards the **River Dionard**. Before the bridge, turn right and follow the river upstream. There is an intermittent anglers' path near the bank and occasional wooden boards across boggy ground and side channels.

After 2.5km reach a track and an **anglers' bothy**. Follow the track southwest for 400 metres to a junction. Turn left up Strath Dionard for 3.5km, passing another **bothy**. At NC 343 526, approximately 900 metres beyond it, turn right off the track and climb towards Foinaven across the southern flank of **Cnoc a' Mhadaidh** (589m). Beyond a broad saddle, tackle the steep, bouldery ascent to **Ceann Garbh** (902m), Foinaven's northernmost summit. The best line tacks slightly left of the crest near the foot of the climb where the ground is grassier and less broken.

The hard work done, savour the swooping ridge as it bears south to the highest point of **Foinaven, Ganu Mòr** (911m). The first, small cairn marks the summit, although it's worth continuing 100 metres east to a larger cairn for the view into the corries and back to the main ridge.

Bear southwest to regain the ridge, which becomes progressively rockier. The trickiest section is around **Lord Reay's Seat** (816m, NC 322 491, unnamed on OS maps). Its east face, 120 metres of vertical rock, plunges to the screes of Coire na Lurgainn. Attempting to scramble over the summit outcrop is not recommended due the difficulty and exposure. Instead bear right to skirt just below it, following the rough path scratched by predecessors over loose, angled scree to rejoin the crest beyond. A steep descent over sharp rocks leads to **Cadha na Beucaich**. Look out for a tiny stone *howff* on the *bealach* – a bolthole of last resort!

Continue south following the rough path up a stony ramp, then a short Grade One scramble through a band of crags to reach the 808m point (NC 325 487). Although it looks intimidating from below, the route is obvious, well worn and straightforward in ascent. Avoid the temptation to bypass the crag on the right as this leads onto uncomfortably loose scree.

From the 808m point bear east then southeast over easy, undulating terrain for roughly 1.25km to reach an unnamed top (NC 339 484). Head southeast gently downhill for 1.5km to reach the headwaters of a burn just west of **Plàt Rèidh**. Shadow the burn gully on its south side for around 500 metres then bear right away from it for another 300 metres to reach the track from Bealach Horn at a sharp bend. Follow the track downhill into Coir' an Dubh-loch.

▲ Descending from Lord Reay's Seat to Cadha na Beucaich

ROUTE 24 – AROUND STRATH DIONARD

▲ Lunar cobbles on the approach to Cranstackie

DAY 2
Coir' an Dubh-loch to Carbreck

Start	Coir' an Dubh-loch (NC 356 463)
Distance	18km (11¼ miles)
Total ascent	990m (3250ft)
Time	7–9hr
Summits	Cranstackie 801m (C), Beinn Spionnaidh 773m (C)

Continue northeast for 1.25km. When the track ends abruptly (NC 362 473), cross the river and keep north on faint deer tracks. After 2.5km reach a **ruin** by Allt nan Carachean Dubh near the northern end of **Loch Dionard**. Climb east for 1km, keeping to the north side of a burn, to reach a broad moorland crest. Bear north up increasingly rocky slopes for 1.5km to **Conamheall** (482m), a moonscape of exposed rock.

Pick your way down from Conamheall. Keep fairly close to the edge above Strath Dionard to maintain the highest ground, turning a few outcrops as you cross a kilometre of broken ground to reach the climb to **Cranstackie** (801m). Once on this slope, the going is straightforward over easy-angled rocks.

For the last 600 metres the climb steepens. Bear right of an outcropped subsidiary top, moving carefully across massive angular boulders. Scramble and boulder-hop to arrive at the summit cairn perched above the north-facing void.

Continuing to **Beinn Spionnaidh** (773m), descend northeast to a grassy col, then tackle the stiff climb to a small cairn at the west end of the bouldery summit plateau. Continue northeast for 300 metres to the trig point inside a circular cairn marking the true summit. Return to the smaller cairn and descend steeply northwest, over awkward rocks at first, to reach a grassy saddle (520m). Cross **Cioch Mhòr**, carefully finding the best line on the steep, outcropped descent, to another grassy shoulder before Cioch Bheag.

Descend left across the hillside towards **Rhigolter** sheep farm. Reach a fence around the 250m contour and another at 150m; look for the gates rather than climbing the fences. Make the last 100-metre descent to Rhigolter on the right side of a burn to reach another gate and the track just before the farmhouse. Turn right and follow the track to the A838 at **Carbreck**.

SCOTTISH WILD COUNTRY BACKPACKING

ROUTE 25
Cape Wrath, Sandwood Bay and the Parph

Start/finish	Parking area at Blairmore (NC 194 600)
Total distance	55km (34 miles)
Total ascent	1425m (4675ft)
Time	4 days
Terrain	Moorland, hill country. There are good tracks around Kervaig and Cape Wrath, but much of the route is pathless and the terrain is rough and boggy in places.
Maps	OS Explorer 446 Durness & Cape Wrath; OS Landranger 9 Cape Wrath
Note	The route crosses the Cape Wrath Training Centre military live firing range and access is prohibited during firing times. Phone in advance of your planned trip: Range Control tel 01971 511242 (8am–5pm).

The far northwestern corner of the Highlands – also known as the Parph – has just about everything the adventurous backpacker could wish for: an expanse of under-visited, geologically stimulating hill country, lonely moors, great towering sea cliffs and no fewer than three MBA bothies. Then there are the area's two main attractions: Cape Wrath and Sandwood Bay. Both are relatively popular with visitors, but this does not detract from the overall feeling of isolation, especially during the walk across the Parph and the coastal walk south from Cape Wrath, where you're unlikely to meet other walkers save for the occasional wild-eyed penitent nearing the end of the Cape Wrath Trail. Indeed, you're more likely to encounter red deer haunting the corries, and golden eagles hunting through the glens.

Don't underestimate this walk; there are a couple of big days and you should be prepared for some rough, boggy and pathless terrain – it is not a walk for bad weather, poor visibility or inexperienced walkers. There is also the small matter of a military live firing range to negotiate (see route information, above).

The route starts with a relatively short walk-in to overnight at Strathan bothy before heading north across the Parph over the summits of Creag Riabhach and Fashven to Kervaig on the north coast. Another long day takes in Cape Wrath and the northwest coast en route to Strathchailleach bothy. The final day is another relatively short walk out via Sandwood Bay.

▲ Kervaig bothy

ROUTE 25 – CAPE WRATH, SANDWOOD BAY AND THE PARPH

DAY 1
Blairmore to Strathan

Start	Parking area at Blairmore (NC 194 600)
Distance	7.5km (4½ miles)
Total ascent	110m (360ft)
Time	2–2½hr

From the car park by **Blairmore**, walk just over 1km southeast, back along the road, to reach the start of the track, on the left. After 1km fork right off the main track to follow an intermittent and often boggy footpath leading to **Loch Mor a' Chraisg** and its smaller satellite. Beyond the lochs the path improves as it continues towards Strathan, descending into **Strath Shinary**. Where the path reaches **Abhainn an t-Srathain** you can cross directly if the river is quiet otherwise there is a wire bridge 200 metres to the northwest. **Strathan bothy** is a former shepherd's cottage with three rooms and a working fireplace – though fuel has to be carried in.

DAY 2
Strathan to Kervaig

Start	Strathan bothy (NC 247 612)
Distance	20km (12½ miles)
Total ascent	1100m (3610ft)
Time	7½–9hr
Summits	Meall Dearg 451m, Meall na Mòine 462m, Creag Riabhach 485m, Cnoc na Glaic Tarsuinn 370m, Fashven 460m, Maovally 302m

From **Strathan bothy** climb steadily northeastwards; the gradient steepens as you gain the spur of Sròn a' Ghobhair with its sandstone outcrops. Continue climbing northeastwards to the *bealach* between An Grianan and **Meall Dearg** (451m), then climb southeastwards for 135 metres to the latter's whale-backed summit. Descend eastwards to the *bealach* and make the short climb to the summit of **Meall na Mòine** (462m). Descend north northwestwards then climb steadily along the ridge of **Creag Riabhach** (485m) with its impressive east- and north-facing cliffs; the summit is marked with a stone shelter wall and trig point. The views are grand, especially southwest over Loch a' Phuill Bhuidhe to tor-crested Grianan.

Head northwest then descend westwards to avoid craggy terrain. On reaching the shallower slopes traverse around to the north of Creag Riabach; the terrain becomes rougher, moving from sandstone to gneiss. Cross Bealach Coir' a' Choin, follow the fence, then drop across the head of Coir' a' Choin to gain the rocky outcrops of **Cnoc na Glaic Tarsuinn** (370m). Continue climbing northeastwards then descend towards the outflow of **Loch na Gainmhich** – the shore is boggy and also has peat hags. Cross the fence into the firing range – indicated by a warning sign – and climb initially on rough ground to gain the long south ridge of **Fashven**, back in sandstone country again. Climb steadily for over 1km to gain the summit (460m). Standing alone, Fashven provides arguably the best viewpoint of the day, taking in north and west coasts, Durness, the surrounding hills and the bigger beasts beyond.

The safest route of descent is northeast avoiding the crags on the northern flank. Once below the crags contour around to the *bealach* between Fashven and **Maovally** (302m); going over this undistinguished-looking hill is a better option than the rough, boggy ground around it. Once over, head north to the track road, turn left and fork right after 2km, continuing downhill to arrive at **Kervaig bothy** perched above the shore. The bothy has two entrances to separate parts of the building, each with a fireplace.

▲ Strathan bothy

ROUTE 25 – CAPE WRATH, SANDWOOD BAY AND THE PARPH

DAY 3
Kervaig to Strathchailleach

Start	Kervaig bothy (NC 292 727)
Distance	17.5km (10¾ miles)
Total ascent	545m (1790ft)
Time	6½–8hr
Summits	Sidhean na h-Iolaireich 230m

From the **bothy** follow the Kervaig River back to the track, turning right across the bridge. The hut is a Ministry of Defence sentry post; during exercises sentries are stationed here to stop walkers straying onto the range. Turn left at a junction where a track leads down to a jetty on the right and follow the road out to the lighthouse at Cape Wrath.

Cape Wrath Lighthouse was built in 1828 by Robert Stevenson and was manned until 1998, when it was converted to automatic operation. It is located at the most northwesterly point on the British mainland, which takes its name from the old Norse *hvarf*, meaning 'turning point'. Looking eastwards from the lighthouse you can see the Clò Mòr sea cliffs – the highest of the British mainland – stretching from Kervaig towards Durness.

From the lighthouse head back along the track for just over 2km. Leave the track heading south towards a grassy area with a stream running through. Cross this and continue southwards across the moor, soon climbing steadily to the col between **Sidhean na h-Iolaireich** – Hill of the Eagles – and **Cnoc a' Ghiubhais** at around 200m. Contour southeastwards along the flank of the latter and Cnoc an Damh at around 200m before descending to the outflow of **Loch Keisgaig** then contouring around to the eastern side of **Loch a' Gheodha Ruaidh**. From there a short walk across the moor brings you to the Strath Chailleach river. Aim for the **bothy** just over the river, bearing in mind that you may have to wade across or go higher upstream to get across.

▲ Old sheep fank and byre at Kervaig

STRATHCAILLEACH BOTHY

The cottage at Strathchailleach was built in the mid 19th century and was permanently occupied until the 1940s. It then mostly lay empty until the winter of 1962, when James McRory-Smith took up residence in this most isolated and basic of dwellings. Also known as Sandy, McRory-Smith had taken to a life on the road in his late thirties after a personal tragedy. His wanderings eventually brought him to Strathchailleach and here he settled, making the cottage his home.

The cottage was six miles across difficult terrain from the nearest habitation, there was no electricity, toilet or bathroom and water was collected from the burn. James gathered driftwood and cut peat from the moor for the fire, snared rabbits and caught fish to supplement a meagre income from odd jobs on the Keodale Estate. It must have been a tough and lonely existence, but it was one that he lived by choice. However, in the winter of early 1979 a storm badly damaged the building forcing him to leave – although he told no-one about his departure.

He failed to collect his pension from the post office in Balchrick and, as time passed, it was assumed he had moved away and perhaps even died. The Mountain Bothies Association had had Strathcailleach on their radar for a long time, but James's occupation of the cottage obviously presented an obstacle. Bernard Heath of the MBA had first visited Strathcailleach in the mid 1950s and, on learning that James had not been seen for 18 months, he journeyed north in the summer of 1980 to inspect the cottage. The MBA could now plan renovations and take over stewardship of Strathcailleach from the Keodale Estate.

However, news came that James was still among the living and had in fact been squatting at Gorton bothy in the Central Highlands, before serving a three-month prison sentence in Inverness. While he was still in detention a deal was struck that would enable James to return to Strathcailleach once renovation was complete. He would have the room with the fireplace and a small back bedroom and the other room would be the open MBA bothy. Work started at Easter in 1981 and the bothy was added to the MBA's list in June that year.

However, problems soon arose with some MBA members reporting that James had refused them entry, although others found him very hospitable – often depending on how much he had had to drink. This behaviour persisted so that members were warned that they might not be able to use the bothy until an amicable arrangement could be found. Unfortunately, none was forthcoming and the MBA dropped Strathcailleach from its maintenance list in 1984. There was some suspicion that James never intended to honour his arrangement with the MBA once the work was completed, and this led to some ill-feeling.

Ten years later when his health deteriorated, James was forced to move to Kinlochbervie. He died in April 1999 aged 75 and was buried at Sheigra Cemetery. Around this time the MBA completed a second major renovation. Today, James's paintings still adorn the walls of the bothy, which he called home for more than 30 years.

See James Carron's biography of James McRory-Smith, *Highland Hermit*

▲ Sandwood Bay from the northeast

ROUTE 25 – CAPE WRATH, SANDWOOD BAY AND THE PARPH

DAY 4
Strathchailleach to Blairmore

Start	Strathchailleach bothy (NC 249 658)
Distance	10.5km (6½ miles)
Total ascent	215m (705ft)
Time	3½–4hr

From the bothy head westwards to Lochan nan Sac in the lee of Cnoc Lochan nan Sac. Continue southwestwards alongside the loch then swing westwards to reach **Sandwood Bay** at the outflow of **Sandwood Loch**. Continue along the bay with a fine view of the huge sea stack, Am Buachaille – Gaelic for The Herdsman – at the southern end of the sands. The sandstone stack was first climbed in 1968 by Tom Patey and Ian Clough.

From Sandwood Bay a path leads south up through the dunes, soon passing an old stone sheep fank. The path, which is the main route taken by day-trippers, becomes a wide gravel track. Follow the track, crossing the outflows of Loch a Mhuilinn and **Loch na Gainimh** en route to **Blairmore** and the parking area.

OUTER HEBRIDES

◀ Looking north to Bàgh Mhiùghalaigh and Cnoc Mhic-a'-Phi (Route 26)

SCOTTISH WILD COUNTRY BACKPACKING

ROUTE 26
A circuit of Mingulay

Start/finish	Landing place (NL 567 828)
Distance	13km (8 miles)
Total ascent	825m (2705ft)
Time	5–6hr
Terrain	There are intermittent trodden paths around the southern half of the island, but fewer around the north. The terrain is generally well-drained although there are some boggy areas. The going underfoot along the rugged clifftops and coastline around the west side is generally good, while around the north and south there are areas of dense heather and creeping willow cover.
Summits	Càrnan 273m, Cnoc Mhic-a'-Phi 223m
Maps	OS Explorer 452 Barra & Vatersay; OS Landranger 31 Barra & South Uist
Note	The usual way to get to Mingulay from Barra is aboard the *Boy James*, skippered by Francis Gillies. Mingulay Boat Trips, tel 01871 810 679 www.mingulayboattrips.com. Visitors are usually landed by tender on rocks a short way southeast of the old schoolhouse, or sometimes on the rocks at the north end of the bay if tides and wind direction dictate.

Lying 12 miles south of Barra, Mingulay has remained uninhabited since it was abandoned in 1912. The National Trust for Scotland has maintained the island's physical heritage and natural environment since 2000.

Today Mingulay is renowned for its seabird populations, which include puffins, razorbills, black-legged kittiwakes and the dreaded great skua or bonxie. Golden and white-tailed eagles are regularly spotted over the hills and sea cliffs while huge numbers of grey seals come ashore to the beach at Bàgh Mhiùghalaigh in the winter and spring. There are no deer and sheep are no longer grazed, which is a boon to the island's botanical diversity. Mingulay's eloquent ruins, its flora and fauna are a big pull for visitors, as are the magnificent sea cliffs and stacks, which are also a mecca for serious rock climbers who like a testing challenge.

This route circumambulates the entire island and takes in its high point, Càrnan (273m). The whole route is seldom less than entirely spectacular. Though not excessively long this is still a fairly demanding walk with some rough terrain; you'll be thankful you're not carrying a heavy pack!

Most visitors to Mingulay will be arriving and departing as part of a day trip from Castlebay, Barra. It is usual for trips to allow 3hr on Mingulay. Overnight camping is permitted and spending a couple of days or so on the island is recommended. There are no facilities and no accommodation excepting the NTS warden's bothy in the renovated old schoolhouse. Good camping ground in the vicinity of the warden's bothy.

ROUTE 26 – A CIRCUIT OF MINGULAY

From the **warden's bothy** follow the path heading south and continue around the coast. For the first 2km around to **Sgiobasdail** the going can be rough through bracken, heather and scrubby willow. A vague path wends its way just above the shore or alternatively follow the line of the old head dyke contouring along at around 50m. The old settlement of Sgiobasdail is a grassy oasis after the rough going and there are fine views across Caolas Bhearnaraigh to the Isle of Berneray with Barra Head lighthouse perched high up above its southwestern cliffs.

Keep following the coast and, where the ground steepens to landward, drop down onto the wide rocky ledge and follow this around to **Rubha Liath** with magnificent views across the rocky islets of **Gèarum Mòr** and Gèarum Beag.

Look out for a horseshoe-shaped dry-stone wall with a small circular aperture built against a rocky outcrop. This is in fact an 'environmental art' work by the artist, Julie Brook, who lived and worked on Mingulay for periods between 1996 and 2011, using the old schoolhouse as a base and studio (see also Route 4).

Head north along the exposed, slabby rock of the clifftops making for the notch in the vertiginous cliffs at the head of Sloc Hèisegeo. Follow the vague path northwest along an old fence line and, shortly after it turns north, you will reach the very narrow isthmus connecting the stack of **Dùn Mhiùghalaigh** (Dun Mingulay). It's worth having a look around as there will be plenty of puffins and razorbills nesting between April and July.

Exercising great caution, lie on your front to look down the north side of the isthmus into the abyss! You can't quite see the tunnel through the Gunamail natural arch, but the basalt dyke connecting the stack to the rest of Mingulay is impressively obvious.

Recross the isthmus and follow the trodden path, climbing steadily northwards along the line of the old fence. There are grand views ahead looking north of Mingulay to the Bishop's Isles and Barra beyond. Eventually the fence path delivers you

▲ *Left*: Ruined croft house above the abandoned village at Bàgh Mhiùghalaigh; *Right*: Heading along the coastline of north-west Mingulay

179

right above the 213m cliffs of **Beul na Creige** (Builacraig), so exercise great care. This is the best point at which to climb south for 300 metres to the summit of **Càrnan** (273m), which is furnished with a stone and mortar trig point. The views are superb, with the jaggedy profiles of the Black Cuillin on Skye and the Rùm Cuillin visible on a clear day.

Head back down to the fence-line path and descend along the cliff edge with care, soon arriving at the narrow gap between Beul na Creige and the cliffs beneath Tom a' Mhaide. The views onto Beul na Creige and the sea below are really spectacular and quite vertiginous; be careful here.

Continue northwest along the old clifftop fence line skirting the broad summit of **Tom a' Mhaide**. In the nesting season (April–July) this area is occupied by great skuas or 'bonxies', which can be very aggressive, so proceed with caution! Bear north and descend towards the head of the sheer-walled inlet of **Sloc Chias Geo**. The views along the geo to the huge stack of **Lianamul** with its enormous cave are mighty impressive. It's also worth continuing northwest to explore the headlands at Guarsaigh Mòr and Guarsay Beag which feature a long natural tunnel between inlets.

Head south, soon climbing alongside a burn. Look out for a path traversing the hillside above to your left and cross the burn at a suitable point to join it and continue northeast along the hillside. There are fine views along the coast as you contour along. The path squeezes between the clifftop and steepening hillside at **Creag Dhearg**, but there is no difficulty.

Cross a *bealach* and climb a short way to the summit of **Tom a' Reithean** (150m). Descend northeast over rough ground to Ard nan Capuill for views over a nerve-shreddingly sheer-sided chasm to the islet of Solon Mòr, alive with nesting seabirds. Climb south then southwest on rough, scrubby terrain to regain the *bealach* between Tom a' Reithean and **Cnoc Mhic-a'-Phì** (223m) then climb south-southwest to gain the summit of the latter. There are fabulous views southwest across Mingulay and northeast along the Bishop's Isles to Barra.

Also known by its anglicised version, Macphee's Hill, this is a fine vantage point with views north across the Bishop's Isles to Barra and east to the Inner Hebrides. The hill was named for the crewman sent ashore when a relief ship was sent by MacNeil of Barra to find out why all communication from Mingulay had ceased. Macphee explored the village and returned to report that the islanders had all died from disease. Fearing that he had been exposed to the plague, his shipmates refused to allow him back on board and abandoned him to his fate. Macphee survived for a year, climbing the hill every day to watch for rescuers. When Mingulay was later re-settled he was given land on the island by the chief of Clan MacNeil of Barra.

Descend west to the island's spine at 150m then descend southwards to return to the environs of the ruined village and the **warden's bothy**.

THE EVACUATION OF MINGULAY

After at least 2000 years of continuous habitation, the evacuation of Mingulay's population began in 1907 in a process that continued until the island was finally abandoned in 1912 – foreshadowing the famous evacuation of Hirta in the St Kilda archipelago in 1930. Just a few decades earlier the island community was thriving, with a population of 150 and a co-operative communal life with a robust fishing-based economy, a school, a mill and a chapel house.

A number of reasons contributed to the evacuation, but the decisive factor was the limit to the islanders' capacity and willingness to endure constant physical hardship when the opportunity for an easier livelihood elsewhere presented itself. Perhaps the greatest difficulty faced by the islanders was the lack of a sheltered landing place, which meant that unloading supply boats could be both strenuous and dangerous. In rough weather the island could be unreachable for weeks at a time. A serious blow to the islanders' morale came in 1897 when a boat from the neighbouring island of Pabbay was lost with its crew of five – more than half of that island's male population.

Furthermore, the population had begun to exceed the capacity of the island's resources, hence three families from Mingulay were among a group of landless cottars from Barra and its neighbouring isles who raided grazing land on Vatersay – a small island close to Barra, with sheltered anchorages – in July 1906. These were followed by more land raiders and, though the landowner took legal action, the judge ruled in favour of the cottars. The following year six more families from Mingulay raided and squatted neighbouring Sandray. Despite the subsequent successful prosecution of the Vatersay raiders, the Congested Districts Board purchased the entire island of Vatersay to provide crofts and by the following summer there were 14 families from Mingulay living there. By 1910 there remained only six families on Mingulay and with the population reduced below a viable number the final abandonment was ensured.

ROUTE 27
Hecla, Beinn Mhòr and South Uist's wild east coast

Start/finish	Parking area near the end of the B890 Loch Sgioport road (NM 827 386)
Total distance	34km (21 miles)
Total ascent	1915m (6285ft)
Time	2 days
Terrain	Rough mountain and moorland terrain, boggy in places.
Maps	OS Explorer 453 Benbecula & South Uist; OS Landranger 22 Benbecula & South Uist
Public transport	Bus W16/W17, request stops at turn-off for B890 Loch Sgioport road. It is a 6.5km walk or hitch-hike to the start of the route.

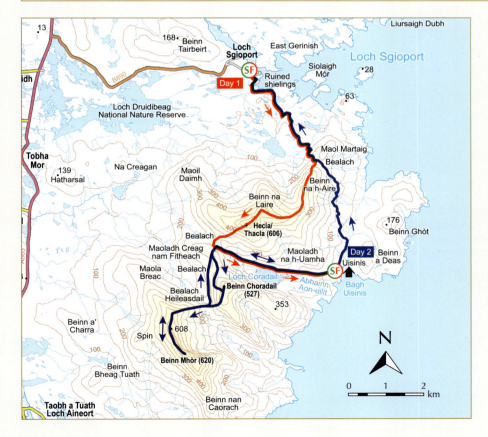

This route traverses the uninhabited hill country on the eastern side of South Uist. This is a challenging route for experienced walkers, involving some rough, pathless terrain. The route starts at the end of a single-track road leading to the shore of Loch Sgioport, from here a path winds out towards the east coast and the long northeast ridge of Hecla, one of the most distinctive hills in the Outer Hebrides. The day ends with a wild camp on the *bealach* between Hecla and Beinn Choradail or, alternatively, continues down through Gleann Uisinis to the MBA bothy above Uisinis Bay. The route continues on Day 2 with ascents of Beinn Choradail and Beinn Mhòr before returning to the bothy or walking back to the start point.

181

DAY 1
Loch Sgioport to Uisinis bothy

Start	Parking area near the end of the B890 Loch Sgioport (Lochskipport) road (NM 827 386)
Distance	12km (7½ miles)
Total ascent	720m (2360ft)
Time	5½–7hr
Summits	Beinn na Laire 564m, Hecla 606m

Where a signpost indicates 'Path to Caolas Mòr 2km, Footway to Hecla 5.5km', follow the maintained path past some old shielings to a ruined croft house where it comes to an end after 1.2km. Thereafter follow an ATV track that bears southeast, keeping to the west (left) of **Loch nam Faoileann** and then winding cross-country making for the obvious notch near the tail of the ridge between Maol Martaig and Beinn na h-Aire. Follow the vague path up the left-hand side of the gully to gain the *bealach* at 200m. Bear south and begin climbing the long ridge that culminates in the summit of Hecla.

The ascent is initially rough going up and over the rugged knuckle of **Beinn na h-Aire**. Here the ridge narrows giving grand views into the deep corries on either side. At Beinn Scalabhat the ridge turns west and rough ground gives way to grassy slopes with a distinct path leading up the ridge to **Beinn na Laire** (564m). A brief descent southwest to Bealach Gaoithe precedes a short climb to the summit of **Hecla** (606m), marked with a pile of stones. To the south, across the head of Gleann Uisinis stands the prow-like summit of Beinn Choradail with the long, whale-backed ridge of Beinn Mhòr looming beyond.

From the summit make for the broad *bealach* at the head of Gleann Uisinis. Head initially westwards along the ridge until clear of the steeper, rockier ground, then descend southwards through a small rocky gully. As the ground levels, gradually descend diagonally southwest towards the *bealach* picking a route on grassy ground between rocky slabs and outcrops. You can camp at the *bealach* or descend into the glen past **Loch Coradail** to the **Uisinis bothy** at the mouth of the glen (1½–2hr from the *bealach*).

To continue to the bothy, head down the glen keeping to the left of the main burn flowing down to the loch, then left and a little above the loch itself. There are sporadic, vague sections of path along the way. Continue east along the outflow of the loch, **Abhainn Aon-uillt**, for about 1km through rough, heathery and boggy terrain, crossing several small burns. As the view down to Bàgh Uisinis opens up, make for a large dry stone-walled enclosure, the bothy sits just below to the east.

The **bothy**, which is maintained by the MBA, sits above **Uisinis Bay** with views on to the Black Cuillin of Skye and the Rùm Cuillin in clear conditions. This wee bothy has 'up and down' sleeping platforms and a wood-burning stove. There is usually plentiful driftwood along the shore.

▲ Hecla from Beinn na Laire

ROUTE 27 – HECLA, BEINN MHÒR AND SOUTH UIST'S WILD EAST COAST

DAY 2
Uisinis bothy to parking area on B890

Start	Uisinis bothy (NF 849 332)
Distance	15km (9¼ miles), including walk out 21.75km (13½ miles)
Total ascent	940m (3050ft), including walk out 1195m (3920ft)
Time	6–7hr (8–9hr)
Summits	Beinn Choradail 527m, Beinn Mhòr 620m

From the **bothy**, retrace your outward route to the **bealach** at the head of Gleann Uisinis. Then from the *bealach* head southwards, through rocky terrain with peat hags, climbing steadily at first and passing two small *lochans*. The ridge rises in a series of steps towards the rocky peak of **Beinn Choradail** (527m). As the climb steepens, skirt around on grassy slopes to the southwest of the buttress crowning the northwest face of the summit. The last 100 metres or so are very steep, but there are no difficulties. Look for an easy way through the crags to gain the summit ridge, then head a short way northeast to the summit, marked with a small stone cairn.

The northeast ridge of Beinn Mhòr is climbed from Bealach Heileasdail, but a direct descent from Beinn Choradail is steep and rocky. Head along the summit ridge for about 500 metres, initially south then trending southeast, before descending south, then west, carefully picking a route through rock bands towards the *bealach*. Caution is required, especially in wet conditions or poor visibility. From the *bealach*, climb gradually at first, keeping to its northern side and making for the grassy slope ascending the ridge between rock bands. Climb steadily for 300 metres to arrive at the northern end of the summit ridge of **Beinn Mhòr**. Reaching the summit entails a superb 1km ridge walk. Heading south, a vague path becomes better defined as you approach the summit. There are fine views on to Beinn Mhòr's north face with its deep, oblique gullies. The ridge narrows to splendid effect just before the summit (620m) which has a trig pillar surrounded by a dry-stone shelter wall. There are excellent views across South Uist and far beyond. About 300 metres further along the ridge a cairn marks its southeastern extremity.

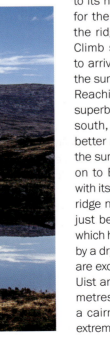

▲ *Top:* Uisinis bothy; *Bottom:* Hecla seen from the north-west

SCOTTISH WILD COUNTRY BACKPACKING

To return to the bothy retrace your outward route though from Bealach Heileasdail skirt northwards along the western flank of Beinn Choradail towards the *bealach* at the head of Gleann Uisinis.

From the **bothy** head north, passing west of the beach and pick up the ATV track. Stay with this track as it winds generally northwards, climbing steadily to arrive at the **bealach** between Beinn na h-Aire and Maol Martaig (200m). As you descend, follow the vague track as it leaves the gully on the right-hand side then continue to head northwest, following the track back to the metalled path and the parking area on the **B890**.

HOWMORE HOSTEL

An ideal base for tackling this route is the nearby Howmore Hostel, which is maintained by the Gatliff Hebridean Hostels Trust (www.gatliff.org.uk). The hostel has a fine location a short walk from the sandy Atlantic shore, which is backed by low-lying dunes and machair that explodes in a floral riot each springtime. The hostel itself is an old 'black house' – a type of thatch-roofed crofters' cottage characteristic of the Outer Hebrides and so-called because of the often-sooty interiors caused by a lack of chimney.

A retired senior civil servant, Herbert Gatliff established the trust in 1961 to promote the hostelling and outdoor movements. Since then, the GHHT has continued to maintain its hostels as well as to promote and support understanding of the cultural life and legacy of the people of the Outer Hebrides.

The Gatliff Trust hostels are a real boon to independent travellers journeying through the islands. In common with the Gatliff Trust's two other hostels on Berneray and Harris, Howmore has simple, but perfectly adequate facilities and a very welcoming atmosphere. There are 13 beds available and plenty of space for pitching a tent in the grounds.

▲ On the summit ridge of Beinn Mhòr

ROUTE 28
Harris Hills, Loch Rèasort and Cravadale

Start/finish	Small layby at the start of Gleann Chliostair access road east of Amhuinnsuidhe Castle (NB 053 077). Also parking 500 metres up the access track by the fish farm turning.
Total distance	36km (22½ miles)
Total ascent	1860m (6100ft)
Time	2–3 days
Terrain	Mountain and moorland. Often pathless, very rough and boggy in places.
Maps	OS Explorer 456 North Harris & Loch Seaforth; OS Landranger 13 West Lewis & North Harris
Note	The route crosses complex terrain and requires competent navigation – it is not a walk for bad weather, poor visibility or inexperienced walkers.

▲ The wild country south of Loch Rèasort

SCOTTISH WILD COUNTRY BACKPACKING

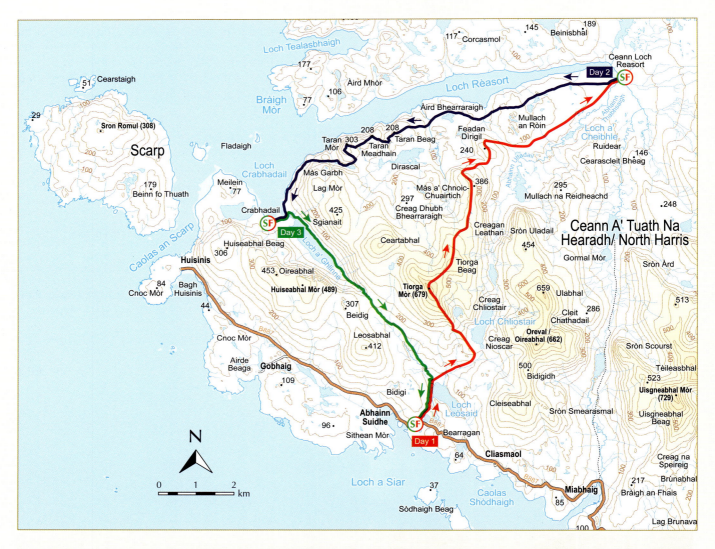

Year on year the Isle of Harris attracts more visitors lured by the astonishingly beautiful white-sand beaches of the west coast, which contrast so pleasingly with the rocky hill country of the island's hinterland. However, with the exception of those minded to bag An Cliseam – at 799m the Outer Hebrides' highest summit – relatively few venture off the beaten track in among the glens and ridges of the Harris Hills.

This route makes the most of the rugged country of the far northwestern area of the Harris Hills, which is seldom visited other than by occasional deer-stalking parties. The outward leg heads north over Tiorga Mòr, along the ridge flanking Gleann Uladail and ultimately to the wilderness at the head of Loch Rèasort and the first night's camp.

The second day's route heads west from Ceann Loch Rèasort above the southern shore of the 8km-long sea loch, traversing rough and rugged country to gain the rocky eminence of Taran Mòr with its commanding views of Loch Rèasort and the wild country of southwest Lewis. The route continues around rough coastline to the second night's magnificent bivouac site above the sandy beaches at the mouth of Glen Cravadale (Crabhadail).

The final half day's route follows the shore of Loch a' Ghlinne through Glen Cravadale before climbing to the *bealach* at the head of Gleann Leòsaid. A long, steady descent brings you back to the Gleann Chliostair track and the short walk back to the start.

186

ROUTE 28 – HARRIS HILLS, LOCH RÈASORT AND CRAVADALE

DAY 1
Amhuinnsuidhe to Ceann Loch Rèasort

Start	Layby at Amhuinnsuidhe (NB 053 077)
Distance	16km (10 miles)
Total ascent	1000m (3280ft)
Time	7½–9hr
Summits	Tiorga Mòr 679m, Tiorga Beag 590m, Màs a' Chnoic Chuairtich 386m, Feadan Dìrigil 240m

From the layby on the **B887**, follow the track road northeast, keeping left at a fork, continuing along the glen past **Loch Leòsaid** and over the bridge across Abhainn Leòsaid. Continue along the track road, passing the hydropower station then climbing steadily up the glen. Just before the track passes beneath the pipeline from **Loch Chliostair**, turn left off the track, climbing northwest on rough ground before gaining a level area just above the loch. Continue climbing steeply up the southeast ridge of Tiorga Mòr, passing above Loch Maolaig, nestled in its corrie. This steepest section of the ridge is rocky and rough, but grassy gullies aid progress. The gradient eases as the rocky ground is cleared and a vague path leads towards the rock-crested summit of **Tiorga Mòr** (679m), with its trig point and dry-stone shelter wall.

From Tiorga Mòr there are fine views all around: to the south the whale-backed hills and sparkling beaches of South Harris; to the east, beyond the peaks of Ulabhal and Oireabhal, rise the summits of Uisgneabhal Beag and Uisgneabhal Mòr; to the north, the hills of West Lewis; and to the west, down through Glen Cravadale to the Flannan Isles on the horizon. On a clear day you may even see the craggy isles and stacks of the St Kilda archipelago on the southwest horizon.

Descend northeast through rocky terrain, then continue across the narrow grassy ridge to the summit of **Tiorga Beag** (590m; NB 062 122). Continue north along the ridge above the rocky cliffs of **Creagan Leathan**, with a good view across the glen to the daunting buttress of Sròn Uladail, hanging menacingly over Loch Uladail. Pass a *lochan* and continue through rocky terrain to gain the summit of **Màs a' Chnoic Chuairtich** (386m), surmounted by a surprisingly substantial cairn.

▲ Approaching the summit of Tiorga Mòr

Descend northwest through rocky terrain, keeping to the ridge for 500 metres until it is possible to turn southeast to contour a short way beneath the crags along the steep northeast flank of Màs a' Chnoic-Chuairtich. Once clear of the steep ground, follow the easiest line of descent northeast over rough ground to a *bealach* then climb north for 75m to gain the modest summit of **Feadan Dìrigil** (240m). There are grand views onto Loch Rèasort and the wild expanse of country beyond.

Descend northeastwards to a *bealach* between Feadan Dìrigil and Mullach an Ròin. Contour round to the southeast flank of Mullach an Ròin and gradually descend over rough ground towards **Loch a' Cheibhle** and **Abhainn Thabhsaigh**. Follow the course of the river northeast to arrive at **Ceann Loch Rèasort**. There is no longer a bridge over Abhainn Mhòr Ceann Rèasort (NB 107 172) where it flows into the loch. However, as long as the river isn't running high, it's worth crossing to the abandoned metal-roofed house on the opposite bank, which offers the best ground to pitch your tent or shelter.

DAY 2
Ceann Loch Rèasort to Cravadale

Start	Ceann Loch Rèasort (NB 107 172)
Distance	12km (7½ miles)
Total ascent	600m (1970ft)
Time	5–6hr
Summits	Taran Beag (208m), Taran Meadhain (208m), Taran Mòr (303m)

Recross Abhainn Mhòr Ceann Reasoirt and pass to the rear of the estate workers' bothy at Luachair, heading due west across rough terrain for 1km. Look out for the flat, diamond-shaped stone marking the old Scholars' Path and follow this intermittent track west-southwest for the next 2km.

The Scholars' Path once linked the settlements of Luachair at the head of Loch Rèasort with Dirascal (or Dìreasgal), 5km to the west on the south shore of the loch. It was built by villagers who had resettled here from the nearby island of Scarp in 1885 after overcrowding had put intolerable pressure on resources. A 'Sgoil nan Leddies' (ladies' school) was established in Luachair under the auspices of the Association for the Religious Improvement of the Remote Highlands and Islands, better known as the Ladies' Highland Association of the Free Church (LHA). The villagers set about building a path for the schoolchildren over the rough and unforgiving terrain. By 1900 it was nearing completion when three crofts were established in the fertile environs of Huisinis for the crofters from Dirascal, rendering the path obsolete. The path is incomplete, intermittent, vague and boggy at times, but it is a cause for some wonder that it has not been entirely subsumed into the landscape during the intervening 12 decades.

Contour around the mouth of the glen above the collection of ruins by the inlet at Dirascal.

Climb gradually southwest then bear west across **Àird Bhearraraigh**. Skirt to the north of **Loch na Gillean** then descend a short way to cross Abhainn Bhearraraigh. Climb initially westwards onto the east flank of **Taran Beag** (208m) and continue generally west-southwest along the ridge to the summit. Descend southwest then west for 60 metres to a *bealach* then climb again northwest to the summit of **Taran Meadhain** (208m). Descend southwest, skirt the upper of two *lochans* before reaching a *bealach*. Climb west-northwest to the summit of **Taran Mòr** (303m),

▲ Looking east along Loch Rèasort from the summit of Taran Mòr

ROUTE 28 – HARRIS HILLS, LOCH RÈASORT AND CRAVADALE

The views from the summit of Taran Mòr are incredible. The entire length of Loch Rèasort winds away to Ceann Loch Rèasort five miles to the east, while the Uig Hills of southwest Lewis loom to the north. To the southwest lie the Isle of Scarp and the beaches of Cravadale.

Head initially south-southwest across the summit plateau then descend southeastwards following a broad gully. Swing southwest to descend to the easternmost end of the Lochan na Sgàil and continue along the northern shores of the first two *lochans*. Cross the burn flowing into the westernmost *lochan* and continue along its south shore. Continue west, climbing a little to the obvious gap between boulders and rocky outcrops. Continue following vague traces of path with the view opening up ahead straight onto Scarp. Descend a gully on the right-hand side of a small, partly subterranean stream with care. Cross over the burn at the obvious point then descend carefully southwestwards avoiding steep ground.

As the gradient eases, follow the easiest line southwestwards above the shore, contouring along at around 50 metres or so before descending to the beach at Haranais. Continue around the coast to Cravadale, crossing the usually shallow outflow of **Loch a' Ghlinne** to arrive at the fine beaches and bivouac site at the head of **Loch Crabhadail**. Several shallow depressions amid the remains of shielings on the machair above the westernmost beach are ideal for pitching a tent or shelter. The greensward surrounding the bay teems with the grown-over corrugations of old lazy beds, which now resemble some form of obscure ancient earthworks.

DAY 3
Cravadale to Amhuinnsuidhe

Start	Cravadale (NB 016 135)
Distance	8km (5 miles)
Total ascent	260m (855ft)
Time	3–3½hr
Summits	Ceartabhal 560m, Huiseabhal Mòr 489m

This is a shorter, easier day benefiting from paths much of the way, though the edge of Loch a' Ghlinne is rough going. If you have the inclination, **Ceartabhal** (560m) can be climbed due north from the *bealach*. **Huiseabhal Mòr** (489m) lies west-northwest of the *bealach*.

Follow the beach around to cross the outflow of **Loch a' Ghlinne** then continue along a vague path by the eastern shore of the loch. The path becomes more defined near the southern end of the loch. Pass some old shielings and then climb up through Glen Cravadale, criss-crossing over Allt a' Ghlinne on the way up. As the gradient eases you'll pass a cairn, then you'll reach a second cairn on the flatter ground at the *bealach* (NB 040 111). Follow the distinct path steadily down through Gleann Leòsaid to rejoin the Gleann Chliostair track. Turn right to return to **Amhuinnsuidhe** (Abhainn Suidhe) and the B887.

▲ *Lochan and lazy beds at Cravadale*

SCOTTISH WILD COUNTRY BACKPACKING

ROUTE 29
Isle of Lewis: Uig Hills and coast

Start/finish	Near the ex-army blockhouse in the village of Brèinis (NA 993 264)
Total distance	24km (15 miles)
Total ascent	1830m (6005ft)
Time	2 days
Terrain	Rough moorland and mountain terrain, boggy in places. Mostly pathless.
Maps	OS Explorer 458 West Lewis; OS Landranger 13 West Lewis & North Harris

This two-day route in the austerely beautiful far southwest corner of Lewis heads south through the rocky hills forming the seaward, western ridge of the Uig Hills. The route traverses a series of rugged summits – including Mealaisbhal, Cracabhal and Griomabhal – before dropping down to the shore of Loch Tamnabhaig. A rough walk along a wild and beautiful stretch of coastline brings the day to a conclusion with a wild camp on the small promontory of Rubha Garbh or at the head of the west-facing inlet of Tamna Sìar. The following day provides a superb coastal walk around to Mealasta, then on around to the starting point at Brèinis.

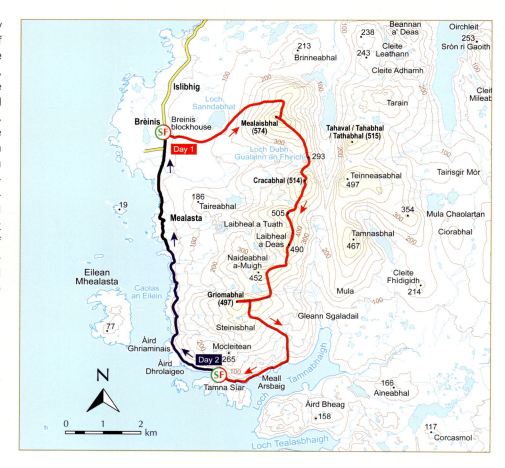

190

ROUTE 29 – ISLE OF LEWIS: UIG HILLS AND COAST

DAY 1
Brèinis to Tamna Sìar

Start	Near the ex-army blockhouse in the village of Brèinis (NA 993 264)
Distance	16km (10 miles)
Total ascent	1305m (4280ft)
Time	7–8hr
Summits	Mealaisbhal 574m, Cracabhal 514m, Laibheal a Tuath 505m, Laibheal a Deas 490m, Naideabhal a-Muigh 452m, Griomabhal 497m

Leave the road by the blockhouse at the north end of **Brèinis** and follow the peat track east for 750 metres to where it runs out amid peat hags. Bear east-northeast, keeping above the boggy terrain with **Loch Sanndabhat** on your left. Climb northeast along the flank of **Mealaisbhal** (574m) before bearing east to gain the saddle between the rocky eminence of Mula Mac Sgiathain and Mealaisbhal.

From here the direct route southwestwards to the summit involves scrambling over boulders, but this can largely be avoided by following a vague cairn-marked grassy path winding its way through rocky terrain to just below and east of the summit. Clamber over boulders then pick up a path leading along the ridge's south side to the summit, which is marked by a large cairn. On a clear day, the views from the top of Mealaisbhal are marvellous, taking in the Harris Hills to the southeast, the Flannan Isles and St Kilda to the west and Uig Sands to the north.

Leave the summit and descend the southeast ridge, picking your route carefully through rocky terrain. Make for the horseshoe-shaped **Loch Dubh Gualainn an Fhirich** sitting on the col at 293m (NB 030 260). From here you can either climb grassy gullies up through the steeper rock on the northern slopes of Cracabhal (514m) to the summit, which looks more difficult than it actually is, or continue southwestwards from the col, keeping left of the loch.

▲ *Climbing Mealaisbhal with Tarain (left) across Gleann Raonasgail and Suaineabhal beyond*

SCOTTISH WILD COUNTRY BACKPACKING

Pass to the right of another *lochan*, descend a broad gully then skirt beneath crags towards Loch Clibh Cracabhal (NB 022 253). Pass to the left of the loch then climb initially south to gain the west ridge of **Cracabhal**. Climb northeastwards to reach the summit (514m), marked with a pile of stones.

Descend southwestwards through rocky terrain with a number of small *lochans* to reach a larger *lochan* in the col (400m) between Cracabhal and Laibheal a Tuath at NB 026 247. Keep to its eastern shore and climb up directly to the summit of **Laibheal a Tuath** (505m). Descend gently southwards to the saddle in the summit ridge before climbing gently again, via a series of small *lochans*, to the summit of **Laibheal a Deas** (490m). Head southwest a short way then descend southwards across the rocky hillside, making for a small *lochan* on the *bealach* below. From the *lochan* head southwest, climbing up to the northeast ridge of **Naideabhal a-Muigh** (452m) then onwards to the summit.

Head west-southwest along the summit ridge passing a few small *lochans* before descending south-southeast following a shallow gully between slabby rocks on the hill's southern flank. From the *bealach* to the east of Loch Bràighe Griomabhal, skirt southeast a short way to pick up Allt Ruadh descending the east ridge of Griomabhal. Follow the burn westwards up along the ridge. Where the gradient eases briefly, pass a small *lochan* and pick up the rocky summit ridge to the top of **Griomabhal** (497m).

Retrace your route from the summit to the *lochan* on the level ground. Head south, passing another *lochan* and pick a route down to Allt na Leoidean Dubha flowing down from Loch Eadar Dha Bheinn. Descend alongside the burn running down the steep gully, until you eventually arrive at a confluence of burns at the head of **Gleann Sgaladail**. Descend through the glen alongside Abhainn Dhubh. Once you reach the shore of **Loch Tamnabhaig**, head west around the edge of the loch just above the shore on the rough, heathery slopes. There is a trodden path, which is fairly well defined.

Beyond the next small bay, avoid the precipitously steep section of coastline by crossing up and over the neck of **Meall Arsbaig**. Continue above the shore to the inlet of Tamna Sear. There are options for camping around the headland to the south of the inlet; Rubha Garbh enjoys fine views of the Isle of Scarp and northwest Harris.

Alternatively, cut across the neck of the headland from Tamna Sear, following the course of an old stone wall to the west-facing inlet of Tamna Sìar. A patch of grassy ground above the head of the inlet benefits from a freshwater spring and plenty of driftwood. However, being west facing, it's not ideal for camping if there's a gale blowing in off the Atlantic!

DAY 2
Tamna Sìar to Brèinis

Start	Tamna Sìar (NA 007 200)
Distance	8km (5 miles)
Total ascent	310m (1015ft)
Time	2½–3hr

From **Tamna Sìar** the route along the north side of the inlet is difficult and hazardous close to the shore, so climb to around 50m keeping a lookout for a vague path, which can be followed much

▲ Negotiating the rough path above Loch Tamnabhaigh

ROUTE 29 – ISLE OF LEWIS: UIG HILLS AND COAST

of the way to the road head south of Mealasta. Pick your route carefully as there are some rocky sections to negotiate and the ground is rough, boggy and heathery; the reward for your endeavour is in the dramatic coastal landscape. Continue around the coast to the inlet on the south side of the rocky headlands of **Àird Dhrolaigeo** and **Àird Ghriaminais** then follow the path, cutting across the low-lying neck of the headlands. Emerging on the west coast of the Uig Peninsula, there are splendid views across the narrow Caolas an Eilein onto Eilean Mhèalasta with an appealing sandy beach at its northeastern end.

Carefully follow the path along and above the shore, traversing several rocky sections and crossing several burns. The coastal scenery here is magnificent. Eventually you will arrive at the road head near Mealasta. Follow the single-track road north for around 2km, passing through **Mealasta** and continuing through a gateway before arriving at **Brèinis**.

MANGERSTA BOTHY

For those with the time to spare at the end of the walk, a visit to the beach and cliffs by the crofting township of Mangersta (Mangurstadh) is recommended. Around 5km along the road north of Brèinis there is a small parking area in an old quarry at NB 012 307 near a sign indicating a path leading down 'To the shore' at Tràigh Mhangarstaidh. Should you be able to tear yourself away from this fine Atlantic-facing beach then cross the dunes backing the beach, follow a path on the north side leading up the grassy slope and make for the prominent cairn on the clifftop. There are fine views back across the bay to Melaisbhal and the Uig Hills.

Continue northwards along the clifftops, which have tremendous views across the coastal landscape of promontories, sea stacks and skerries, with Eilean Molach to the north. After a kilometre or so you'll reach a rocky area of exposed Lewisian gneiss on the clifftop south of Lèirigeo. Here, tucked in against a rocky outcrop at the top of a sheer cliff face, is the most remarkably conceived and impressively located bothy in all of Scotland. Designed in the style of the ancient monastic beehive cells dotted around the Hebrides, the bothy was built more than 30 years ago by local crofters, John and Lorna Norgrove. Over the years a slow trickle of people made the pilgrimage to stay at the tiny timber-framed and stone-walled structure, but in the last few years it has become popular to the point that overnight stays need to be booked a long way in advance. Even so, just visiting to admire the bothy in its remarkable setting makes for a very worthwhile excursion.

The bothy also serves as a memorial to the Norgroves' daughter, Linda, an aid and development worker who was kidnapped in Afghanistan in 2010 and died during an attempted rescue by US forces. Linda was a highly qualified and dedicated environmental expert who had worked in Afghanistan since 2005, initially as an environmental and rural development officer for the UN. In Linda's memory and to continue her work, John and Lorna established the Linda Norgrove Foundation in October 2010, a trust that funds education, health and childcare for women and children affected by the war in Afghanistan. To learn more about the work of the Linda Norgrove Foundation, visit www.lindanorgrovefoundation.org. You can either return by your outward route or head east to the road at the north end of Mangersta and walk back down to the beach from there. There are working crofts all around the township, so please close all gates and be aware of livestock.

▲ Tamna Sìar and Rubha Garbh with the Harris Hills beyond

SCOTTISH WILD COUNTRY BACKPACKING

ROUTE 30
Isle of Lewis: Pairc Peninsula

Start/finish	Parking area near Eishken Lodge (NB 325 124)
Total distance	45.5km (28¼ miles)
Total ascent	2155m (7070ft)
Time	3 days
Terrain	Rough mountain and moorland terrain, largely pathless, boggy in places.
Maps	OS Explorer 457 South East Lewis; OS Landranger 14 Tarbert and Loch Seaforth

The Pairc region of southeast Lewis is a landscape of rough, rolling hill country, moorland and bog with a rugged coastline riven by a series of sea lochs. It is a huge area of land all but cut off from the rest of Lewis and Harris by the ingress of Loch Shìophoirt (Seaforth) to the south and west and Loch Eireasort (Erisort) to the north. The northern part of Pairc is home to 11 scattered townships and a population of 400 while the area south of Loch Sealg (Shell) has been devoid of inhabitants since the land was cleared to make way for the Pairc Sheep Farm during the early 19th century. In a pattern repeated all over the Highlands and Islands, sheep eventually gave way to red deer when the area became Park Deer Forest, a sporting estate, in 1886. In 1924 the southern part of Pairc became the Eishken Estate which is still a sporting estate today.

Such a vast expanse of wild land is of course good for wildlife. As well as a large population of red deer, Pairc is home to one of the highest densities of breeding golden eagles in Europe and there are also nesting white-tailed eagles.

▲ Looking southeast to the head of Loch Bhrolluim

ROUTE 30 – ISLE OF LEWIS: PAIRC PENINSULA

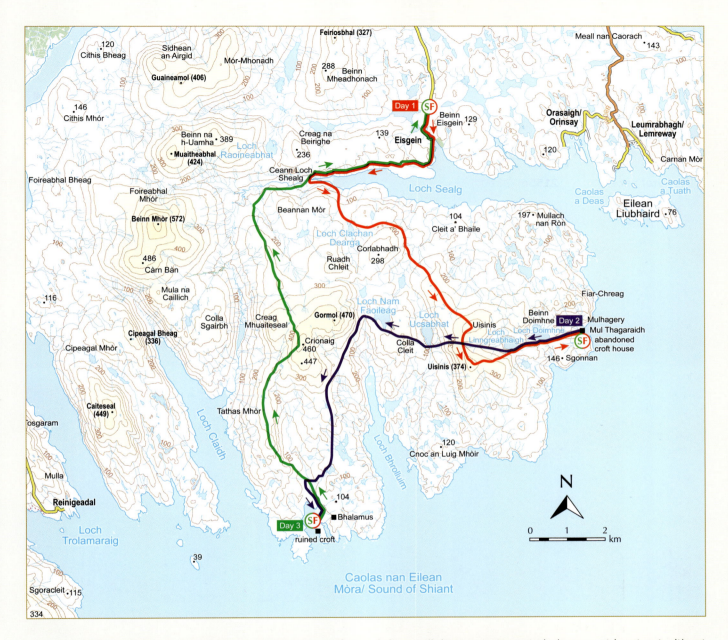

In recent years there have been several proposals for wind farms to be established on the Eishken Estate. None have come to fruition – in part because of the threat turbines pose to the eagle population. Whether this remains the case is another matter.

This route is a rough, tough and challenging walk taking in remote, seldom-visited country. It is largely pathless and navigation can be tricky, especially if visibility isn't good. It is a walk best not attempted alone or at least not without a personal locator beacon (PLB). Warnings dispensed with, this is also a hugely rewarding walk through some magnificent wild landscapes with splendid views across the Minch to the Shiant Isles and the mountains of the western seaboard, beyond. There are plenty of options for elaborating on the route described here with a number of extra-curricular hills to climb, should you wish.

195

DAY 1
Eisgein to Mul Thàgaraidh

Start	Parking area just north of Eisgein (NB 325 124)
Distance	16.5km (10¼ miles)
Total ascent	725m (2380ft)
Time	7–8hr
Summits	Uisinis 371m (north), 374m (south)

From the parking area walk down the road towards the lodge, bear left alongside metal railings and go through an electric gate leading into the grounds of Eishken Lodge. Bear right, past the nursery and hedge-enclosed garden, then turn right past the front of the lodge and continue through another gate. The track initially leads down the west side of Tòb Eisgein then bears west – look out for the estate ponies, which can often be found here. The path continues above the north shore of **Loch Sealg**, passing through a gate in a deer fence. The track narrows to a path but remains distinct, if muddy in places, crossing several culverted burns and a couple of footbridges en route to Ceann Loch Shealg.

Cross the footbridge over the Abhainn Gleann Airighean Dhòmhnaill, continue for 200 metres to a path junction, turn left and continue to the site of **Ceann Loch Shealg**, a township on the south side of the loch – several ruins and grassy terrain are all that remains. Continue southeastwards, on rough ground, crossing the outflow of a burn to join another gravelled track climbing steadily from the shore to around 140 metres before it runs out. Head southeast, cross the outflow of **Loch Clachan Dearga** and climb to the flank of **Corlabhadh** (298m). Contour initially eastwards around the rough hillside at about 180 metres, steering around to the eastern flank and descending to cross the glen through which Abhainn Chòrlabhaidh flows.

Cross the burn before gaining the northwest ridge of **Uisinis** and climbing steadily for 2.5km to the cairn-marked north summit (371m). Descend southwestwards to a *bealach* before climbing to the south summit (374m). Descend northeastwards into Glean Linngreabhaigh making for the outflow of **Loch Linngreabhaigh**. Continue eastwards to **Loch Doimhne**, cross the outflow and follow Abhainn Mol Chadha Gèarraidh out to the coast at **Mul Thagaraidh** (Mulhagery). The greensward around the abandoned croft house here is an ideal bivouac site.

▲ Heading west from Eisgein to Ceann Loch Shealg

ROUTE 30 – ISLE OF LEWIS: PAIRC PENINSULA

FIAR-CHREAG PLANE CRASH

On 31 July 1942 a Lockheed Hudson bomber flying in over the The Minch in foggy weather crashed into the summit of Fiar-Chreag, the rocky hillside framing the north side of the glen above Mul Thàgaraidh (Mulhagery). The bomber – FH375 – was flown by Coastal Command and was engaged in anti-submarine operations; it had had its radar repaired and was carrying out an air-test when it crashed. That day the weather at Stornoway airfield was poor and there was dense, low cloud cover. All aircraft were grounded, but inexplicably the Hudson was allowed to take off. Fiar-Chreag rises very steeply from the coast and there would be little warning for the crew flying in blind in the fog. Had the pilot managed to climb another few metres the plane would have cleared the top of the hill.

When the Hudson failed to return a sea search was started, followed by an air search when the weather improved, but after three weeks the bomber had still not been found and the search was wound down.

Nearly four weeks after the crash the crew of a civilian passenger flight from Glasgow to Stornoway spotted likely wreckage and a land search was carried out, albeit initially too far south in the hills around Bhalamus. On 29 August, a search party was landed at Mulhagery and soon the wreckage was found scattered over a wide area along with the bodies of the three crew. Extensive remains of the bomber, including its engines remain on the hillside today.

The Hudson's crew were pilot, F/O Derek Rigby, radar operator, P/O Frank Hancock, and radar technician, Sgt Bernard Rixon.

DAY 2
Mul Thagaraidh to Bhalamus

Start	Mul Thagaraidh (NB 366 066)
Distance	12.5km (7¾ miles)
Total ascent	715m (2345ft)
Time	6–7hr

From **Mul Thagaraidh** head back up the glen to **Loch Linngreabhaigh** then climb to the *bealach* between the two summits of **Uisinis**, skirting to the left (south) of the peat hags at the head of the glen. From the *bealach* descend westwards quite steeply, aiming for the outflow of **Loch Ucsabhat**. Cross the outflow, skirt round to the eastern shore then take the easiest line westwards climbing up along the ridge of **Colla Cleit** to the aptly named Creag na h-Iolaire – Eagle's Crag.

Descend northwestwards, making for the western side of **Loch Nam Faoileag**. From its westernmost point descend a short way west to cross Abhainn Gleann Chrionaig at the head of Gleann Chrionaig. The view down to the head of Loch Bhrolluim with the steep flank of Creag Mhosgalaid Mhòr rising on the western side is splendidly dramatic. Now head southwestwards along the eastern flank of **Gormol** (470m), initially contouring beneath rocky outcrops then climbing steadily to the shoulder on the hill's south ridge at around 280m.

Descend south along the ridge on the eastern side of Coire Dubh then bear southwestwards skirting along the eastern flank of Crionaig Mhòr above Coire Buidhe. Make for the obvious *lochan* and then follow its outflow as it descends initially southwest, then northwest before turning south into the head of Gleann Bhalamuis. Continue through the *gleann* following Abhainn Gleann Bhalamuis – the going is much easier on the eastern side of the burn.

▲ Ruined barn at the long-abandoned settlement of Bhalamus

197

Pass beneath Creag Glas Bhalamuis to reach the abandoned settlement of **Bhalamus** with its ruined croft house and roofless barn. As at Mul Thagaraidh the greensward around the croft house is ideal for pitching a tent.

DAY 3
Bhalamus to Eisgein

Start	Bhalamus
Distance	16.5km (10¼ miles)
Total ascent	720m (2365ft)
Time	6½hr–7½hr
Summits	Tathas Beag 186m, Tathas Mhor 305m, Crionaig 460m

From **Bhalamus** head northwestwards along Gleann Bhalamuis, passing beneath Creag Ghlas Bhalamuis. Cross the burn and climb the slope to the gap between rocky outcrops. Climb north over Tathas Beag (186m). Continue northwestwards then north again along the rocky ridge, crossing a couple of outcrops before gaining **Tathas Mhòr** (305m). Drop a little, passing *lochans* then climb again heading northeastwards to reach the summit of **Crionaig** (460m). Descend northwestwards following the ridge along Druim Sgianadail and pick up the gravelled path heading northeastwards from near the foot of the ridge.

Cross a footbridge and continue for another 500 metres to a junction. Keep right (straight ahead) and stay with the graveled path for a further 1.25km as it continues down towards the head of Loch Sealg. Where the path forks take the left-hand branch and follow it for 200 metres to cross the bridge over the Abhainn Gleann Airighean Dhòmhnaill at **Ceann Loch Shealg**. Retrace your outward route above the north shore of **Loch Sealg** to return to **Eisgein**.

▲ *Top:* Looking north towards Gleann Bhalamuis; *Bottom:* Trout weathervane on the Gleann Airigh an Domhnuill path;
▶ *Opposite:* Beinn Mhòr (left) with An Cliseam in the distance seen from Beinn na h-Uamha

APPENDIX A
Table of Munros and Corbetts

The 'Munros' are the 282 Scottish hills over 3000 feet (914.4m), named after Sir Hugh Munro, who first listed them. 'Corbetts' are the 222 Scottish hills of between 2500 and 3000 feet (762–914.4m) that also have a descent of 500 feet (152.4m) on all sides, a list compiled by John Rooke Corbett.

SUMMIT	HEIGHT	MUNRO/CORBETT	ROUTE	PAGE
A' Chailleach	997m	Munro	18	137
A' Ghlas-bheinn	918m	Munro	12	108
A' Mhaighdean	967m	Munro	19	141
An Coileachan	923m	Munro	18	137
An Ruadh Stac	892m	Corbett	17	132
An Socach	921m	Munro	13	112
Aonach Beag	1116m	Munro	7	78
Aonach Buidhe	899m	Corbett	14	117
Baosbheinn	875m	Corbett	20	145
Beinn a' Bhuird	1197m	Munro	10	95
Beinn a' Chlaidheimh	914m	Corbett	19	141
Beinn an Eòin	855m	Corbett	20	145
Beinn Bhàn	896m	Corbett	15	121
Beinn Bheòil	1019m	Munro	7	78
Beinn Bhreac	912m	Corbett	8	83
Beinn Dearg	913m	Corbett	20	145
Beinn Dronaig	797m	Corbett	16	125
Beinn Eibhinn	1102m	Munro	7	78
Beinn Fhada	1032m	Munro	12	108
Beinn Fhionnlaidh	1005m	Munro	13	112

SUMMIT	HEIGHT	MUNRO/CORBETT	ROUTE	PAGE
Beinn Leòid	792m	Corbett	22	156
Beinn Liath Mhòr	926m	Munro	17	132
Beinn Liath Mhor Fannaich	954m	Munro	18	137
Beinn Mheadhonach	901m	Corbett	8	83
Beinn nan Aighenan	960m	Munro	1	46
Beinn Spionnaidh	773m	Corbett	24	166
Beinn Tarsuinn	937m	Munro	19	141
Beinn Tharsuinn	863m	Corbett	16	125
Ben Alder	1148m	Munro	7	78
Ben Avon	1171m	Munro	10	95
Ben Klibreck	962m	Munro	23	160
Ben Starav	1078m	Munro	1	46
Bidein a' Choire Sheasgaich	945m	Munro	16	125
Braeriach	1296m	Munro	9	89
Braigh nan Uamhachan	765m	Corbett	3	55
Càirn Toul	1291m	Munro	9	89
Càrn Bàn Mòr	1052m	Munro	9	89
Càrn Dearg	1034m	Munro	7	78

APPENDIX A – TABLE OF MUNROS AND CORBETTS

SUMMIT	HEIGHT	MUNRO/CORBETT	ROUTE	PAGE
Càrn Eige	1183m	Munro	13	112
Cranstackie	802m	Corbett	24	166
Faochaig	868m	Corbett	14	117
Foinaven: Ganu Mòr	911m	Corbett	24	166
Fuar Tholl	907m	Corbett	17	132
Geal Chàrn	1132m	Munro	7	78
Glas Bheinn Mhòr	997m	Munro	1	46
Leathad an Taobhain	902m	Corbett	8	83
Lurg Mhòr	987m	Munro	16	125
Màm Sodhail	1181m	Munro	13	112
Maol Chean-dearg	933m	Munro	17	132
Meall a'Chrasgaidh	934m	Munro	18	137
Meall Gorm	949m	Munro	18	137
Meall nan Eun	929m	Munro	1	46
Meallach Mhòr	769m	Corbett	8	83
Mullach Clach a' Bhlàir	1019m	Munro	9	89
Mullach Coire Mhic Fhearchair	1019m	Munro	19	141
Mullach na Dheiragain	982m	Munro	13	112
Ruadh Stac Mòr	918m	Munro	19	141
Sgòr an Lochan Uaine	1258m	Munro	9	89
Sgòr Gaoith	1118m	Munro	9	89
Sgorr Craobh a' Chaorainn	775m	Corbett	2	50

SUMMIT	HEIGHT	MUNRO/CORBETT	ROUTE	PAGE
Sgorr Ruadh	962m	Munro	17	132
Sgùman Còinntich	879m	Corbett	14	117
Sgùrr a' Chaorachain	792m	Corbett	15	121
Sgùrr an Airgid	841m	Corbett	12	108
Sgùrr Bàn	989m	Munro	19	141
Sgùrr Breac	999m	Munro	18	137
Sgùrr Gaorsaic	839m	Corbett	12	108
Sgùrr Ghiubhsachain	849m	Corbett	2	50
Sgùrr Mòr	1108m	Munro	18	137
Sgùrr na Ceathramhnan	1151m	Munro	13	112
Sgùrr na Feartaig	862m	Corbett	16	125
Sgùrr na Lapaich	1036m	Munro	13	112
Sgùrr nan Clach Geala	1093m	Munro	18	137
Sgùrr nan Each	923m	Munro	18	137
Stob a' Bhealach an Sgriòdain	770m	Corbett	2	50
Stob Coir' an Albannaich	1044m	Munro	1	46
Stob Coire a' Chearcaill	771m	Corbett	2	50
Streap	911m	Corbett	3	55
The Devil's Point (Bod an Deamhain)	1004m	Munro	9	89
Toll Creagach	1054m	Munro	13	112
Tom a' Chòinnich	1112m	Munro	13	*112*

APPENDIX B
Glossary

GAELIC	ENGLISH
abhainn	river
àird	height, promontory
allt	burn, stream
bàgh	bay
beag, bheag	small
bealach	pass, gorge
beinn	mountain, peak
buidhe	yellow
camas	bay
caolas	kyle, strait, sound
cladach	beach, shore, coast
cnoc	round hill, knoll
coire	corrie, steep-sided hollow
creag	crag, rock, cliff
cruach	stack, heap

GAELIC	ENGLISH
dearg	red
dubh	black
eilean	island
garbh	rough
geodha	steep-sided inlet
glas	grey, green
gleann	glen, valley
lag	hollow
lochan	small loch
mòr, mhòr	big
port	port, harbour, ferry
rubha	promontory, headland, point
tràigh	beach
uamh	cave
uisge	water

APPENDIX C
Further reading

Neil Ansell, *The Last Wilderness*, Tinder Press, 2018

John Bainbridge, *The Compleat Trespasser*, Fellside Books, 2020

Alastair Borthwick, *Always a Little Further*, Vertebrate, 2015

Theresa Breslin, *An Illustrated History of Scottish Folk and Fairy Tales*, Floris Books, 2012

Dave Brown and Ian Mitchell, *Mountain Days and Bothy Nights*, Luath Press Ltd, 1987

James Carron, *Highland Hermit: The Remarkable Life of James McRory Smith*, CreateSpace Independent Publishing Platform, 2012

Mike Cawthorne, *Wilderness Dreams: The Call of Scotland's Last Wild Places*, In Pinn, 2007

Mike Cawthorne, *Wild Voices: Journeys Through Time in the Scottish Highlands*, Birlinn Ltd, 2014

Peter Drummond, *Scottish Hill and Mountain Names*, Scottish Mountaineering Press, 1st ed 1991

James Hunter, *The Making of the Crofting Community*, Birlinn Ltd, 3rd ed 2010

John Lister-Kaye, *Gods of the Morning: A Bird's Eye View of a Highland Year*, Canongate, 2016

John Lister-Kaye, *Song of the Rolling Earth: A Highland Odyssey*, Abacus, 2017

Alan McKirdy, *Set in Stone: The Geology and Landscapes of Scotland*, Birlinn Ltd, 2015

John Murray, *Literature of the Gaelic Landscape*, Whittles Publishing, 1st ed 2017

W.H. Murray, *Mountaineering in Scotland*, Vertebrate, 2015

W.H. Murray, *Undiscovered Scotland*, Vertebrate, 2015

Scottish Rights of Way and Access Society, *Scottish Hill Tracks*, Scottish Mountaineering Trust, 2011

Sydney Scroggie, *The Cairngorms Scene and Unseen*, Scottish Mountaineering Trust, 1989

Ralph Storer, *Exploring Scottish Hill Tracks*, David and Charles, 1994

Mike Tomkies, *A Last Wild Place*, Birlinn Ltd, 2021

Tom Weir, *Highland Days*, Steve Savage Publishers Ltd, 2010

Andy Wightman, *The Poor had No Lawyers*, Birlinn Ltd, 2011

▲ *Clockwise from top left*: Stornoway Coastguard SAR helicopter en route to rescue a walker fallen from cliffs, south-west Lewis (photo: James Lyne); Drift-engulfed ruin in the abandoned village at Bàgh Mhiùghalaigh (Route 26); The climb eases on Sgùrr a' Chaorachain (Route 15); On Sgùrr Ghiubhsachain (Route 2); A quick pitch before the weather comes in, South Glen Shiel ridge;

▶ *Opposite:* Rugged going on the traverse of the Bealach nan Arr

DOWNLOAD THE ROUTES IN GPX FORMAT

All the routes in this guide are available for download from:

www.cicerone.co.uk/904/GPX

as standard format GPX files. You should be able to load them into most online GPX systems and mobile devices, whether GPS or smartphone. You may need to convert the file into your preferred format using a conversion programme such as gpsvisualizer.com or one of the many other such websites and programmes. When you follow this link, you will be asked for your email address and where you purchased the guidebook, and have the option to subscribe to the Cicerone e-newsletter.

www.cicerone.co.uk

LISTING OF CICERONE GUIDES

BRITISH ISLES CHALLENGES, COLLECTIONS AND ACTIVITIES
Cycling Land's End to John o' Groats
The Big Rounds
The Book of the Bivvy
The Book of the Bothy
The C2C Cycle Route
The Mountains of England and Wales:
 Vol 1 Wales
 Vol 2 England
The National Trails
Walking The End to End Trail

SCOTLAND
Backpacker's Britain: Northern Scotland
Ben Nevis and Glen Coe
Cycle Touring in Northern Scotland
Cycling in the Hebrides
Great Mountain Days in Scotland
Mountain Biking in Southern and Central Scotland
Mountain Biking in West and North West Scotland
Not the West Highland Way
Scotland
Scotland's Best Small Mountains
Scotland's Mountain Ridges
Skye's Cuillin Ridge Traverse
The Ayrshire and Arran Coastal Paths
The Borders Abbeys Way
The Great Glen Way
The Great Glen Way Map Booklet
The Hebridean Way
The Hebrides
The Isle of Mull
The Isle of Skye
The Skye Trail
The Southern Upland Way
The Speyside Way
The Speyside Way Map Booklet
The West Highland Way
The West Highland Way Map Booklet
Walking Ben Lawers, Rannoch and Atholl
Walking Highland Perthshire
Walking in the Cairngorms
Walking in the Pentland Hills
Walking in the Scottish Borders
Walking in the Southern Uplands
Walking in Torridon
Walking Loch Lomond and the Trossachs
Walking on Arran
Walking on Harris and Lewis
Walking on Jura, Islay and Colonsay
Walking on Rum and the Small Isles
Walking on the Orkney and Shetland Isles
Walking on Uist and Barra
Walking the Cape Wrath Trail
Walking the Corbetts
 Vol 1 South of the Great Glen
 Vol 2 North of the Great Glen
Walking the Galloway Hills

Walking the Munros
 Vol 1 – Southern, Central and Western Highlands
 Vol 2 – Northern Highlands and the Cairngorms
Winter Climbs Ben Nevis and Glen Coe
Winter Climbs in the Cairngorms

NORTHERN ENGLAND TRAILS
Hadrian's Wall Path
Hadrian's Wall Path Map Booklet
The Coast to Coast Walk
The Coast to Coast Map Booklet
The Dales Way
The Dales Way Map Booklet
The Pennine Way
The Pennine Way Map Booklet
Walking the Dales Way
Walking the Tour of the Lake District

NORTH EAST ENGLAND, YORKSHIRE DALES AND PENNINES
Cycling in the Yorkshire Dales
Great Mountain Days in the Pennines
Mountain Biking in the Yorkshire Dales
St Oswald's Way and St Cuthbert's Way
The Cleveland Way and the Yorkshire Wolds Way
The Cleveland Way Map Booklet
The North York Moors
The Reivers Way
The Teesdale Way
Trail and Fell Running in the Yorkshire Dales
Walking in County Durham
Walking in Northumberland
Walking in the North Pennines
Walking in the Yorkshire Dales: North and East
Walking in the Yorkshire Dales: South and West

NORTH WEST ENGLAND AND THE ISLE OF MAN
Cycling the Pennine Bridleway
Cycling the Reivers Route
Cycling the Way of the Roses
Hadrian's Cycleway
Isle of Man Coastal Path
The Lancashire Cycleway
The Lune Valley and Howgills
Walking in Cumbria's Eden Valley
Walking in Lancashire
Walking in the Forest of Bowland and Pendle
Walking on the Isle of Man
Walking on the West Pennine Moors
Walks in Silverdale and Arnside

LAKE DISTRICT
Cycling in the Lake District
Great Mountain Days in the Lake District
Joss Naylor's Lakes, Meres and Waters of the Lake District

Lake District Winter Climbs
Lake District: High Level and Fell Walks
Lake District: Low Level and Lake Walks
Mountain Biking in the Lake District
Outdoor Adventures with Children – Lake District
Scrambles in the Lake District – North
Scrambles in the Lake District – South
The Cumbria Way
Trail and Fell Running in the Lake District
Walking the Lake District Fells –
 Borrowdale
 Buttermere
 Coniston
 Keswick
 Langdale
 Mardale and the Far East
 Patterdale
 Wasdale

DERBYSHIRE, PEAK DISTRICT AND MIDLANDS
Cycling in the Peak District
Dark Peak Walks
Scrambles in the Dark Peak
Walking in Derbyshire
Walking in the Peak District – White Peak East
Walking in the Peak District – White Peak West

SOUTHERN ENGLAND
20 Classic Sportive Rides in South East England
20 Classic Sportive Rides in South West England
Cycling in the Cotswolds
Mountain Biking on the North Downs
Mountain Biking on the South Downs
Suffolk Coast and Heath Walks
The Cotswold Way
The Cotswold Way Map Booklet
The Great Stones Way
The Kennet and Avon Canal
The Lea Valley Walk
The North Downs Way
The North Downs Way Map Booklet
The Peddars Way and Norfolk Coast path
The Pilgrims' Way
The Ridgeway National Trail
The Ridgeway Map Booklet
The South Downs Way
The South Downs Way Map Booklet
The Thames Path
The Thames Path Map Booklet
The Two Moors Way
The Two Moors Way Map Booklet
Walking Hampshire's Test Way
Walking in Cornwall
Walking in Essex
Walking in Kent
Walking in London
Walking in Norfolk

Walking in the Chilterns
Walking in the Cotswolds
Walking in the Isles of Scilly
Walking in the New Forest
Walking in the North Wessex Downs
Walking on Dartmoor
Walking on Guernsey
Walking on Jersey
Walking on the Isle of Wight
Walking the Jurassic Coast
Walking the South West Coast Path
Walking the South West Coast Path Map Booklets:
 Vol 1: Minehead to St Ives
 Vol 2: St Ives to Plymouth
 Vol 3: Plymouth to Poole
Walks in the South Downs National Park

WALES AND WELSH BORDERS
Cycle Touring in Wales
Cycling Lon Las Cymru
Glyndwr's Way
Great Mountain Days in Snowdonia
Hillwalking in Shropshire
Hillwalking in Wales – Vols 1&2
Mountain Walking in Snowdonia
Offa's Dyke Path
Offa's Dyke Path Map Booklet
Ridges of Snowdonia
Scrambles in Snowdonia
Snowdonia: 30 Low-level and easy walks – North
Snowdonia: 30 Low-level and easy walks – South
The Cambrian Way
The Ceredigion and Snowdonia Coast Paths
The Pembrokeshire Coast Path
The Pembrokeshire Coast Path Map Booklet
The Severn Way
The Snowdonia Way
The Wales Coast Path
The Wye Valley Walk
Walking in Carmarthenshire
Walking in Pembrokeshire
Walking in the Forest of Dean
Walking in the Wye Valley
Walking on Gower
Walking on the Brecon Beacons
Walking the Shropshire Way

INTERNATIONAL CHALLENGES, COLLECTIONS AND ACTIVITIES
Canyoning in the Alps
Europe's High Points

AFRICA
Kilimanjaro
The High Atlas
Walking in the Drakensberg
Walks and Scrambles in the Moroccan Anti-Atlas

ALPS CROSS-BORDER ROUTES
100 Hut Walks in the Alps
Alpine Ski Mountaineering
　Vol 1 – Western Alps
　Vol 2 – Central and Eastern Alps
Chamonix to Zermatt
The Karnischer Hohenweg
The Tour of the Bernina
Tour of Monte Rosa
Tour of the Matterhorn
Trail Running – Chamonix and
　the Mont Blanc region
Trekking in the Alps
Trekking in the Silvretta and Ratikon Alps
Trekking Munich to Venice
Trekking the Tour of Mont Blanc
Walking in the Alps

PYRENEES AND FRANCE/SPAIN CROSS-BORDER ROUTES
Shorter Treks in the Pyrenees
The GR10 Trail
The GR11 Trail
The Pyrenean Haute Route
The Pyrenees
Walks and Climbs in the Pyrenees

AUSTRIA
Innsbruck Mountain Adventures
The Adlerweg
Trekking in Austria's Hohe Tauern
Trekking in the Stubai Alps
Trekking in the Zillertal Alps
Walking in Austria
Walking in the Salzkammergut:
　the Austrian Lake District

EASTERN EUROPE
The Danube Cycleway Vol 2
The High Tatras
The Mountains of Romania
Walking in Bulgaria's National Parks
Walking in Hungary

FRANCE, BELGIUM AND LUXEMBOURG
Chamonix Mountain Adventures
Cycle Touring in France
Cycling London to Paris
Cycling the Canal de la Garonne
Cycling the Canal du Midi
Mont Blanc Walks
Mountain Adventures in the Maurienne
Short Treks on Corsica
The GR20 Corsica
The GR5 Trail
The GR5 Trail – Benelux and Lorraine
The GR5 Trail – Vosges and Jura
The Grand Traverse of the Massif Central
The Loire Cycle Route
The Moselle Cycle Route
The River Rhone Cycle Route
The Way of St James – Le
　Puy to the Pyrenees
Tour of the Queyras
Trekking in the Vanoise
Trekking the Robert Louis Stevenson Trail
Vanoise Ski Touring
Via Ferratas of the French Alps
Walking in Provence – East
Walking in Provence – West
Walking in the Ardennes
Walking in the Auvergne
Walking in the Briançonnais
Walking in the Dordogne
Walking in the Haute Savoie: North
Walking in the Haute Savoie: South
Walking on Corsica

GERMANY
Hiking and Cycling in the Black Forest
The Danube Cycleway Vol 1
The Rhine Cycle Route
The Westweg
Walking in the Bavarian Alps

IRELAND
The Wild Atlantic Way and Western Ireland
Walking the Wicklow Way

ITALY
Italy's Sibillini National Park
Shorter Walks in the Dolomites
Ski Touring and Snowshoeing
　in the Dolomites
The Way of St Francis
Trekking in the Apennines
Trekking in the Dolomites
Trekking the Giants' Trail: Alta Via 1
　through the Italian Pennine Alps
Via Ferratas of the Italian
　Dolomites Vols 1&2
Walking and Trekking in the Gran Paradiso
Walking in Abruzzo
Walking in Italy's Cinque Terre
Walking in Italy's Stelvio National Park
Walking in Sicily
Walking in the Dolomites
Walking in Tuscany
Walking in Umbria
Walking Lake Como and Maggiore
Walking Lake Garda and Iseo
Walking on the Amalfi Coast
Walking the Via Francigena
　pilgrim route – Parts 2&3
Walks and Treks in the Maritime Alps

MEDITERRANEAN
The High Mountains of Crete
Trekking in Greece
Treks and Climbs in Wadi Rum, Jordan
Walking and Trekking in Zagori
Walking and Trekking on Corfu
Walking in Cyprus
Walking on Malta
Walking on the Greek Islands
　– the Cyclades

JAPAN, ASIA AND AUSTRALIA
Hiking and Trekking in the Japan
　Alps and Mount Fuji
Hiking the Overland Track
Japan's Kumano Kodo Pilgrimage
Trekking in Tajikistan

HIMALAYA
Annapurna
Everest: A Trekker's Guide
Trekking in Bhutan
Trekking in Ladakh
Trekking in the Himalaya

NORTH AMERICA
The John Muir Trail
The Pacific Crest Trail

SOUTH AMERICA
Aconcagua and the Southern Andes
Hiking and Biking Peru's Inca Trails
Torres del Paine

SCANDINAVIA, ICELAND AND GREENLAND
Hiking in Norway – South
Trekking in Greenland – The
　Arctic Circle Trail
Trekking the Kungsleden
Walking and Trekking in Iceland

SLOVENIA, CROATIA, SERBIA, MONTENEGRO AND ALBANIA
Mountain Biking in Slovenia
The Islands of Croatia
The Julian Alps of Slovenia
The Mountains of Montenegro
The Peaks of the Balkans Trail
The Slovene Mountain Trail
Walking in Slovenia: The Karavanke
Walks and Treks in Croatia

SPAIN & PORTUGAL
Camino de Santiago: Camino Frances
Coastal Walks in Andalucia
Cycle Touring in Spain
Cycling the Camino de Santiago
Mountain Walking in Mallorca
Mountain Walking in Southern Catalunya
Portugal's Rota Vicentina
Spain's Sendero Historico: The GR1
The Andalucian Coast to Coast Walk
The Camino del Norte and
　Camino Primitivo
The Camino Ingles and Ruta do Mar
The Camino Portugues
The Mountains of Nerja
The Mountains of Ronda and Grazalema
The Sierras of Extremadura
Trekking in Mallorca
Trekking in the Canary Islands
Trekking the GR7 in Andalucia
Walking and Trekking in the Sierra Nevada
Walking in Andalucia
Walking in Menorca
Walking in Portugal
Walking in the Algarve
Walking in the Cordillera Cantabrica
Walking on Gran Canaria
Walking on La Gomera and El Hierro
Walking on La Palma
Walking on Lanzarote and Fuerteventura
Walking on Madeira
Walking on Tenerife
Walking on the Azores
Walking on the Costa Blanca
Walking the Camino dos Faros

SWITZERLAND
Switzerland's Jura Crest Trail
The Swiss Alpine Pass Route
　– Via Alpina Route 1
The Swiss Alps
Tour of the Jungfrau Region
Walking in the Bernese Oberland
Walking in the Engadine – Switzerland
Walking in the Valais
Walking in Zermatt and Saas-Fee

TECHNIQUES
Fastpacking
Geocaching in the UK
Map and Compass
Outdoor Photography
Polar Exploration
The Mountain Hut Book

MINI GUIDES
Alpine Flowers
Navigation
Pocket First Aid and Wilderness Medicine
Snow

MOUNTAIN LITERATURE
8000 metres
A Walk in the Clouds
Abode of the Gods
Fifty Years of Adventure
The Pennine Way – the Path, the People,
　the Journey
Unjustifiable Risk?

For full information on all our
guides, books and eBooks, visit our
website: www.cicerone.co.uk

CICERONE

Trust Cicerone to guide your next adventure, wherever it may be around the world...

Discover guides for hiking, mountain walking, backpacking, trekking, trail running, cycling and mountain biking, ski touring, climbing and scrambling in Britain, Europe and worldwide.

Connect with Cicerone online and find inspiration.

- buy books and ebooks
- articles, advice and trip reports
- podcasts and live events
- GPX files and updates
- regular newsletter

cicerone.co.uk